Northumberland County, Virginia

Deed and Will Book

1658–1662

Ruth and Sam Sparacio

HERITAGE BOOKS
2020

HERITAGE BOOKS
AN IMPRINT OF HERITAGE BOOKS, INC.

Books, CDs, and more—Worldwide

For our listing of thousands of titles see our website
at
www.HeritageBooks.com

Published 2020 by
HERITAGE BOOKS, INC.
Publishing Division
5810 Ruatan Street
Berwyn Heights, Md. 20740

International Standard Book Number
Paperbound: 978-1-68034-970-2

NORTHUMBERLAND COUNTY, VIRGINIA
RECORD BOOK
1658-1662

256. From 1658 to 1666. Memorand: JNO. CLARKE sale of Land to RALPH ( ); THOS:
    JONES Es. THO· HOBSON, Janry. 17( ) Recorded p me.
    THO. HOBSON his Book Anno Domini 1701
    JOHN BAYLES Will p 52. 1659. OB 1658-1666. THO: HOBSON
    KNOW ALL MEN by these presents that I WILLIAM SHORTE of County of Northum-
berld   THO: HOBSON

p   Mr. WM. PRESLY his Accompt upon the Estate of Coll. JNO: MOTTROM deced.
1   The Estate of Coll. JNO: MOTTROM deced. Dr. Tobco. Imprs. Paid Mr. MADDOCK by
        order; To Mr. FRANCIS CLAY by Ordr., To Mr. HAWLEY in pt. of his Order; To Mr.
MADDOCK & BAILY; To JAMES MAGREGOR by Order; To Capt. BRENT by Order; To Squire
ROCKE concerning the ( ); To THOMAS HASELIP for 1 barrell of Corne; To Coll. TRUS-
SELL for Levies ye last yeare; To GRINSTED for Payle & Tubbe; To 2 gall. Drams laun-
ching the Sloop; To Mr. HENRY VINCENT for sayieing ye Sloop; To Mr. PETER KNIGHT pt.
of Order; To Mr. ASHTON in pt. of his order; To 4 paire of shooes to ye Servants; To
Sherr· Fees to Mr. LITTLE; To THOMAS HASELIP for his clothes; To Coll. TRUSSELL for a
pr. of Oares. To Levies this yeare; To 5 p:sons tithes to the Minister; To Sherr. Fees due
to me; To bushell of Salt; To 2 dietts for the Servants; To THOMAS HASELIP for his ( ); To
Mr. RICHARD FLYNT for ( ); To FRANCIS SIMMONS by Order; To HENRY RAYNER in pt.
of ( ); To me by order for my ( ); To expence at JAMES ( ); To JNO: MOTTROM for his ( );
To WM. BEDLAM for sayle ( ), To GEORGE SUTTON; Paid to Mr. CLAY for se( ); To ser-
vants had of him; Paid to Old SUTTON by m( );
    Contra is Credr. By Tobco. Imprs. of Mr. MICHAELL, of EDWARD COLES, of RICHARD
ILAND, of WALTER WEEKES, of WM. WALKER; of JOHN ROBINSON; of Mr. MADDOCK, of
Mr. ALLENSON for TAINTORs Debt.. of ROBERT BRADSHAWE; of BRADSHAWE & CLAUGH-
TON for a Bull; of JAMES CLAUGHTON by order; of Squire ROCKE; of JOHN EARLE, of Mr.
HAWLEY. of Mr. HUGH LEE; of THO; SHEPPARD for ye Debt; two hhds. Tobco, pd. out of ye
Crop to Mr. CLAY; of Mr. VINCENT for the fraught of ye Sloope; of ROBT. SMITH, of
JAMES WILLIS. to 1 hhd. paid out of ye crop to CLARKE; of ANTHONY LINTON; of HUGH
LEE debt of Coll. SPEKE of STEVEN NEWMAN; of Mr. JNO: TEMPLE for a fraught; of Mr.
( )LOR of C( )LIUS ROBINSON; of Mr. NICHOLAS MORRIS; of THOMAS SAFFALL; of JNO:
WOOD for ye ( )ookes; of Hogshds. more out of the crop; ( ) of the 3d. part of 8000;
( )DMAN's Bill for 800 for fraugh ( ) ye Sloope not reced but ancepted; ( ) GIBBLE for
fraught; of HENRY HURST; of DANIELL CROSBY; of WM. BEDLAM; of SIMON RICHARD-
SON. of NICHOLAS BUTLER. of Mr. COLCLOUGH ye 3d. pt. of charges
                      July ye 20th 1658
( ) & just Accompt of what debts & dues ( ) of Coll. JNO: MOTTROM Estate and what ( )
the sd. Estate; Witnes my hand   Errors Excepted   WM. PRESLY
    Jurat in Cur et Recordat

p.   ( ) Witnesseth yt: I SETH FOSTER doe bargaine & ( ) pr:sents have bargained
1   & sold unto FRANCIS ( ), Servant named WILLIAM COUPTER nowe in MRS. ( )
        for the full tearme & time of two ( ) oblige my selfe my Exers. Admrs. or
assignes ( ) two yeares service unto the sd. CLAY his heires assignes & alsoe to send or
bring downe ( ) to the sd. CLAY by the last of March at time ( ) from the claime of any
p:son or p:sons whatsoever; In Witness whereof I the sd. SETH FOSTER have hereunto

sett my hand this 27th day of January 1657
Testes   ANN WRIGHT.   SETH FOSTER his marke
         THOM: HARFORD
  20th July 1658. This Writeing was recorded.

p.   KNOWE ALL MEN by these prsents that I HENRY RAYNER of CHICOKACONE,
2   Planter, doe constitute elect ordaine & chouse my welbeloved Wife, MARY RAY-
         NER, my true and lawfull Attorney to aske & demand to sue & recover all such
debts as shall be made appear to be mine, Likewise to pay acquit and discharge in as full
& ample manner as if I my selfe were here in p:sone; Witnes my hand this 23th day of
May 1658
Witness the marke of WM: HOPKINS,   HENRY RAYNER
         ye mke. of FRANCIS SIMMONS
   3d June 1658 This Lre. of Attor: was recorded

p.   A True Accott of the Cattle of THOMAS CANE left to his Children: Imprs. WIL-
2   LIAM his Sonne 2 cows, 2 yearlings, the one a heyfer the other a Steere & a
         Steere Calfe: THOMAS hath nowe instant 1 Cow, 1 Heyfer & ( ) Steere & one
Steere 4 yeares old & advantage; SUSANNA hath one Cowe & one St( ) of Cowe Calves &
a yearling heyfer; this years increase; The increase of WM. CAINEs Cattle ( ); The
increase of THOMAS Cattle 2 ( ), of SUSANA's 3 head. 3d. June 1658
   MARY RAYNER de( ) & then recorded

p.   The Orphans of WM: REYNOLDS deced. their part of Cattle.
2   A true list of the female Cattle ( ) the Orphans of WM. REYNOLDS ( ) severall
         names. JAMES REYNALDS his Cattle: 7 Milch Cowes, 3 two yeare old h( ), 4 year-
ling cowes, 1 young cowe, 1 yearling St( ); WM. REYNALDs his Cattle. 4 Cowes, 1 yearling hey( ); 2 cowe calves ( ); ANN REYNOLDS her Cattle; 2 Cowes, 1 yearling st( );
ANN & ELIZABETH MEDCALFE their Stock of Cattle; The Accot. presented by NICHOLIS
OWEN. ANN MEDCALFE hath 2 Cow ( ) 1 cowe calfe, 1 bull calfe ( ); ELIZABETH MED-
CALFE hath 1 Cowe, 1 cowe calfe;   NICHOLAS OWEN
   3d. Junii 1658. Jurat in Cur et record:

p   HENRY MOSELEYs Childn: their Stock of Cattle.
3   HENRY MOSELEY hath 2 cowes, 1 steere Calfe -3; JOHN hath 2 cowes, 1 yearling
         Steere -3: WILLIAM hath 1 yearling heyfer -1; ANNE hath 1 Cowe -1; This is the
whole Estate of these Children   JOHN TINGEY
   3d. Junii Jurat in Cur et record. 1658

p.   Purchased by WALTER WEEKES, Admr. of the Estate of Mr. JNO: RADFORD for the
3   use of the Children of the sd. RADFORD, 1658. ( ) 4 Cowes, ( ) cowe calfe -5;
                                             WALTER WEEKES
3d June 1658. This was recorded

p.   Accompt of WM. BASHAWEs Cattle. vizt. ( ) yeares increase 2 calfes -5; ( )
3   Cattle vizt.) _ Heyfer -2; ( ) increase   p me JAMES HAWLEY
         3d June 1658 Jurat in Cur et Recordatr:

p.   ( ) the Cattle of HENRY MEDCALFE the ( )EDCALFE, ( ) Cowe & a yearling hey-
3   fer; ( ) this is the whole stock of   WILLIAM DAVIS
         ( )rat in Cur et Recordatr:

p.   ( ) of the Cattle of JANE MEDCALFE. Imprs. 3 ( ), & 3 cowe calves and a heyfer
3   3 yeares old -7; This is the whole stock of JANE MEDCALFE
                                                        JOHN CLARKE
3d. Junii 1658. Jurat in Cur et recordatr.

p.   An Accott: of Cattle belonging to the Children of (blank) POLLHAM. Whereas
3   there were two Orphans bequeathed to me by their Parents upon their death
        beds & they left them a Cowe & a Sowe wth: Piggs by her side in my possession, I
have sold the Sowe & Piggs & p:duced a heyfer for them; And move they have 2 cowes &
a heyfer of 3 yeares and another of 2 yeares old & one yearling heyfer and a heyfer of
4 yeares old, wch: hath valued this yeare; and all the rest are barron, wch: cattle are not
as yett in the right marke but I shall Endeavour to gett them into the right marke as
soone as possible I can, And this is accompt of there Estate wch: was left me wch: will be
disposed upon my Oath by me   SAMUELL NICHOLAS
    3d. Junii Jurat in Cur & Recordatr.

p.   ELLENOR DOBBINS her Stock of Cattle. Acknowled: one Cowe and Calfe be-
3   longing unto ELENR: DOBBINS, the Daughter of JAMES DOBBINS, the Cowe black
        marked a hole in the left eare & a slitt in the right & the upper peice tooke off;
the Calfe of the same marke & one browne Cowe wth: a hole in th ( ) & cropt in the
right,   ANDREW POWLTER
    Cattle in Court to the proper ( ) and then recorded

p   ANDREW POWLTER's Gift to JOHN WADDY . I ANDREW POWLTER doe give unto
3   JOHN WADDY one Cow Calfe ( ) on both eares, the female to ( ) make to be for
        his ffather ( ) till he cometh to age: ( )
    3d. Junii 1658 This Deed ( ) in Court by the sd. ANDREW ( ).

p.   JUSTINIAN TENNIS. his Guift to HEN: HURST JUNIOR;
3   KNOWE ALL MEN that I ( ) HENRY HURST, Sonne of ( ) cropt the left ( ) taken
        out afore ( ) her increase mal( ) if the sd. Childe ( ) sd. Heyfer with ( ) HURST
Daughter ( ): As Witness ( )
    the marke of ( ) Witness JOHN G( )
    3d Junii 1658 ( )

p   Cattle wch: did belong to JUSTINIAN GRESHAM. An Accompt of all cattle ( )
3   JUSTINIAN GRESHAM deced. Imprs. 1 cowe & cowe calfe, 1 heyfer & bull hey-
        fer, 1 yearling heyfer ( ) living   JUSTINIAN TENNIS his marke
    3d. Junii 1658 Jurat in Cur et recordat

p.   All the Cattle belonging to JOHN PLAYER (vizt.) 1 cowes, one two yeare old hey-
4   fer, 1 yearling heyfer & 2 cowe calves -6; wch: is a just & true accompt. As Wit-
        ness my hand this 3d of June 1658   the marke of HENRY HURST
    3d. Junii 1658 Jurat in Cur et recordat

p.   ELIZABETH WEST her marke of Cattle. To ye Worpll. Comrs. of Northumberland
4   An Accot. of one Cowe belonging to ELIZABETH WEST wch: is in my ( ) there is
        one cowe & one cowe calfe, this is a true Accompt.
                                                JOHN BENNETT
    3d. Junii 1658 Jurat in Cur et recordat

p.
4

KNOW ALL MEN by these pr:sents that I THOMAS BREWER for a valuable consideracon to me in hand paid by THOMAS HOPKINS at & before the signeing &
delivery of these p:sents, wherewith I acknowledge my selfe to be contented &
paid have bargained & sold & by these p:sents doe fully & absolutely sell unto the sd.
THOMAS HOPKINS one Heyfer of colour red wth: white starr in the forehead, white in
the flanke, being marked vizt., Cropt in ye right eare wth: a strik on the upper side &
the left ( ) halfed, shee being about the age of fourteene ( ); To have & to hold the sd.
Heyfer Calfe as ( ) with all the increase that shall come of her ( ) sd. THOMAS HOPKINS
his heirs Exrs. Admrs. and ( ) to his & their proper uses & behoofe for ( ) and I the sd.
THOMAS BREWER my Exrs. Admrs. & ( ) the sd. Calfe unto the sd. THOMAS ( ) Admrs. &
assignes agaisnt all ( ) will warrant acquitt & for ever defend ( ) In Witness whereof I
have hereunto ( ) this 3d. of June 1658
Witnessed by RI: FLYNT   ( ) his marke
( ) doe hereby assigne & transferr ( ) title & interest of this Bill ( ) specified unto
THOMAS BREWER ( ) THOMAS BREWER SENIOR, ( ) JUNIOR being my God Sonne ( )
female as witness my hand this 3d. of June 1658

THOMAS HOPKINS

3d of Junii 1658 this assignemt. together with the Bill of Sale was recorded

p
4

Mr. MALLERY, Gaurdian to THOMAS OLDIS, Execucon agst. Capt. STREATER.
Whereas it was ordered at a Quarter Court held at JAMES CITTY the 17th day of
March 1657 that the difference depending betweene PHILLIP MALLORY, Clerk.
Gaurdian of THOMAS OLDIS, & Capt. EDWARD STREATER, whoe married the Relict of Coll.
THOMAS BURBAGE deced., should by consent of p:ties be referred to ye arbitracon of
Messrs. WM. WORLICK, Capt. JNO: POWELL, Mr. WM. BATTE & RICHARD HULL, within ten
dayes after the expiracon of the sd. Court & in case the sd. Arbytrators disagreement
that they to chouse an Umpire whose Umpirage should be a finall ( ) thereof & if the
sd. CAPT. STREATER should not appeare upon sufficient notice given him by the sd. Mr.
MALLORY, then the Arbytrators to proceed upon the Accompt delivered to them by the
said Mr. MALLORY; And Whereas the sd. Capt. STREATER notwithstanding notice given
him according to the sd. Order, made no appearance; the sd. Arbitrators haveing p:sued
the Accompt provided by the sd. MR. MALLOR & proofes thereof made p:ceeded in the
Arbitracon & did thereby award that the sd. Capt. STREATER should satifie & pay unto
the sd. Mr. MALLORY the quantity of Twenty five thousand two hundred & fifty pounds
of Tobco: & Twenty eight barrells of Corne, as alsoe to deliver unto the sd. Mr. MALLORY
all the Cattle ( ) & being upon the Plantacons at KE( ) WICOCOMOCO male & female included sold by Mr. GEORGE COLCLUGH & ( ) deliver unto the sd. Mr. MALLORY Ele( ) of
soe many Sheepe sold by the sd. ( ) part of all the moveables according ( ) of Mr. THO:
OLDIS deced., & the Inventory ( ) the time of his decease; & that the ( ) should pay all
costs expended in the ( ) Capt. STREATER hath altogether ( ) thereof according to the
tear. of ( ) the Quarter Court bearing date ( ). These are therefore according to the ( )
named of His Highness, the Lord ( ) to make seizure & de( ) as also to make ( ) Estate of
the sd. ( ) for the sd. 25250 lbs. of ( ) part of the moveables ( ) suit & after valuab( )
sufficient men accordi( ) to the same into ( ) without baile ( ) yor: p:rll; Given and ( )
1658 To ye Sheriffes of NAN( ), YORKE, ELIZABETH CITTY, NORTH( ) & LANCASTER
Counties or their Deputies
16th July 1658. This ( ) was recorded

p.
4

Mr. MALLORY's Attorns: Rect. to Mr. ASHTON
Reced. ye 16th of July 1658 of Mr. PETER ASHTON, High Sheriffe of Northumberland Thirty five head of Cattle vizt., two steares of 6 yeares old, 4 steares of 3 & 4

yeares old, one steare of 2 yeares old, 2 yearling heyfers, one Bull, 1 & 1/2 yeares, 2 yearling heyfers, 1 yeareling steare, two 2 yeare old heyfers, 2 steares 3 yeares old, 9 cowes, 5 steare calves, 3 cowe calves, all marked at these 2 markes, the old cowes cropt on the right eare, the rest 2 halfe moones on the right eare & a hole in the left; I say reced. by the appointmt. of PHILLIP MALLORY, Clerk, Gaurdian to THOMAS OLDIS, p mee

JNO: LEAR

16th July 1658 This Rect. was recorded

p.   BE IT KNOWNE unto all men by these pr:sents that I PHILLIP MALLORY, Clerke,
5   Gaurdian to THOMAS OLDIS, doe hereby constitute ordaine & appoint my loveing
       Friend, Mr. JNO: LEAR, my true & lawfull Attorney for me & in my name to act as
Gaurdian in managemt. & p:socuson of the execucon lately obtained against Capt.
EDWARD STREATER and upon receipt of the same or any pt: thereof to give discharge or
discharges if occasion require & whatsoever my sd. Attorney shall lawfully doe in my
name I doe hereby ratifie confirme & ( ) unto my sd. Attorney all my power and
authority in the pr:misses; Witnes my hand & seale this 27th day of June 1658
Signed in pr:sence of
       JOHN ( ); ROGER MALLORY   PHILLIP MALLORY ye Seale
   16th July 1658 This Lre. of Attorney was recorded

p.   WM. BACON's Bill Mr. CLAY wth: his State bound over
5   KNOW ALL MEN by these pr:sents that I WM: BACON doe for me my heires Exrs.
       Admrs. or assignes confesse my selfe to stand indebted unto FRANCIS CLAY or
his Exrs. Admrs. or assignes in the just sume & quantity of Seaven thousand ( ) hundred pounds of merchantable Tobco: payable according to Act of Assembly with sufficient caske to containe the sd. quantity of Tobco: ( ) the true p:formance of this Debt
abovesd. I the sd. WM: BACON doe by these pr:sents bind & make over unto the sd. FRAN-
CIS CLAY my Plantacon wch: I doe nowe live on wth: such houseing fenceing as nowe is
upon it & all other grounds that doth belong to my Plantacon, And likewise I doe bind
and make over unto the said FRANCIS CLAY foure Cowes, the wch: Cowes called or
knowne by the names of the one Blackbird, the other Buck, & the 3d. Pye, the fourth
Nancey; the wch: cowes ( ) upon the Plantacon wth: their future increase ( ) absolutely agreed betweene the p:ties abovesd. the sd. ( ) Tobco. of 7500 lbs. is to be paid betweene this pr:sent Christmas next come twelve moneth, or else the sd. Estate the Plantacon & cowes aforesaid ( ) & it is further agreed betweene the p:ties sume of Tobco: is
to be paid 3500 on the ( ) next after this pr:sent date and 4000 ( ) Christmas, the wch:
will be in the yeare 1659; ( )formance hereof I have hereunto sett my ( ) July 1658;
Moreover I WM: BACON with ( ) doe hereunto sett my hand & seale ( ) 1658
Delivered in the pr:sence of us
       ( ); WILLIAM THOMAS,   WILLIAM BACON, the seale
                                            ( ) her marke, the seale
( ) desire you for to record this Writeing ( ) & I doe hereby wth: MARGARETT ( )ledge
it to be as authentique as if it were ( ) selfe wth MARGARETT my wife to acknowledge it
in the next Cort ( ) Northumberland County   Yor: Friend
                                                  WILLIAM BACON

   24th July 1658 This Writeing was recorded

p.   BE IT KNOWNE unto all men that I HEN: ROCKE doth make Mr. THOM: BROUGHTON
5   my lawfull Attorney to plead any case in Northumberland Court betweene RICE
       MADDOX and the sd. ROCKE as Witness my hand this 19th day of July 1658

Witness DA: LINDSAY   HENRY ROCKE
   20th July 1658. This Lre. of Attor: was recorded

p.   To all &c., Whereas &c. Now Knowe yee that I the sd. RICHARD BENNETT Esqr.,
5   &c. Give & grant unto Mr. NICHOLAS JERNEW Six hundred & fourteene acres of
           land scituate in County of GLOUCESTER upon the East, South East side of PORO-
PATANCK CREEKE begining at the mouth of a small Branch or Swamp wch: devides this
land and the land of Mr. OLIVER GREENE, extending East South East into the Woods,
North North East upon the land of Mr. WEBB & Mr. PATE, North West by West along a
Swamp wch: devideth this land & the land of the aforesd. PATE & WEBB, binding along to
the Creeke, and West North West upon POROPATANCK CREEKE: This Land being due unto
the sd. NICHOLAS JERNOW by & for the transportacon of Eleven p:sons into this Colony,
all whose names are on Records menconed under this Pattent &c. Dated the 3d day of
July 1653   RI: BENNETT
                                                 W: CLAIBORNE, Secr.
   Be it Knowne unto all men by these pr:sents that I NICHOLAS JERNOW acknowledge
that there is due to Mr. THOMAS BLANCKETT his heires Exrs. & assignes for ever ( )
hundred acres of land out of this Pattent lyeing on PEROPATANCK CREEKE begining at
the marked trees of ( )LIVER ( ) and ending at a Swamp by the land of ( ) hundred
acres I doe acknowledge ( )THOMAS BLANCKETT and his heires for ever ( ) this 23th of
Septr: 1654
per me SAMUELL DOBSON, ROGER ST( )
   21th July 1658. This Acknowledgemt. of ( ) recorded with the Pattent

p.   Mr. JERNEWs Assmt. of a Pattent to Mr. GAYLARD
5   KNOWE ALL MEN by these pr:sents that I ( ) & made over & by these pr:sents ( )
           to mee in hand paid ( ) doe assigne & make over all my ( ) & the Land therein
menconed unto ( ) to hold to him & to his heires ( ) warrant the same to be ( ) any
claime thereto ( ) Admrs. or Assignes or by ( ) Witness whereof I have ( ) of March
1657
Witness WILLIA: WYATT   Sig: ( )
   20th July 1658. This ( ) by RICHARD FLYNT ( ) JAMES GAYLARD &c.
   Mr. GAYLORD's Assignmt. of that Pattent to MICHAELL CRAFTON. KNOWE ALL MEN by
these pr:sents ( ) & made overby the ( ) my right & title ( ) menconed dunto
MICHAELL ( ) Witnes my hand this ( )
Witness JON: LEWIS, THOMAS EL( )
   20th July 1658. This Assignmt. was acknowledged in Court by the sd. JAMES GAYLARD &
is recorded

pp.   Mr. JERNEWs Lre. of Attorney to RI: FLYNT
5-   KNOWE ALL MEN by these pr:sents that I NICHOLAS JOURNEAW have constituted
6   appointed & ordayned & by these pr:sents doe constitute appoint & ordayne my
           trusty & well beloved Friend, Mr. RICHARD FLYNT, my true & lawfull Attorney
for mee in my name stead & place in the County Court of Northumberland County in
Virginia, to acknowledge a Pattent & five hundred acres of land (lyeing in POROPA-
TANCKE CREEKE in the County of GLOUCESTER in Virginia aforesd.) together with the
Assignemt. thereof thereon endorsed unto JAMES GAYLARD his heires & assignes fore
ever ratifying & confirming ehat my sd. Attorney shall act or doe in the p:misses in as
ample manner to all intents & purposes as if I my selfe were p:sonally pr:sent & did the
same: In Witness whereof I have hereunto sett my hand & seale this Nineteenth day of
July 1658

Witness THOMAS SHAWE,   the marke of NICHOLAS JEARNEAW
         WILKES MAUNDER
20th July 1658   This Lre. of Attor: was recorded

p.   To all &c., Whereas &c., Now Knowe yee that I the sd. RICHARD BENNETT Esqr.
6   &c. give & grant unto Mr. HENRY WICKER 250 acres of Land scituate upon the
          South side of GREAT WICOCOMOCO RIVER, West Northwest side of a Maine Branch
( ) VULCANS CREEKE abutting North Northeast upon ( ) FRANS CREEKE, East South East
upon the head of the sd. Branch & upon the Land of JEFFERY GOCKE ( ) Southwest into
the woods; the sd. Land being due unto the sd. HENRY WICKER by & for ye Transportacon of Five psons into this Colony all whose names are in ye Records menconed under
this Pattent &c., Dated the 20th of Novembr: 1651   RI: BENNETT
                                                     W. CLAIBORNE Secr.
     KNOWE ALL MEN by these prsents that I HENRY WICKER wthin menconed for & in
consideracon of Two hundred & fifty acres of land at the head of WICOCOMOCOE RIVER &
a House &c., doe hereby sell alienate & assigne over from mee and my heirs Exrs. or
Admrs. unto GERVASE DODSON of WICOCOMOCO RIVER for the 250 acres of land wthin
specified wth: the House & all priviledges to the sd. House & Land belonging; wth: all
writeings that any way concerne the same; wch: I the sd. HENRY WEEKER engage as
aforesd. to deliver to the sd. DODSON or his assignes; wth: the Pattent thereto belonging
at the next Court Court & to assigne over the Pattent & acknowledge the sale to the sd.
DODSON his heires or assignes; To have & to hold to him & them for ever and I the ( )
further bind my selfe my heirs Exrs. or Admrs. to ( ) this sd. Sale the sd. House & Land
from any claime ( ) pson or psons whatever that shall lay any claime ( ) by vertue of
any sale assignemt. bargaine & sale this ( ) Aprill 1658 & have delivered possession ( )
Witness my hand & seale in presence of
     ( )HOUS, THOMAS JONES   HENRY WEEKER, his marke, ye Seale
   ( ) This Sale of Land was acknowledged by HENRY WEEKER unto GERVASE DODSON &c.

p.   JOSEPH HORSLEY aged 22 yeares or thereabouts sworne & examined saith That
6   hee delivered the right Bull belonging to the Estate of JANE BASHAWE unto
          THOMAS ORLEY's man for her use, to the best of this Deponts. knowledge & fur-
ther saith not   JOS: HORSLEY
20th July 1658 Jurat in Cur.

P.   THESE PR:SENTS Witness that I GERVASE DODSON for & in consideration of 250
6   acres of Land granted by Pattent to HENRY WICKER at a Branch of WICCOCOMOCOE
          RIVER called VULCANS CREEKE wch: the sd. HENRY WICKER hath sold untome &
the House & all rights & priviledges belonging thereunto, I ye sd. GERVASE DODSON (in
consideration thereof) doe hereby sell & assigne over unto the sd. HENRY WICKER two
hundred and Fifty acres of Land at or neare a Maine Branch of the head of the sd. WICO-
COMOCO RIVER & bounding Southerly upon the sd. Branch, Westerly upon a line running Northerly from the said Branch of the head of the River by the outside of the
fence a mile into the woods & soe by opposite sides & angles makeing a course including
the said quantity of Two hundred & Fifty acres; wth: the House & all thereto belonging
excepting halfe the Corne & halfe the trees vizt., I to chouse two trees & then the sd.
HENRY WICKER to chouse two, then I &hee two till all is devided both Apple trees &
other fruit trees & I engage myselfe my heires or Admrs. to warant this Sale from any
claime from any pson or psons wch: shall prtend or show right thereto by vertue of
any bargaine or contract saile or assignemt. from me or my assignes; Witness my hand

& seale ( ) 1658 being Easter Munday & to acknowledge it ( ) Court
Witness JOHN GATEHOUSE   GERVASE DODSON
      THOMAS JONES
  20th July 1658. This Sale of Land ( ) Court by the sd. GERVASE DODSON unto ( ) & is
recorded

p.   JNO: MOTLEY's Deed of Land to MATH: WILLCOCKS)
6   KNOW ALL MEN by these prsents that ( ) WICOCOMOCOE in County of ( ) in
        consideracon of the Marriage of ( ) doe freely give unto MATHEW WILL( )
County his heirs or assignes for ever One hundred cres of ( ) Six hundred granted to
( ) being bounded upon the ( ) ALLEN, I the sd. MOTLEY ( ) assignes to acknowledge
( ) my hand this 19th day of July ( ).
Test JOHN FAWSETT
  20th July 1658. This ( ) sd. JNO: MOTLEY unto ( )

p.   MATHEW WILLCOCKS Assignmt. of Land to GEORGE ALDRIDGE.
6   I MATHEW WILLCOCKS ( ) right title & interest ( ) ALDRIDGE or his assigns ( )
        1658.   MATHEW WILLCOCKS
Witness PETER ASHTON
  20th 9ber: 1658. This ( ) by the sd. MATHEW WILL( )

P.   The Deposicon of AMY BOND aged 20 yeares or thereabouts sworne & examined
6   this 8th of July 1658, saith that about February last to the best of this Deponts.
        remembrance, Mr. JNO: TEMPLE being in discourse wth: ROBT. LAND, the
Tincker, about HENRY HAYLER, hee the sd. Mr. TEMPLE called him the sd. HENRY HAY-
LER Rogue & said hee would prove him a Rogue & further sayeth not
Taken before me JOHN TRUSSELL   Sigd. AMY BOND
  20th July 1658 This Depo: was recorded

p.   KNOWE ALL MEN by these prsents that I WM: BACON for a good & valuable con-
7   sideracon already in hand received have bargained & sold unto WILLIAM THO-
        MAS his heires Two hundred acres of land more or lesse with wch: satisfacon I
am fully contented, lying & being in YEACOMOCO NECK joyning upon my Land, Begining at ye Creeke side running to a white oake soe by marked trees till you come to a
marked Gumm, then upon a line to the Land of RICHARD HOLDEN & along ( ) to the land
of WM: JEFFER; To have & to hold the sd. Land with all priviledges as in my Pattent is
specified; tohim his heires Exrs. & Admrs. & assignes for ever; from me my heires Exrs.
and assignes; To hold the sd. Land from all psons whatsoever that shall lay claime or
interest unto the same and I doe binde my selfe my heires to acknoweldge it in Court
unto WM. THOMAS his heires whenever they shall demand the same; Witness my hand
Novembr: 3d. 1657.
Test WILLIAM JEFFARS   WILLIAM BACON
      JAMES CLAUGHTON
  20th July 1658. This Sale of Land was acknowledged in Court by THOMAS PHILPOTT,
Attorney of the sd. WILLIAM BACON, & is recorded

  KNOWE ALL MEN by these prsentsthat I WM. BACON of the County of Northumberland doe constitute & appoint my Friend, THOMAS PHILLPOTT for me & in my name to
assigne & settover unto JOHN WOOD or any Attorney or Attorneys of his, one Pattent of a
Thousand acres that I the sd. WILLIAM BACON had of JOHN WOOD from my my heires to

him his heires & further I doe appoint my loveing Friend to acknowledge sd. pr:cell of land with the Bill of Sale unto WM. THOMAS or his assignes; And what my Attorney shall doe I retify & confirme in as full & ample maner as if I my selfe were present; In Witness whereof I have set my hand this 19th of July 1658

( )LIAM COLEMAN   WILLIAM BACON
( ) This Lre. of Attorney was recorded

( ) I WILL: THOMAS doe bind my selfe my heires ( ) wayes to trouble or molest STE-PHEN BAILY ( ) in or about the Land that hee nowe possesses ( ) him quietly & peace-ably enjoy the same ( ) my selfe my heires or assignes that ( ) Agreemt. the sd. WM. BACON have made ( ) HEN: BAILY in or about the sd. Land ( ) Lease for Eleven yeares, I do by ( ) my selfe my heires to ratify & ( ) set forth as if my selfe did make ye Lease ( ) Novembr: 3d. 1657

( ) CLAUGHTON,   WILLIAM THOMAS
WILLIAM JEFFARS
( ) 1658. This Writeing was acknowledged in Court ( ) WM. THOMAS & is recorded

KNOW ALL MEN by these pr:sents that I JOHN WOOD doe bind my selfe to deliver unto WM. THOMAS or his assignes both my Bills of one & twenty hundred pounds of Tobco: & Caske & all Bills that Mr. WM. BACON past to him; Moreover I JOHN WOOD doe bind my selfe to deliver all these Bills upon the 21th day of January 1657. Witness my hand this 16th of Novembr: 1657

Test ye marke of JAMES MAGREGER   JOHN WOOD
ye marke of HUGH FOUCH
20th July 1658 This Writeing was recorded

p.   An Inventory of the Estate of JNO: HEWETT of YEOCOMICO in the County of
7   Northumberland deced. taken in the presence of us whose names are subscribed
Imprs. 2 feather beds & bolster, 1 rugg & white blankett, 1 Catt-taile bed, 1 fea-ther bolster, 1 white blankett, 1 flock bed, 2 feather pillowes, 1 old red rugg, 1 iron ket-tle, 3 iron potts, 1 iron spitt, iron drippin pan, frying pan, 2 paire pott hookes & hookes to hang potts on; 2 iron pestles, smoothing iron, 1 box wth: severall old writeings; 3 plaines, 1 handsaw, 1 small auger, 1 cooprs: adds, 1 broad chissell & 3 narrow ones; 2 pricker, 1 small square, 2 rumbletts, 1 pricer bitt, 1 plaine, 1 staple, great ffro; 1 small ffro, 1 ffiles, 1 markeing iron, 3 old hilling hoes, 3 old weeding hoes, 1 hamer, 2 old narrowe axes, a pce: of old iron, 2 gunns, a shott bagg & powder; 1 bedstead, 1 crosse sawe, iron wedges, 2 chests, 2 old chaires, 1 stoole, 1 table, cutting knife, 3 pewter dishes, 2 porringers, 1 salt seller, 1 sawcer, 1 brasse candlestick, 8 pewter ( ), 2 old sifters, 2 old milke trays, 1 churne, 1 old chamber pott, 4 cowes, 5 yearling heyfers, 3 young calves, 2 being cowes, 1 brasse sunn diall   PEETER LEFEBUR
THOMAS SHAWE

20th July 1658 ( )

p.   JNO: HILLER Gent., aged 50 yeares or thereabouts examd. saith that this ( )
7   hundred pounds of Tobco: & ( ) Collo. MOTTROM bought ( ) saith not
22 Decem: 1657. Jurat in Curat   Teste me ( )
20th July 1658 ( )
Coll. MOTTROM's Acquit to Mr. HILLER; I Coll. JOHN MOTTROM ( ) HILLER from fowre-teen ( ) due unto ABRAHAM MO( ) Witness my hand this 12th ( )
Witness JO: ROSIER. THOMAS SPEKE   JOHN MOTTROM
20th July 1658. This Acquit was recorded

p. 7 THOMAS SHEPPARD's ccot. Charges upon JOHN WOOD

1657. JOHN WOOD Dr. To severall paymts. made for Land by THOMAS SHEPPARD. Imprs. to himselfe one cowe wth: calfe, one gunn, to JNO: STEELE 300 lbs. Tobco: to Mr. VINCENT 600 lbs. Tobco:, To more 100 lbs. Tobco.

THO: SHEPPARD his marke

20th July 1658 Jurat in Cur

p. 8 GEORGE DURANT aged 25 yeares or thereabouts doth testifie and am ready to be disposed: That arriveing in HOLLAND & in the Province of ZEALAND in the Ship "PATOMACK MECHT.," Mr. ROBERT CLARKE Commander, Mrs. HANNAH LEE had in the sd. Ship about 30 hoggsd. of Tobacco whereof about 29 of them were delivered at MIDLEBURGH, shee supposeing they were or had taken well in the sd. Ship; where yor: Depont: did sound or see the Pump of the sd. Ship where the sd. Ship sounded every day during the sd. Voyage and I ( ) sawe ( ) or 8 inches water or thereabouts in the well ( ) further yor: Depont: being p:sent at the ( )ing of the sd. Tobco: where the Tobco: was crusted ( ) the ballast as severall others was but soe farr as I knowe nott verse, for the hoggsd. of Tobco wch: they say was totally spoyled your Depont. did see & the condicon of it to ye best knowledge was not spoyled by the shipp nor ballast but it seem'd to me to be House b( )nd for it was black & dry & soe spotted that I doe verily believe I could not lay the breadth of a Shilling between them, neyther did they the viewers weigh or seperate that wch: was damaged from the rest but as they sett it downe by aime: And further yor: Depont. sayth tht Mr. SEAVERNE told mee that when some of Mr., LEE's Tobco: was brought aboard the sd. Ship, the heads of some of them fell out & hee sawe it was soe bad hee would not stow it before Mr. LEE know of it, sending up WM. SMITH to him, the sd. LEE, hee sent to them and ( ) them stow it and this the sd. SEAVERNE said ( ) would be deposed when occasion served

GEO: DURANT

( ) July 1658. Jurat in Cur

p. 8 ( ) PEOPLE to whome these pr:sents shall come ( )KER send Greeting. Now Knowe yee yt: ( )DORE BAKER who married wth: ELIZABETH ( ) Daughter of JOHN INGRAM, late of the ( ) NEKE in the County of Northumberland and ( ) Virginia deced., doe acknowledge to have ( ) from Mr. THOMAS HOPKINS (who married ( ) the Relict of sd. JNO: INGRAM) p:cell of the Estate due or beloning ( ) INGRAM my nowe lawfull Wife, eyther ( ) sd. JNO: INGRAM or any otherwaies ( ) myu Wife due or belonging unto her, And ( ) for mee my heires Exr. &c. remise acquitt & discharge & for ever acquit Mr. THOMAS HOPKINS his heires, Exers, Admrs. ( ) of & from the sd. Estate & every part of ( ) excepting one mare filley which is due to my ( ) by the Will of the sd. INGRAM when shee shall attaine to the age of Eighteene yeares: In Witness whereof I the sd. THEODORE BAKER have hereunto sett my hand & seale this 26th day of July 1658

Signed Sealed & Delivered in the presence of us

SAML: SMYTH, RI: FLYNT   THEODORE BAKER ye Seale

28th July 1658. This Acquit was recorded

p. 8 KNOW ALL MEN by these pr:sents that wee GEORGE COLCLOUGH and URSULA his Wife, Gaurdians of RICHARD & SARAH THOMPSON, have granted bargained & sold & doe hereby grant bargaine & sell unto JOHN CURTIS one iron grey Mare; To have & to hold the sd. Mare & all her future increase unto the sd. JNO: CURTIS his Exrs. Admrs. & assigns, warranted by us our Exrs. Admrs. or assignes for ever by these pr:-

sents. In Witness whereof wee have hereunto put our hands and seals the 29th day of
September 1657

        FRANCIS CLAY,   GEO: COLCLOUGH ye Seale
        ANN WRIGHT   URSULA COLCLOUGH ye Seale
13th August 1658 This Bill of Sale was recorded

p.   KNOWE ALL MEN by these pr:sents that I WILLIAM CLAIBORNE, Surveyor, doe
8   for my selfe my heires Exrs. Admrs. & assignes & every of them acquit & dis-
      charge SAMUELL SMITH his heires Exrs. and Admrs. & every of them from all
manner of dues & demands whatsoever from ye beginning of the World to this day as
Witnessmy hand this ( )
Testibus GEO: LYDDALL,   WILLIAM CLAIBORNE
    JAMES DASHIEL, JNO: BRO( )
 August 23th 1658 This Acquit was ( )

p.   ANNE HAMMONDs Sale of Goods to DANLL. HOLLAND
8   KNOWE ALL MEN by these pr:sents that I ( ) Province of MARYLAND have ( )
      & more especially for One thousand ( ) Tobco & caske by me received ( ) fully &
amply satisfied have ( ) HOLLAND of the County of ( ) Virginia two featherbeds, ( ) &
one bolster & one ( ) beds & one boulster ( ) alsoe two iron pots, one pewter dish,
( ) doe from me my ( ) sell alienate & ( ) Exrs. Admrs. & assignes ( ) as his or theire
owne ( ) quiett & peaceable ( ) molestacon ( ) p:sons whatsoever ( ) demand, as Witness my ( )
Signed & delivered in ( )
    the marke of RALPH ( )
 28th August 1658 This ( ) was recorded

p.   Goods of EDWARD ROBERTS sold at an Out Cry. August ye 7th day 1658.
8   Goods of Mr. EDWARD ROBERTS appointed & ordered by the Court to be sold at an
      Out Cry. One feather bedd & boulster & rugg bought by mee, and one iron pott at
560 lgbs. tobco. SAMUEL NEALE; one Pettecoate & wastcoate bought by mee at 250 lbs.
tobco. the make of NICHOLAS BANISTER; one wrought wastcoate bought by mee at 81 lbs.
tobco; THOMAS HAILES his marke; one old Trunck bought by mee at 21 lbs. tobco.
HENRY HAYLER his marke   312 lbs.
 20th 7br: 1658 This was recorded

p.   A Subpena against Mr. COLCLOUGH
9   These are in the name of his Highnes the Lord Protector to will & require you
      to sumon the appearance of Coll. JNO: TRUSSELL, Lt. Coll. SAMUEL SMYTH, Capt.
RICHD: BUDD; Mr. WM. NUTT, Mr. WM. PRESLY, Mr. PETER PRESLY, Mr. EDW: COLES,
Mr. THO: HOPKINS, Mr. NICHOLAS MORRIS, THO: BREWER, SIMON COX, Mr. GERVASE
DODSON, ABRAHAM JOYCE, JOSEPH HORSLEY, MARY RAYNER to the next Court holden
for this County at the House of HUGH FOUCH & JAMES MacGRIGER the 20th of Septr. next
then and there to testifie their severall knowledges (upon interogatories) in differences depending betweene severall of the Inhabitants of this County and by them to
be articled, exhibited agt. Mr. GEORGE COLCLOUGH hereof faile not &c. Given under my
hand this 5th of Aug: 1658   PETER KNIGHT
 20th 7br. 1658 This Subpena was recorded

p.
9
The marke of a yearling heyfer that was given by a Bill from ROBERT NEWMAN to WM. RAVEN, Sonne of JOHN RAVEN, is nowe delivered unto the sd. WM. RAVEN by WM: PRESLY Exer. of the sd. NEWMAN's Estate, vizt., cropt on both eares & slitt & a piece taken away from the under side of the left eare & a peice taken away from the upper side of the right eare & is of a red brindled colour, this yearling I have reced., of WM: PRESLY, Exr. of ROBT. NEWMAN for the use of my Sonne, WM. RAVEN,
Testes WILKES MAUNDER,   the marke of me   JOHN RAVEN
        RICHD: LEE
( ) 7br: 1658. The Rect. of this Heyfer was acknowledged in Court by the sd. JNO: RAVEN & is recorded

p
9
( ) by these presents that I JOHN HUGHLETT, Admr. of THOMAS READE deced., have sold unto THOMAS GASCOINES of GREAT WICOCOMO ( ) of Northumberland & to his heires forever One thousand acres of Land ( ) between GREAT WICO-COMOCOE ( ) the Branches of the said River, Southerly ( ) & the Branches of COROTO-MAN RIVER ( ) County & bearing Easterly & Southerly from ( ) the said River; which sd. Land with all the ( ) belonging I the sd. JOHN HUGHLETT doe warrt. unto the sd. ( ) heires & assignes for ever agt. any ( ) that shall thereto make claime or demand ( ) manner according to the tenor of ye ( ) Law can be required & doe likewise ( ) to make an acknowledgmt: of this Sale ( ) Pattent for the abovesd. Land upon ( ); Witness whereof I have sett to my hand this 28th ( ) 1658
In psence of us JOHN HAYNIE,   Sig.   JOHN HUGHLETT
        JEFFERY GOCKE
20th 7br: 1658. This Sale of Land was acknowledged in Court by the sd. JOHN HUGHLETT unto the said THOMAS GASCOINES and is recorded

p.
9
I doe relinquish all Letters of Attorney nowe upon record in Northumberland County made from SETH FOSTER to me FRANCIS CLAY
Sept. ye 23th (58) Record

pp.
9-
10
A Note of Bills belonging to the Estate of Coll: JNO: MOTTROM taken July ye 19th 1658. One Bill of WM: DENBIGHs 30 armes length of roanoke; SIMON RICHARD-SONs Bill for 20 lbs. of Beaver; JOHN RAVEN's Condicon concern Ploughs & Carts; Mr. MOONEs Note for 160; JOHN RAVEN's Bill for 1015; THO: SHEPPARD ye re-maindr: of a Bill -83; THO: ( ) his Bill -562; WM. COX Bill -2146; A Bill of Sale from Mr. HOPKINS for a Sloope, Servant and Cowe; EDWARD HULLs Fee; ROGER BAXTERs Bill; a Note of ()ONEYs & POWELL for Sack; Bill of Sale on RICHARDSONS & JNO: LEEs for 2 Bar-rells Corne; one Bill of ZACHARI: WADEs; a Bill of JOHN EARLEs, Accompt of JOHN WIN-CHESTER, a Judgmt. agt. NATH: HICKMAN; JNO: KELLYs Bill, Bill of Mr. ROBERT FORN-HAM's, a Verdict of a Jury agt. Mr. HOPKINS; a Bill of THO: ATTWELLs; Bill of JAMES CLAUGHTON, JOHN ( ) & HENRY CARTWRIGHTs for 200 lbs.; Bill of SIMON RICHARDSON, Bill of ROBT. BERREYs, Bill of HENRY MORGAN; Note for severall ( ); Note of Mr. MANNI( ) CLAUGHTON & CLAREs ( ); THO: SWAINEs Bill; an Assignmt. of ( ) Mr. PETER KNIGHTs re( ); JOHN WADDYs Note; ( ) WALTER WEEKES, CHARLES WILLIAMS, Mr. BATCHELLERs Bill; Mr. FRANCIS POSIEs; Mr. FRANCIS CLAYs; a Note of JOHN W( ); THO: SHEPPARDs Bill; To JNO: INGRAMs Bill; Mr. CLAYs Bill; WILLIAM ABRAHAM Bill; THO-MAS MORGANs Bill; SAMLL. CHEWs Bill; CHARLES WILLIAMS Bill; THOMAS MAN's Bill; ROBERT BRADSHAWEs Bill; Mr. GERVASE DODSONs Bill; JOHN ASHLEYs Bill; CHARLES SCARBOROUGHs Bill; Mr. PETER ASHTONs Bill; Mr. BROUGHTONs Bill; Coll. SPEKEs Bill; ANTHO: DONEYs Bill for a paire of shooes & stockins & 50 lbs. Tobco: RANDALL CROWEs

Bill: RICHARD LUCUS & WM: WHEATLEYs for 620; Mr. WALTER BRODHURSTs Bill, two Bills
of WM. MEDCALFE; Capt. FLEETs Bill for 12 lbs. of Beanes; Mr. WM. THOMAS his Bill; 1
Bill of ROBT. NEWMANs; 1 Bill more of the sd. NEWMAN, PRICE & BOOTHEs Writeings; Mr.
RICHARD BENNETTs Note; Coll: BURK( ), a Note for 33 paires of Shooes; Coll: YARDLEYs
Lre. to Coll. MOTTROM; Coll. SPEKEs rect. for JACKSONs Bills, Coll. SPEKEs Rect.; RICHARD
BENNETTs ( ); ( ) SMOOTEs Bill for six barrells of Corne; WM. SALE his Engagemt. two
pounds one shilling halfe ( ); brasse gun & 1 case of Sack; THO: DEACONs Bill; SPEKEs
Acct. for one Bill of THOMAS BAKERs & THO: KNIGHTs; oneBill of JNO: LANCELOTTs, one
Bill of JAMES HAREs, and two pounds of Beaver; one Bill of RICHARD HILLs; one Bill of
RICHARD BROWNEs; Bill of ROBT. MAPHEN ( ) MASONs Bill & Accot., ( ) Bills be-
longing due from Mr. TURNEY, likewise Bills of JNO: WALTONs & CORBETT PEDLE; ( )
HALLOWES for Tobco; writeing concern Capt. JOHN JACOBE; ( ) for BILLINGSLEYs busi-
ness; ( ) Mr. THOMAS BRERETON; ( ) WESTMORELAND Court has granted agst. ( ) for
what was due from him to this Estate; ( ) this Court for what was found due ( ) SAMLL:
SMYTH; ( ) items that were returned to Mr. ( ) belonging to the Estate of Coll: ( ); the
rest of the Writeings being ( ) by Order to the severall p:sons ( ) appeare paid
                                        WM: PRESLY
( ) This Accompt of these Bills & other ( ) recorded

p.   The Cattle belonging to ye Children of Coll: JNO: MOTTROM deced. ( ) Eig( ),
10   three Oxen, twelve ( ) & seaven calves; three Bulls, fower yearling heyfers, two
            yearling steers -39; being ordered p ye Cort. of Northumberland to view the
Cattle belonging to the Estate of the Children of Coll. JNO: MOTTROM which is thirty two
of all sortes & the Calves; As Witness our hands the 14th of August 1658
                    JOHN MOTTRAM   ROBERT SECH
                                           RICH: WRIGHT

    The Cattle abovesd. I have reced. in my possession
    20 7br: 1658. This Writeing was recorded

p.   Mr. WM. THOMAS his Assignmt. of a Pattent to WM: BETT
10.   KNOWE ALL MEN by these pr:sents that I WM: THOMAS doe assigne & transfer all
            my title & interest of this Pattent of Land unto WM. BETS his heires & assignes
for ever & doe warrant the sd. Land (according to the sd. Pattent) unto him the sd. BETS
his heires & assignes for ever; Witness my hand this 31th of August 1658
Teste PETER ASHTON,   WM: THOMAS
        ye marke of THOMAS TREPE
  20 7br: 1658. This Assignemt. was acknowledged in Court by the sd. WM. THOMAS &
recorded. The Patt: was originally granted to THO: MOULTON by him assigned to JNO:
WOOD; from him to Mr. THOMAS & is recorded in WESTMORELAND Records ye 20th of Feb:
1657.

p.   To all &c., Know yee that I the sd. RICHARD BENNETT Esqr. &c., grant unto JOHN
10   HULL Five hundred acres of land scituated in Northumberland County & upon
            the South side of the DEVIDEING CREEKE abutting South upon ye Land of GEORGE
COLCLOUGH, West upon a White Marsh or glade wth: High Land called the MOUNTAINEs,
North upon a Branch of the head of the sd. Creeke & East upon the DEVIDEING CREEKE,
the sd. Land being formerly granted unto the said JOHN HULL by Pattent dated the 5th
of ( ) 1651, & order of ( ) for the renewing thereof by the Governr: & Councell dated
the 6th of June 1654; To have & to hold &c., dated the ( ) of June 1654
        W. CLAIBORNE, Secr,   RI: BENNETT

KNOW ALL MEN by these pr:sents that I ( ) Wife ANNE HULL (for a valuable ( ) the Receipt whereof wee doe hereby acknowledge due for us our heires ( ) THOMAS BREWER his heires Exrs. Admrs. ( ) our right title & interest of this ( ) menconed & doe further warrant the ( ) from all former grants, As Witness ( ) Anno 1658
Witness RI: FLYNT   JOHN HULL
                                                     ANN HULL

20th 7br: 1658. This Assignemt. ( ) the sd. JOHN HULL & ANNE his Wife ( ) and recorded with the ( )

p.   FRANCIS ROBERTS his Pattent
10   To all &c., Whereas &c. (MATHEWES Esqr. &c. ( ) hundred acres of ( ) bounding
          ( ) above the sd. SPEKEs ( ) MACKGREGERY his Land ( ) 123 poles & Norther( )
into the Woods to ( ) being due unto ( ) transportacon of ( ) are in the Recor( ) the
15th of July ( )
          FRANCS: ROBERTS Assignemt. of this Pattent to JOSEPH FEILDING & JNO: GARNER
    KNOWE ALL MEN by these pr:sents that ( ) a valuable consideracon ( ) my selfe to be
fully ( ) paid doe for me my heires ( ) title & interest of this Pattent & the land ( ) into
JOSEPH FEILDING & JOHN GARNER & their heires & assignes for ever; Together with all
rights thereunto belonging; And further I the sd. FRANCIS ROBERTS my heires & every
of us the sd. Pattent & Land unto the sd. JOSEPH FEILDING & JNO: GARNER their heires &
assignes against all people will acquitt & for ever defend by these pr:sents from any
claime or title thereunto (INDIANS onely excepted); In Witness whereof I the sd.
FRANCIS ROBERTS have hereunto sett my hand this 20th day of September 1658
Signed & delivered in the pr:sence of
          THO: BROUGHTON   FRANCIS ROBERTS his marke
          JNO: HULETT his marke
    20th 7br: 1658. This Assignemt. was acknowledged in Court by the sd. FRANCIS
ROBERTS & recorded wth: the Pattent

p.   WILLIAM BEDLAM aged 35 yeares or thereabouts sworne and examined sayth
11   that being in the Sloope of Coll: JNO: MOTTROMs deced., & haveing full power
          from ye Admr. of the sd. Estate to agree for Fraight in the sd. Sloope & the sd.
WM. BEDLAM agreed wth: Mr. HUGH LEE for a turne of Cattle from KENT in MARYLAND
to CHICACOAN & to have for my hire of the Sloope & paines one able good sufficient
cowe bigg wth: Calfe, or one by her side, or otherwise Six hundred pounds of tobco: &
caske; to the best of my knowledge wch: was to be delivered or paid after ( ) p:formed
wch: was truly p:formed and as yett noe satisfaction made by the sd. LEE to my knowledge & further sayeth not
  Sworne before us PETER KNIGHT,   WILLIAM BEDLAM
          JAMES HAWLEY
  20th 7br: 1658 This Dept. was recorded

p.   BE IT KNOWNE unto all men by these pr:sents that Lt. Coll. HENRY FLEETE doth
11   constitute & appoint my Friend, JOHN STEVENS, to be my lawfull Attorney to aske
          and demand of any p:son or p:sons whatsoever that are indebted unto mee
eyther by Bills or Accompts or in any other obligation whatsoever wth:in the County of
Northumbld., Likewise I doe give power to my sd. Attorney to implead or discharge or
make any agreemt. wth: any p:son or p:sons whatsoever wth:in the said County as well
as if I my selfe were then & there p:sent; In Witness my hand this 22th of September
1657

Teste ye marke of WM: CLAPHAM   HENRY FLEETE
        THO: MANSOY
    20th 7br: 1658. This Lre, of Attor: was recorded

p.   THIS BILL Bindeth mee WM. DAVISON my heires Exrs. and ( ) cause to be paid
11   unto EDWARD HENLY his heires ( ) or assignes the sum of Two thousand ( )
            good tob: cleare of ground leaves with caske ( ) upon the Tenth of Octobr: next
for the payml. of the aforesd. sum of Two ( ) tob: with caske, I the sd. WM. DAVISON ( )
my crop or crops of Tobco. now ( ) whereof I have hereunto sett my hand ( )
September 1658
    ( ) in presence of DANIELL ROBERTS   ye marke of WM. DAVISON
    ( ) this Writeing was acknowledged in Court ( ) DAVISON & recorded

p.   ( ) about the age of Thirty yeares deposeth ( ) CLAY came to yor: Depont. be-
11   Xtmas: ( ) Depont. was stripeing Tobco. that hee had a ( ) from Mr. LEE or that
            hee could have it, your ( ) not which instly: & yor: Depont. told the sd. Mr. ( )
tobacco wch: hee was then stripping was towards ( ) satisfacon of that Bill & the sd. Mr.
CLAY came after wards ( ) upon two hogsds. of tobco: then struck & for ( ) yor: Depont.
knowes liked them for hee reced. them & marked them but not weighed them but a long
time afterwards the said Mr. CLAY came to yor: Depont. and left one of the hogsds. of
tobco: upon yor: Deponts. hands & desired yor: Depont. to dispose thereof & that hee
would forbeare yor: Depont. till the next yeare   SAMUELL NICOLLS
    20th 7br: 1658. Jurat in Cur & Record

p.   I RICE MADDOCKS of NOMINY, Chyrurgin, for my selfe & assignes doe hereby
11   assigne over unto MRS. ANNA COLE, the Wife of RICHARD COLE, of SALISBURY
            PARKE in the County of Northumberland, Mercht., by his owne consent an
IRISH Girle named MARY DOWRY about the age of seaven yeares for the terme of Fourteene yeares from the tenth day of Novembr: next: Witnes my hand this 30th day of
August one thousand six hundred Fifty eight
Witnessed by us
        sign   JOHANIS WILLSON   RICE MADDOCKE
        sign   THOMAS ARPIN
    I RICHARD COLE am content with this Guift of the Girle to my Wife, ANNA COLE, to her
her heires & assignes for ever the day & yeare abovesd. p. RICHARD COLE
    20th 7br: 1658. This ( ) from RICE MADDOCKE of MARY DOWRY to MRS. ANNA COLE was
acknowledged in Court by the said MADDOCKE as also ( )tentmt. therewth: was acknowledged in Court by the abovesd. RICHARD COLE & are recorded

p.   I MARTINE COLE & ALICE COLE doth freely give unto MARY LAMKIN, Daughter
11   of THOMAS LAMBKIN one Cow Calfe marked &c. coloured as followeth; with a
            slitt downe the right eare & cropt on the left eare with a slitt in the crop alsoe;
wee give unto the said MARY the increase of the Cow Calfe ( ) male & also wee have
delivered the Calfe unto THO( ) the Father of MARY LAMKIN, & if in case ( ) out of this
County to live that the sd. ( ) Calfe with her increase both male & female ( ) honest
man or otherwaies to put in good ( ) that the Calfe & her increase maynot be ( ) further wee MARTINE COLE & ALICE COLE ( ) this is our good free & lawfull Guift ( ) day of
Septembr: 1658
Witness the marke of NI(   )   the marke of MARTINE COLE
                                             the marke of ALICE COLE
    20th 7br: 1658 This Deed of Guift ( ) by the sd. MARTINE COLE & recorded

p.   BYRAM, BENNETT, HOPPER & HULETT, their declaracon concern Mr. RICHARD
11   COLE. Wee underscribed doe by ( ) required DAVID LYNDSEY ( )ning some
        differa( ) sd. DAVID LINDSAY ( ) any Councell or ( ) sd. Mr. COLE but ( )
publiquely speke ( )   sig: ABRA: BYRAM
                                                   ( ) HULETT

   21 7br: 1658 ( )

p.   THO: PHILPOTTs Sale of a Cowe to RICH: HOLDEN
11   To all &c. to whome &c. ( ) PHILPOTT hath in ( ) hath bargained sold ( ) or to
        his assignes ( ) followeth, vizt., cropt on the left eare & a peice ( ) cut of from
the right eare with ( ) wh( ) udder & a white tip of the tayle with her increase, I the
said THOMAS PHILPOTT doth ( ) ye molestacon or incumbrance of mee my heires Exrs.
or any p:son or p:sons whatsoever that shall claime title or interest unto the sd. Cowe or
of her increase, As Witnes my hand this 21th day of 7br: 1658
Test DANIELL ROBERTS,   THOMAS PHILLPOT
     WILKES MAUNDER
   I RICHARD HOLDEN doth assigne all my right & title of this in mentioned Bill of Sale
unto FRANCES ROBERTS, Daughter of EDWARD ROBERTS, and EDWARD ROBERTS JUNIOR
vth: the increase of the cowe both male & female; As Witnes my hand this 21th day of
7br· 1658
Test THOMAS PHILPOTT,   the marke of RICHARD HOLDEN
     WILKES MAUNDER
   21th 7br: 1658 This Assignemt. was rcorded wth: the Bill of Sale

p.   JAMES NEPPERS of the Parrish of WICOCOMOCO in the County of Northumber-
12   land & Colony of Virginia doth give for his marke of Cattle & hoggs Vizt. a
        swallowe forke in the right eare with the tip of the sd. eare taken of and a
flower de luce on the left eare
   12th Octobr: 1658. This Marke was recorded

p.   KNOWE ALL MEN by these pr:sents that I JOHN LORD of HARFORT in NEW ENG-
12   LAND, Mercht., the Lawfull Attorney of my Brother, RICHARD LORD, and of MRS.
        ALICE ( ) ALCOTT of the same place aforesd., doe by these pr:sents make & or-
daine my well beloved Friend ( ) WM. THOMAS my lawfull Attorney in all cases concerning any debts due tome or my aforesd. Brother or Mrs. ( ) ALCOTT in Virginia
giveing and granting to my sd. Attorney my full power & authority as any Attorney can
have; Witnes my hand this 24th Decembr: 165( )
Witnes WM: PRESLY   JOHN LORD
       ISAAC ALLERTON JUNIOR
   12th Octobr: 1658 The Lre. of Attor. was recorded

p.   DAVID SPILLER his Last Will and Testament
12   IN THE NAME OF GOD Ame. I DAVID SPILLER being weake in body yett in p:fect
        memory, I bequeath my body to the Earth & my Soule to God that gave it, I doe
make my Last Will & Testamt. as followeth: As for my worldly goods I bestowe as followeth:
   Imps. I give my whole Estate to be equally devided betweene my Sonnes, JNO: SWAN-
SON, RICHARD DENNIS, PASCO DENNIS, JNO: DENNIS, excepting one Cowe called Florence
wch: I alsoe give to my youngest Sonne, JNO: DENNIS;
   Item; I give unto SUSANNA HOLLING, my Brothers Childe, the ( ) Cowe Calfe which is

calved of any of the Cowes which ( ) to my Estate; this her saith & noemore as concer( )
his Estate:

Item. I desire that my Debts be paid (to witt), ( ) one hogsd. of tobco:, 5 empty caskes
due ( ) his debt; ( ) tobco. to JAMES MAGREGORY; ( ) one gallon of Vinegar & a quart
( ) 107 lbs. tobco;
( ) THOS: GALIN,   ye marke of DAVID SPILLER
     JOHN TAYLOR ye marke
( ) Will was proved in Cort: by the oathes ( ) & ANDREW POULTER

p.   (Most of this entry is missing)   by NATHANIELL HOLLING -465 lb..
12   Inventory (the last three items) SIMON ( ) his halfe part is to be paid in Corne,
     248 lbs. 3 empty hoggsds.
  21 8br: 1658. This was recorded

p.   Copy of HENRY BRADLEYs Will   (Copia)
12   IN THE NAME OF GOD Ame. I HENRY BRADLEY being sick in body but of p:fect
     memory thanks be to God, knoweing the certainty of death & frailty of mans
Estate here upon Earth, doe make this my last Will & Testamt. in manner following; I
bequeath my Soule into the hands that gave it, and my Body to the Earth from whence it
came;

I doe here order & ordaine my welbeloved Wife, FRAUNCES BRADLEY my full Executrix
of all goods chattells lands & whatsoever else during the time of her Widdowhood and
after it shall please God shee shall marry agine, that wch: belongs to the Children to be
sett forth & improv( ) profitt of my said Children in equal proport( ) full power and
authority unto my sd. Executrix to ( ) full meanes for the enjoymt. of the sd. Estate; And
( ) heareby declare this to be my last Will & Testament utterly ( )ring all other Wills;
Witnes my hand this ( ) of Aprill 1650
Witness EDWARD DEINES,   HENRY ⊥ BRADLY
     NICHOLAS /V CHURCH   his marke
     THO: MADESTONE
In Vera Copia Test Will. 21th 8br: 1658. This Copy was recorded

p.   JOHN & ANN TAYLOR their Attestacon concerning BRADLYs Children
12   This is to certifie you that Mrs. B( ) did desire that her Sonne, JOHN ( ) tuicon
     of the two little b( ) owne Brother to them & desired ( ) and he carefull over
them & what ( ) you take it into consider( ) his Mother desired him ( ) their Father in
Law ( ) Oath   JOHN TAYLOR
  22th 8br. 1658 This ( )

p.   Mr. COLCLOUGHs Guift of Heyfer to URSULA RICHARDSON
12   KNOWE ALL MEN ( ) for diverse considera( ) enfeoffee & confirme unto ( )
     RICHARDSON one Heyfer (.) being cropt on the ( ) left haveing a who( ); To
have & to hold the sd. Heyfer & all her fut( ) forsoever, excepting one ( ) SIM( ) the
male incr( ) dureing the minority of ( ); Witness my hand ye 29th day of July 165( ).
in pr:sence of ISAAC FOXECROFT   ( ) COLCLOUGH
     JAMES AWSTEN
  21 8br. 1658. This Deed of Guift was acknowledged in Court by the sd. GEO: COLCLOUGH &
recorded

p.   KNOWE ALL MEN by these prsents that THOMAS ROE of CHICACOAN Parish in
12   Northumberland County doth give for his marke of cattle and hoggs, vizt., cropt
        & slitt in the left eare & a hole in the right eare
20th 9br. 1658. This marke was recorded

p.   RICHARD ILANDs Assignmt. of a Patt: to GEO: MARKES and THOMAS SWAINE
13   The Pattent is recorded in the other Books of Records in folio 79; May 1656.
        I RICHARD ILAND doe assigne over all my right title and interest of this Pattent
of Land unto GEORGE MARKES and THOMAS SWAINE or their assignes; As Witnes my
hand this 21th 7br: 1658
Witnes HENRY CLARKE, JOHN SHAW   Sig. RI: ILAND
  21th 7br. 1658. This Assignemt. was acknowledged in Court by the sd. RICHARD ILAND
& is recorded

p.   GEO: MARKES & THOMAS SWAINE their Assignemt. of a Patt: to SIMON RICHARD-
13   SON.   Wee GEORGE MARKES & THOMAS SWAINE doe assigne over unto SIMON
        RICHARDSON his heires Exrs. & assignes all our right & title of ( ) & Land there-
in menconed for ever; Witnes ( ) this 13th of 9br: 1658
Test RI: ( )   GEO: MARKES
        SIMON COX his marke   THO: SWAINE his marke
  20th 9br: 1658. This Assignemt. was acknowledged in Court by the said THOMAS
SWAINE & RICHARD FLYNT, Attorney of the sd. GEORGE MARKES, & is recorded
  The Pattent for this Land is recorded in the other Books of Records in folio 7; originally granted to THOMAS ( )AYLES & THOMAS SHEAPARD

KNOWE ALL MEN by these prsents that I GEORGE MARKES doe constitute & appoint
RICHARD FLYNT my true & lawfull Attorney for mee & in my name to acknowledge all
my right & title of a Pattent unto SIMON RICHARDSON as relacon being had to the Endorsemt. on the back side thereof bearing date with these prsents; the Land lying &
being in Northumberland County upon PATOMACK RIVER, Eastward from CUPIDS
CREEKE containing 300 acres by the sd. Patt. originally granted to THOMAS HAYLES &
THO: SHEPPARD ( ) one halfe thereof being assigned to mee & THO: SWAINE from
RICHARD ILAND, And whatsoever my said Attorney shall lawfully doe in the acknowledgemt. of the prmisses in Northumberland County Court I doe hereby ratify as if I
were prsent & did the same; Witnes my hand this 13th of 9br: 1658
        ( )NRY CARTWRIGHT.   GEO: MARKES
( ) This Lre. of Attorney was recorded

p.   ( ) that I GEORGE COLCLOUGH of WICOCOMOCOE ( ) of Northumberland in Vir-
13   ginia Gent., ( ) my Exrs. Admrs. &c. to deliver unto Mr. ( ) Exrs. Admrs. &c. one
        good sufficient ( ) exceeding the age of seaven yeares ( ) first day of March
next in LITTLE ( ) for the sole use & proper benefitt as ( ) vizt., the sd. Mare & all her
future ( ) the sd. MORRIS during his naturall life and ( ) case ( ) to the sole use & Benifitt
lof JANE ( )ter of: the sd. Mr. NICHOLAS MORRIS & nowe ( ) JOHN HAYNIE of the sd.
Parrish & County ( ) excepting the first Mare foale which shall fall from the sd. Mare
and her increase to be for the onely use & behoofe of the sd. JANE HAYNIE & her heires
for ever; Witnes my hand this 20th of 9br: 1658
Signed & delivered in presence of us
        PETER ASHTON, RI: FLYNT   GEO: COLCLOUGH
  20th 9br: 1658 This Writeing was recorded

p.   THOMAS BREWER his Patt: for Land
13   To all &c., Whereas &c., Now know yee that I the said EDWARD DIGGES Esqr. &c.
       give & grant unto THOMAS BREWER One thousand acres of land scituated in
Northumberland County upon the North side of DENNIS his CREEKE, Begining at a
marked Pine tree standing in the mouth & West side of a Branch of the sd. CREEKE
deviding this Land & the Land of Mr. RICHARD BUDD, & extending along the sd. Branch
& Swamp along the Land of Mr. BUDD three hundred & twenty poles to a marked Oake
standing on North side of a Valley & from thence West four hundred poles to another
marked Oake to the West side of a Valley, South upon a Branch ( ) Swamp upon the head
of the sd. Creeke, extendinging along the sd. Creeke to the place where it began; the sd.
Land being due unto him the said THOMAS BREWER by & for transportation of Twenty
p:sons into this Collony; whose names are on the Records menconed under this Pattent;
Dated the 1th of March 1656
                   EDWARD DIGGES   W. CLAIBORNE, Secr.
        THOS: BREWERs Sale of 400 acres of Land to JENKIN PRICE & JNO: MOUTON
KNOWE ALL MEN by these pr:sents that I THOMAS BREWER have for my selfe my heires
Exrs, Admrs. &c. hath for a valluable consideracon to mee in hand satisfied, sold & sett
over and due by these pr:sents sell & set over unto JENKIN PRICE & JOHN MOUTON & their
heires ( ) Pattent ( ) being that pt. wch: is left ( ) HOPPER ( ) & JOHN HOPPER, together with all ( ) & built with all other ( ) granted unto mee by the ( ) of the pr:misses I
doe bind ( ) the sd. Land wth: every pt. ( ) sold & transferred ( ) that shall thereto
make ( ) manner as Law may ( ) to my hand this 17th ( )
In presence of us JOHN ( )   THOMAS BREWER
  20th 9br: 1658. T( ) by the sd. THOMAS BREWER

p.   RICHARD RICE his Pattent
13   To all &c. Whereas &c., ( ) Esqr. &c., give & grant ( ) of land scituate ( ) on the
       Southwest ( ) Easterly upon the ( ) North Westerly upon ( ) DAMERON & a
Maine ( ) Southeasterly upon the ( ) the lands of Mr. THOMAS BROO( ) first menconed
lands three hundred & ( ) the Maine Swamp for length into the Woods, ( ) being due
unto him the sd. RICHARD RICE by & for the transportacon of Eight p:sons into this
Collony whose names are in ye Records menconced under this Pattent &c., Dated the ( )
January 1656
                   EDWARD DIGGES   W. CLAIBORNE, Secr.
BE IT KNOWNE unto all men by these pr:sents that I RICHARD RICE with the consent of
my Wife assigne & sett over all my right title & interest of this Pattent with all priviledges of ye Land herein menconed to THOMAS HARDING & JAMES JOHNSON their heires
& assignes for ever; Witnes our hands the 2th of Novembr: 1658
Witnes THOMAS BROUGHTON,   RICHARD RICE his marke
       ROBERT KEMPE   ANNE RICE her marke
  22d. 9br. this Assignemt. was acknowledged in Court by the sd. RICHD: RICE unto the sd.
THOMAS HARDING & JAMES JOHNSON and is recorded with the Pattent

p.   KNOWE ALL MEN by these pr:sents that I RICHD: GIBLE for a valuable consider-
14   acon reced. have bargained & sett over & do by these pr:sents sell & sett forth
       from me my heires Exrs. & Admrs. unto RICHARD SMYTH his heires Exrs. or
assignes a moyety or small pr:cell of land amounting unto Thirty acres be it more or
lesse, Begining at a markt. tree in the Valley belowe the Springs standing in the midle
of the first Branch betweene the sd. GIBLEs House & Mr. WM. NUTTs & thence according as ye trees are marked unto the Land formerly sold by the sd. GIBLE unto ROGER

WAR( ) SMYTH, haveing a sufficient out lett for ( ) of the sd. GIBLE tohave free egress
& ( ) out lett is to be adjoyneing unto the sd. ROGE( ) Land, & from thence bounding
onthe Land of GE( ) & Mr. WM. NUTT including the Land that he ( ) properly unto the
sd. GIBLE outward in ye Woods from the first marked trees, And I the sd. GIBLE doe
warrt. ye sd. Land wth: all priviledges thereunto belonging unto the sd. SMYTH his
heires & assignes for ever from any molestacon or trouble that may or shall arise by or
from any pson whatsoever & doe bind my selfe to acknowledge this sale in the next
County Court, As Witnes my hand this ( )6th of March Ano: 1657
Witnes: WM. THOMAS   Sig: RICH: GIBLE
       JOSEPH FEILDINGE
( ) 1658. This Sale of Land was acknowledged in Court by RICHARD GIBLE & recorded

p.   ( ) by these prsents that I DANIELL HOLLAND doe ( ) my heires Exrs. Admrs. or
14   assignes sett lett & ( ) unto RALPH KEY one prcell of land for one ( ) yeares, the
        bounds thereof as followeth; from a ( ) CREEKE Northerly till it come to a corner
( ) from the corner marked tree due East ( ) the sd. Land already marked out & if ( )
shall live longer, to enjoy it for his life ( ) quietly without any molestacon or ( )
DANIELL HOLLAND or by his Procuremt. wth: all ( ) belonging to the sd. Land; ( ) this
15th day of November 1658
Witnes JOHN HULL   DANIELL HOLLAND his marke
       ( )GHAM
( ) Writeing was acknowledged in ( ) DANIELL HOLLAND & recorded

p.   ( ) all men by these prsents that I JOHN ( ) instituted & made & doe hereby
14   ( ) make Mr. JNO: HAYNIE of WICOCOMOCO in ( ) true & lawfull Attorney for mee
        and ( ) receive recover arest & take all such ( ) are to mee due & oweing within
ye County of Northumberland in Virginia by any pson or psons granting unto my sd.
Attorney my full power to sue for & receive and upon paymt. to acquitt & discharge any
pson or psons to mee indebted; & to dispose of my goods as it is to me belonging within
the County of Northumberland in as full & ample manner as if I my selfe were prsent;
As Witnes my hand & seal the 21th of June Ano: 1658
Test EDWARD COLTON,   JOHN HANSFORD ye Seale
       GER: DODSON
20th 9br: 1658. This Lre of Attorney was recorded

p.   I MICH: BROOKE doe testifie that I did drawe a discharge or a release some nine
14   yeares since for WILLIAM WILDEY for some certaine parcell of Bills & Writeings
        which was left in the hands of the sd. WM. WILDEY by CORBELL PIDWELL and to
the best of my knowledge am able to depose the same, As Witnes my hand this 26th of
March 1658
Witnes: WM: THOMAS   MICH: BROOKE
20 9br: 1658   This Attestacon was recorded

p.   ROGER WALTERS Assignemt. of Land to MATHEW WILCOCKES
14   I ROGER WALTERS for a valuable consideracon to mee in hand payd ( ) WILL-
        COCKES doe assigne & sett over unto the sd. M( ) his Exrs. Admrs. or assignes
from mee my heires ( ) for ever; all my right title and interest of this ( ) Sale & the
Land therein menconed; Witnes ( ) of 9br: 1658
Witnes: RICH. ( )   Sig   ROGER WALTERS
The Bill of Sale is recorded in the other Booke of Records in folio 140, ye ( ) of May
1658, granted from & by RICHARD GIBLE to the sd. ROGER WALTERS

p. I JOHN WALKER for a valuable consideracon doe give unto JARNINGHAM
14 LAMPKIN, Daughter of ( ) LAMPKIN, one Cowe Calfe being under keeld & ( )
    crop on the right eare & slitt down ( ) increase the male excepted ( ) Father till
shee be married ( ) 8th of October 1658
 20th 9br: 1658. This Deed of Guift ( ) by HENRY CLARKE, Attorne( )
 JNO: WALKER's Lre. of Attor: to HEN: CLARKE. I JOHN WALKER doe authorize ( ) this
Deed of Guift in my ( ) LAMPKIN as witnes my ( )
Witnes: Sig: FRAN: ( )   JOHN WALKER
20th 9br: 1658. Th( )

p. ANN GIBLEs Acknowledgemt. of Land to DAN: HOLLAND
14 This shall engage ( ) HOLLAND the Land ( ) GIBLE the next Court ( ) 1658
    Witnes JOHN HUDNALL   the marke of ( )
 22th 9br. 1658. ( ) the sd. ANNE GIBLE ( )

p. ANNE GIBLEs Assignemt. of Land to WM. CORNISH
14 I ANNE GIBLE doe ( ) & interrest of 400 acres of Land ( ) and unto WM. CORNISH
    or his assignes ( ) this ( ) of 9br. 1658
 23 9br. This Assignemt. was acknowledged in Court by the sd. ANNE GIBLE & is recorded

p. JOHN MOTTROM sworne May ( ) 1658 saith Vizt. That about September last this
14 Depont. came to the House of MARTINE COLE & the sd. COLE his Wife told him this
    Depont. that THOMAS PRYER of RAPAHANOCK had him at worke with the sd. COLE
but howe many dayes this Depont. knowes not, and for his Labour the sd. MARTINE COLE
sett the sd. PRYER to MARY LAND thus farr this Depont. deposeth & further saith not
Witnes his hand signed & supro:
Sworne before me WM. PRESLY   JOHN MOTTERAM
 23 9br: 1658. This Depo: was recorded

p. The Deposition of THOMAS SWAINE aged 21 yeares or thereabouts taken this
15 28th of 9br: 1658. This Depont. saith that MARTINE COLE transported one THOMAS
    PRYER in his Boate from YEOCOMOCO to PINEY POINT in MARY LAND (being about
the moneth of July in the yeare 1657) & there left the sd. PRYER & further this Depont.
saith not   Sig: THOMAS SWAINE
 23d. 9br: 1658 Jurat in Cur et Record

p. MR BROUGHTONs Sale of Land to SAMLL. MAN & ROBT. KEMPE
15 TO ALL TO WHOME these presents shall come, THO: BROUGHTON of MATTAPONY in
    the County of Northumberland, Mercht., send Greeting. Now Know yee that I
the sd. THO: BROUGHTON for & in the consideracon of the sum of Five thousand Five
hundred pounds of tobco: & caske to mee in hand paid have sold & doe sell unto SAMLL.
MAN & ROBT. KEMPE all that p:cell of land scituate & being in the County aforesd.
bounding upon the Land of ROBT. BRADSHAWE, Eastward upon the Creeke called BROAD
CREEKE, Northward upon a certaine p:cell of Land heretofore in the tenure of Mr. WM.
BACON, Westward containeing by estimacon Foure hundred twenty one acres of land
which sd. Land is now in ye possession of the sd. THOMAS BROUGHTON; To have & to hold
the said Land with all its rights & priviledges to them the sd. SAMLL. MAN & ROBT.
KEMPE their heires & assignes for ever; And the said THOMAS BROUGHTON doth by these
pr:sents for him his heires & every of them covenant & agree with the sd. SAMLL. MAN
& ROBT: KEMPE their heires & assignes & every of them to warrant & keepe harmlesse

the sd. Land from incumbrance or molestacon whatsoever and doth covenant to acknowledge this Deed of Sale in Northumberland County Court; In Witnes I have hereunto sett my hand and seale this ( ) day of Novembr: 1658
Witnes: WILLIAM WILLDEY   THO: BROUGHTON, ye Seale
  ( ) Sale of Land was acknowledged in Court by THOMAS BROUGHTON & is recorded

p.   ( ) these pr:sents that I WILLIAM HOPKINS ( ) unto ANNE HENLEY, Daughter of
15   EDWARD HENLEY ( ) Cowe Calfe about three quarters of a ( ) the right eare &
          one slitt in the crop ( ) under keeled on the left eare; To have & to hold the sd.
Calfe & her increase for ever & if ( ) doth dye before shee is married ( ) shall belong to
her Sister, SUSAN ( ) her increase & to dispose of them how ( ). The said WM. HOPKINS
doth warrant this ( ) from all p:sons soever, As Witnes my hand this 3th of November
1758
Testes   SIMON RICHARDSON,   WM. HOPKINS, ye marke of
         JOS: HORSLEY
  23d. 9br: 1658. This Deed of Guift was acknowledged in Court by the sd. WM. HOPKINS &
is recorded

p.   There is due to THOMAS ORLEY from Lt. Coll. HENRY FLEETE by agreemt., of
15   Mr. STEPHENS, his Attorney, the full sume of 800 lbs. tobco. & caske for a run-
          away Servant & its endorsed on the back side of his Covenant
  23 die 9br: 1658   Jurat in Cur et Recor:

p.   IN THE NAME OF GOD Amen. I THOMAS HALES being dangerous sick & weake
15   but in p:fect sence & memory, thanks be to almighty God, doe bequeath my
          Soule to God and my Body to the Mother Earth from whence it came; this being
the Last Will & Testamt., desire of the Worpll. Comrs. that my whole Estate may be sold at
an Out Cry, that the Tobacco to pay my Debts & then the remainder I freely bequeath to
my loveing Wife, ANNE HALES, moreover, I desire that I may have a Christian buriall
out of my Estate; Witnes my hand this 3d. of Septembr: 1658
Witnes: JOHN WALKER,   .   the marke of THOMAS HALES
        WILLIAM PIGGOTT
  23 9br: 1658. This Will was proved in Court by the oaths of WM. THOMAS & W( ) the
Will recorded

p.   An Inventory of THOMAS HALES Estate. In Tobco:
15   Imprs. One cowe ( ) two young steares & a heyfer, six hoggs, one bed, boulster,
          one rugg & a blankett, three kettles and a skillett, all the old iron, two chests,
one gun, one shott bagg, two potts & the appurtenances; one drippin pan, one frying
pan, one hide, halfe a dozen spoones & a chamber pott, seaven boles, three sifters, three
payles, a jugg, all his clothing, three old hogsds., five Turkies, the crop of Tobacco, 2
hoes, 5 shotes, 2 canvas baggs, Poultrey, 1 share of Cor( ), 1 feather bolster ( )
  23 9br: 1658. T( )

p.   Mr. JNO: TEMPLE his Last Will & Testamt.
15   IN THE NAME OF ( ) in body but of ( ) same doe make my ( ) day of October
          16( ) the earth; Imprimis I doe give ( ) the Earth from whe( ) Item I doe give
( ) all my Estate both ( ) chattles Bills, Bonds Lands & ( ) her and her heires forever
  Item, I doe constitute ( ) afsd. Wife my sole Executrix of this my last Will & Testamt. In
Witness thereof I have hereunto sett my hand and seale the day & yeare above written

Signed Sealed & published in ye presence of
    GEORGE NORSWORTHY,   JOHN TEMPLE ye Seale
    THO: NORSWORTHY
    JA: GAYLARD, ROBT: SELFE his marke
  24th 9br: 1658. This Will was proved in Court by the Oathes of Mr. JAMES GAYLARD &
ROBT: SELFE to be the Last Will & Testament of the sd. JOHN TEMPLE and execucon thereof committed to the sd. ANNE TEMPLE, and the Will is recorded

p.   KNOWE ALL MEN by these prsents that I HENRY WATTS with the Consent of my
16   Wife, ELIZABETH, for diverse good consideracons mee thereunto moveing have
      freely & absolutely aliened & given & bythese prsents doe alien transferr &
give to RICHARD SPAN one p:cell of Land by estimacon fourty acres (more or lesse)
scituate in LITTLE WICOCOMOCO in the County of Northumberland, bounding on a
Branch & Swampe by marked trees to a Gum, thence along a Glade, thence on the Land
of THO: DORRELL, finally on the Land of RICHD. SPAN aforesd., To have & to hold the sd.
Land wth: all priviledges thereto from me my heires & assignes to the sd. RICHD. SPAN
his heires & assignes for ever; without the let or molestacon of any psons whatsoever;
In Witnes whereof I HENRY WATTS with my Wife have sett our hands & seals this ( )5th
of January 1658
Witnes: THO: ( );   HENRY WATTS ye Seale
    JOHN KNIGHT   ELIZABETH WATTS ye Seale, her marke
  20 January 1658. This ( ) was acknowledged in Court by the sd. HENRY WATTS and is
recorded

p.   KNOW ALL MEN by these pr:sents that I WM: CORNISH doe for my selfe my
16   heires for a valuable consideracon already reced., have bargained & sold, & doe
      by these pr:sents bargaine and sell unto ROBERT SMITH his heires Exrs. Admrs. &
assignes one black Cowe called by the name of Broad Hornes, cropt & slitt in the left
eare & under keeled on the right eare, and one yearling heyfer cropt & slitt in the
right eare & cutt over & under the left eare, and further bind my selfe my heires that
ye sd. SMITH shall peaceably & quietly enjoy the aforesd. with their whole increase
without any trouble of any psons whatsoever; to him and his heires for ever; As Witnes my hand this 20th of ( ) 1658
  Witnes JOHN HULL,   WM: CORNISH his marke
    ANDREW COCKERIN his marke
  ( ) January 1658. This Bill of Sale was acknowledged in Court by WM. CORNISH unto
ROBT. SMITH & is recorded

p.   ( ) by these pr:sents that I JACOB CONTANCEAN ( ) Sonne JACOB CONTACEAN &
16   to my Sonne ( ) three Cowes a peice, the one called Black ( ) & slitt on the left
     eare, another ( ) on both eares, one Calfe cropt on ( ) in the right eare; ( )
WMs. one Cowe named White Foote cropt ( ) browne heyfer cropt on both eares; one
Cowe Calfe called Starr ( ) a hole in the left eare; This I doe ( ) from any psons what-
soever ( ) & WILLIAM the sd. Cattle within ( ) female & their male for the House; As
Witnes my hand this 20th of January 1658.
Testes ( ); ROBERT SECH   SARAH CONTANCEAN
                     JACOB CONTANCEAN
  ( ) shall none have till they come in age ( ) have all the Cattle in possession, I ( )
CONTACEAN, the Father, order soe to be enrolled in the Court Booke
  20th January 1658. This Deed of Guift was recorded

p.   KNOWE ALL MEN by these pr:sents that I JACOB CONTANCEAN JUNIOR doth give
16   for his marke of Cattle & hoggs, Vizt., crop on both eares & a hole in the right
    eare
20th January 1658 This marke was recorded
     KNOWE ALL MEN by these pr:sents that I WM. CONTANCEAN, ye Sonne of JACOB
CONTANCEAN SENIOR, doth give for his marke of Cattle & hoggs vizt., cropt in both eares
and a hole in the left eare
   20th January 1658 This marke was recorded

p.   KNOWE ALL MEN by these pr:sents that I GEORGE DAY have nominated & ap-
16   pointed FRANCIS CLAY my true & lawfull Attorney for mee & in my name to
    answere the suite of Capt. RICHARD COLE in Northumberland County Court,
ratifying & confirming what my sd. Attorney shall doe in the p:misses; Witnes my hand
15th January Ano: 1658
Witnes: JAS: GAYLARD, ANN TEMPLE   GEORGE DAY
   20th January 1658 This Lre. of Attor: was recorded

p.   I doe hereby impower & invest RICHARD FLYNT wth: as full power to answere
16   upon the suite of Capt. RICHARD COLE agt. GEORGE DAY as is wth:in expressed to
    ( ) shall doe therein this shall bind mee to confirme. Witnes ( ) this 19th day of
January 1658
Witnes: ( ); ISAAC ( )   FRANCIS CLAY
    GEO: HALE his marke
   20th January 1658; This Lre. of Attor: was recorded

p.   KNOWE ALL MEN by these pr:sents that I FRANCIS CLAY have nominated & ap-
16   pointed RICHARD FLYNT my true & lawfull Attorney to doe act & p:sent my
    business for or concerning mee at the next County Court held for Northumber-
land and what my sd. Attorney shall act and doe therein I shall & will allow of as if I
were p:sonally p:sent; & did the same; Witnes my hand this 19th day of January 1658
Witnes. ISAAC FOXCROFT;   FRANCIS CLAY
    GEO: HALE his marke
   20th January 1658. This Lre. of Attorney was recorded

p.   Mr. FLYNT. I pray doe mee that favour ( ) in any cause or causes whatsoever
16   ( ) my behalfe I will ratify & ( ) pr:sent & remaine yors: to ( )
    Jan: 20, 1658   ( ) WRIGHT
  20 January 1658. This Lre. of Attor: was recorded

p.   JNO: BENNETTs Lre. of Attor: to his Wife
16   KNOWE ALL MEN by these pr:sents ( ) ordayne & ( ) made my lo: Wife ( ) for &
    in my name ( ) upon the Estate of ( ) deceast nearest of eyther (this my Attor-
ney ( ) firmly as I my selfe ( ) January 16( )
In p:sence of R( ); GEO: DURANT   JNO: BENNETT
   20th January 1658. This Lre. of Attor: was recorded

p.   KNOWE ALL MEN by these pr:sents ( ) JAMES CLAUGHTON of MATTAPONY in
16   Northumberland County doe ( ) marke of Cattle & hoggs Vizt., Cropt on the
    right eare a hole in the same eare, and the left eare underkeeld;
  2d. February 1658. This marke was recorded

p.   KNOWE ALL MEN by these pr:sents that JOHN AIRES of YEOCOCOCO in Northum-
16   berland County doth give for his marke of Cattle and Hoggs, vizt., cropt on the
      right eare & slitt on the left eare
  3d. February 1658   This marke was recorded

p.   TO ALL TO WHOME these pr:sents shall come, I ROBT. NEWMAN of the County of
17   Northumberland send Greeting in our Lord God everlasting; Knowe yee that I
      the sd. ROBT. NEWMAN for diverse good & valuable consideracons to me already
satisfied & paid & wherewith I hold my selfe amplie & fully contented, have bargained
sold & made sale of and doe by these pr:sents sell of from mee my heires Exr. Admrs. &
assignes unto ROBT. SMYTH of the aforesd. County & to his heires forever all that tract &
Neck of Land lying agt. ye Land ( ) Begining at a point which ( ) comonly is called ( )
PLACE agt. the LANDING PLACE of ye sd. JNO: HULL extending Westerly into the Woods
( ) unto the ( ) Branch wch: runneth into a Creeke ( ) that devideth ( ) from the Land
of THOMAS HAYLES and THOMAS ( ) & from the head of the sd. Branch extending
Southerly upon a line of marked trees unto a small Branch wch: runneth into CHO-
TANCK CREEKE & down the sd. Branch Easterly into the sd. CHOTANCK then downe the sd.
Creeke Northeasterly into the point or LANDING PLACE where it first began; wch: sd.
tract of land being in estimacon Fifty acres or thereabouts be it more or lesse, together
with all appurtenances and hereditaments thereon or thereunto belonging. I the sd.
ROBT. NEWMAN doe for my selfe my heires sell & make sale of unto the sd. ROBT. SMYTH
& to his heires & assignes forever; to use as his or their own ppr: goods & Estate; further
grnt sd. ROBT: SMYTH & his assignes all immunities of regresse & egresse for any his or
their stocks or flocks upon the sd. Fifty acres ( ) that as freely as ever I might have
done ( ) Grand Pattent; And I the sd. ROBT. NEWMAN my heires unto the sd. ROBT.
SMYTH his heires agt. any p:sons that make any claime ( ) lawfully demanded satisfie &
pay ( ) for theholding of the sd. Fifty acres ( ), I the said ROBERT NEWMAN have hereunto sett my hand and seale the ( ) 1652

                         Signum   ROBERT NEWMAN ye Seale
                                      ELIZ: NEWMAN Sig.
( ), This Sale of Land from ROBT. NEWMAN to ROBT: SMYTH was acknowledged in Court
by Mr. WM: ( ) of the Last Will & Testamt. of the said ( ) for soe farr forth as the sd. Mr.
PRESLY hath ( ) thereunto; And the sd. Sale is recorded March the 21th 1658

      I ROBT. SMITH doe for my selfe my heires & assignes assigne over all my right
title & interest of this Writeing unto WILLIAM CORNISH his heires Exrs. & assignes as
witnes my hand this 20th day of January 1658
Witnes: JOHN HULL,   ROBERT SMITH
      ANDREW CORBERILL his marke
20th January 1658. This Assignemt. was acknowledged in Cort: by ROBT. SMITH unto
WM. CORNISH and is recorded March the 21st 1658.

      I WILL: CORNISH doe assigne over all my right title & interest of this Convey-
ance of Land unto JNO: RAVEN; And in case of the non payment of the tobco: for the sd.
Land, I the sd. WM. CORNISH to reenter the sd. Land againe; As Witnes my hand this 21th
of March 1658
Witnes: HENRY CLARKE   WM; W CORNISH
  21 Maii 1658. This Assignemt. was acknowledged in Court by the sd. WM. CORNISH unto
JNO: RAVEN and is recorded
The Conveyance of this Land is recorded in the present Leafe being originally granted
from ROBT. NEWMAN to ROBT. SMITH and him assigned to WM. CORNISH

KNOWE ALL MEN by these pr:sents that I JOHN RAVEN doe bind my selfe my heires to pay or cause to be paid unto WILLIAM CORNISH or his assignes the full & just sume of One thousand pounds of good sound merchantable tobco: & caske at or before the 11th of November nxt ensueing the date hereof & JNO: RAVEN is likewise to pay for the recording of a Conveyance of Land wch: WM: CORNISH bought of ROBERT SMYTH & hath now sold it to mee; And for the better security of payment of the abovesd. Debt, I doe binde over unto WM. CORNISH the sd. Land & in case of non paymt. to be esteemed his ( ) Witnes my hand March the 7th 1658
Test WM. PRESLY, SAMUELL NIC( )   JOHN RAVEN
  21 March 1658. The Writeing was acknowledged in Court by the sd. JNO: RAVEN & is recorded

p.   Mr. HOPKINS his Sale of a Mare to THO: BREWER
17   KNOWE ALL MEN by these pr:sents ( ) CREEKE in the County of Northumberland
          ( ) valuable consideracon ( ) of DENNIS CREEKE in ( ) before the Enfea( ) my selfe to be ( ) bargained & sold & by ( ) white with a red patch ( ) in ( ); To have & to hold ( ) shall come of her ( ) assignes to his & ( ) sd THOMAS HOPKINS ( ) Mare unto the sd. ( ) agt. all people ( ) pr:sents; In Witnes ( )
Signed sealed and delivered in the presence of
          HENRY BENTLEY,   ye marke of THO: HOPKINS
          KNOWE ALL MEN by these pr:sents that I THOMAS BREWER of GREAT WICOCOMOCO in County of Northumberland assigne all my right title & interest I may have in this Bill of Sale for a Mare unto Mr. CHRISTOPHER GARLINGTON his heires & assignes for ever & I the sd. THOMAS BREWER doe warrant this Bill of Sail against all p:sons whatsoever; In Testimony whereof I sett my hand this 2d. of February Anno Dom: 1658
Witness JOHN TAYLER,   THOMAS T B BREWER ye marke of
          ye marke of FRAUNCES ALLCUTT
  21 March 1658 This Assignmt. was recorded wth: the Bill of Sale

p.   Wee JAMES MACGREGER and HUGH FOUCH doe assigne over all our right title &
18   interest of this Pattent of Land unto JOHN WATTS or his assignes; As Witnes our
          hands this 21th day of March 1658
Test ROBT. BURRELL,   JAMES T MAGREGER his marke
     RICHD. GIBBLE his marke   HUGH F FOUCH his marke
  21d Maii 1659 This Assignemt. was acknowledged in Court by the sd. JAMES MACGREGER & MIRIAN his Wife & HUGH FOUCH and is recorded
  The Pattent for this Land is recorded in the other Booke of Records in folio ( ) of 9br: 1655, there being but 350 acres du( ) Assignement & left unsold by THOMAS SAFFAL( ) Proprietor thereof & then by him sold to the sd. ( ) & FOUCH & recorded in folio 134 in the other Booke ( ) January 1657

p.   Lt. Coll. SAMUELL SMYTH aged 40 yeares or thereabouts sworne and examined
18   sayth; That on the ( ) day of January 1658, This Depont. being at the House of
          JAMES MAGREGER, at night, Capt. RICHD. COLE being there in Bed, some words passed betweene the said COLE and JAMES GAYLARD, the said GAYLARD goeing out of the roome did say unto the sd. COLE, "thou are a rogue, thy ( )ther is a whore & thou art a Bastard," And that on the morrowe morning he would bast his sides & further this Depont. sayth not
  22 die Jan: 1658 Jurat in Cur
  22 March 1658. This Depo: was recorded

p.   WM. WILLDEY aged 40 yeares or thereabouts sworne & examined saith the very
18   same verbatim with the sd. SAMLL. SMYTH & further this Depont. sayeth not
      ( ) This Depo. was recorded

p.   ( ) aged 28 yeares or thereabouts sworne & examined January the 22th 1658
18   ( ) in bed with Capt. RICHARD COLE at the House of ( )REGER, on the 21th of
      January 1658 at ( ) passed betweene the sd. COLE & JAMES ( ) ( )nt. did heare the
sd COLE say unto the sd. ( ) nitty Rogue but before that the ( ) unto the sd. COLE thou
are a Cuckold ( ), the sd. COLE offering to gett up, this ( ) to lye still but the sd. COLE
replyed ( ) pushed that hee had much a doe to ( ) this Depont. to prsuade the sd. GAY-
LARD ( ) come & wth: much difficulty of per( ) urgeing the sd. GAYLARD to be gone
( )oing out of doore alsoe said unto the ( ) Rogue & a Bastard & I will prove ( ) morning
I will bang thy Eares & make ( ) further this Depont sayth not
   ( )58. This Dep· was recorded
   ( )st. Deposicons were not sworne unto

p.   KNOWE ALL MEN by these prsents that RICHARD ILAND of the Parish of WICO-
18   COMOCO in the County of Northumberland doth give for his marke of Cattle &
      hoggs Vizt., cropt on both eares a peice cutt out over the right eare and a peice
cutt out under the left eare
   21th March 1658. This marke was recorded

p.   KNOWE ALL MEN by these prsents that I JEFFERY GOCKE of GREATE WICOCOMO-
19   COE in the County of Northumberland for & in consideracon of the love &
      affeccon I beare unto SAMUELL GOCKE, Sonne of my Brother, JOHN & KATHERINE
GOCKE. doth freely give & grant & by these prsents have given unto the sd. SAMUELL
GOCKE all my Lands being more or lesse lying & being on the Westerne side of a Creeke
commonly called by the name of CUPIDS CREEKE, with all the imunities & priviledges
that are specified in the Grant Pattent of mee the sd. JEFFERY GOCKE, lying & being on
the South side of GREAT WICOCOMOCO RIVER, All which I give to him the sd. SAMUELL
GOCKE & his heires or heire males for ever; hee the sd. SAMUELL GOCKE to run South
West from the head of the sd. Creeke to ( ) for the better pformance of lthis my
meaning & ( ) is the sd. JEFFERY GOCKE doe give all my right of the aforesd. NECK or
NECKs of Land to him the sd. SAMUELL GOCKE & his heires or heire males for ever; In
Witnes whereof ye before menconed prmisses I the said JEFFERY GOCKE hereunto set
my hand & seale this 21th day of March 1658
Sealed & Delivered in the presence of
      PETER KNIGHT.   JEFFERY GOCKE   the Seale
      HEN: WATTS
   21th March 1658 This Writeing was acknowledged in Court by the sd. JEFFERY GOCKE
and is recorded

p.   I doe hereby in the behalfe of Mr. JNO: HARTFORD (?) of YOREE County acquitt
19   & discharge Mr. WM: THOMAS ( ) a Bill of ( ) thousand lbs. of tobco. in caske &
      the ( ) of Pork; Witnes my hand the 3d. of Feb: 1658
Witnes PAUL BAYLIE,   JOHN HAYNIE
      Sig: THOMAS ( )
   21th March 1658 This Quit was recorded

p.   An Inventory of the Estate of THO: PRICKETT
19   An Inventory of all ye goods of THO: PRICKETT appraysed by JNO: HUGHLETT
          and JNO: ( ). Imprs. 3 Milke treys, 1 small, 3 pewter spoones, 1 old ( ), 1 old
wooden bottle, ( ), 1 hominey sifter, ( ), 1 pewter beaker, ( ), 1 halfe butt( ); 1 old
( ); 1 smootheing iron

                              JNO: ⅃ H HUGH( ) Signum
                              JNO: ⅂ H HOPPER Signum

    21th March 1658. ( )

p.   Witnesseth these prsents that I THO: CORNWALEYS doe authorize my loveing
19   freind, THOMAS PHILPOTT, to be my lawfull Attorney to demand & receive ( ) as
          is due to mee from JOHN AYRES & ROBERT SM( ) from RICHARD HOULDEN and
MARTINE COLE, and for non payment to sue and implead the sd. parties or other lawfull
acts for the recovery of the sd. Debts for wch: this shall be his warrant: Witnes my
hand this 18th of Novembr: 1658
Witnes WILKES MAUNDER,   THO: CORNWALEYS
        JOHN ABINGTON
    21th March 1658. This Lre. of Attorney was recorded

p.   KNOWE ALL MEN by these prsents yt: wee WM: PRESLY, Executor of the Estate of
19   ROBT. NEWMAN deced., & JNO: HAYNIE have sold & made sale of and doe by these
          prsents sell unto DANIELL HOLLAND a prcell of land lying at the Mouth of
CHINGOHAM CREEKE & upon the Easterly side of the same being a Neck of Land whereon
the sd. NEWMAN was seated at his decease, & is now left unsold; together with all the
houses & ediffices therein erected & built, onely prvided that JNO: RAVEN be admitted to
plant this ensueing crop at the lowermost cleare land in the sd. Neck, paying the sd.
HOLLAND a reasonable rent and yt: ELIZABETH NEWMAN have land sufficient for the
ensueing crop for no land ( ) for the same; and wee doe hereby further engage ( ) our
heires to warrant the prmisses unto the sd. DANIELL HOLLAND & his heires & assignes
for ever agst. any prsons yt: shall thereto make claime or demand & likewise to acknowledge this sale at the next Court holden for this County if sd. HOLLAND shall require the
same; Witnes our hands in Northumberland County ye 18th of Febry: Ano: 1658
                              WM. PRESLY
                              JOHN HAYNIE
    I doe allowe of ( ) firme ( ) abovesd. sale, ELIZ: NEWMAN, Sig.
    There is at the South of CHOTANK CREEKE & on the Northwest side thereof a small
prcell of land left unsold with the Marsh adjoyning wch: wee within named doe likewise make sale of to the sd. HOLLAND within mentioned; dated March ye 21th 1658
                              JOHN HAYNIE
                              WM: PRESLY
    21th March 1658. The Sale of these Lands was acknowledged in Cort: by the sd. WM.
PRESLY, JNO: HAYNIE & ELIZ: NEWMAN, unto the sd. DANIELL HOLLAND &c. and is
recorded

p.   A Cow cropt on the left eare & slitt in the same & the right eare whole, being
19   red in colour is here put in lieu ( ) formerly recorded to JOSEPH WHITE by mee
          on the ( ) Estate of ROBT. NEWMAN, deced., wch: former ( ) barren
March ye 21th 1658   WM: PRESLY
    ( ) 1658. This was recorded

p.   KNOWE ALL MEN by these pr:sents that I MILES COOKE, Marrin r:, doe ordaine
19   my well beloved Freind, HENRY (   ) lawfull Attorney to use any lawfull meanes
        (   ) a Debt due to mee from Mr. NICHOLAS (   ) giveing my sd. Attorney by these
presents power to sue implead & upon receipt to discharge & what my sd. Attorney shall
doe in the pr:misses I doe binde my selfe to ratifie & confirme as if my selfe had bin
p:sonally p:sent: As Witnes my hand the 18th ( ) 1658
(   ) RICHD. WRIGHT,   MILES COOKE
(   ) This Lre. of Attorney was recorded

p.   Deposicon of Capt. JNO: ROGERS
19   (   ) that he heard Mr. HUGH LEE confesse in (   ) & paid 150 lbs. of tobco. to WIL-
        LIAM (   ) of the Assignemt. of an Indenture (   ) SHAWEs & some clothing ye sd.
ALLENSON (   )RETT BASHAWE with, which sd. Tobco. was paid out of the sd. MARGA-
RETTs Estate or out of the rest of the Orphans & further sayth not
(   ) 1658 Jurat in Cur   JOHN ROGERS
 21th March 1658 Recorded

p.   The Deposicon of MARY EARLE, Saith that shee heard Mr. LEE confesse in Court
19   publickly that hee bought the Indenture hee had of MARGARETT BASHAWEs
        from WM. ALLENSON & that hee had given him One hundred & fifty lbs. of tobco.
in consideracon thereof; And that this tobco. was allowed him in Court & was paid out of
the Childrens owne Estate
 21 7br. 1658. Jurat in Cur   MARY }{{ EARLE
 21th March 1658 Recorded

p   The Deposicon of RICHARD WHITE aged 80 yeares or thereabouts taken this
19   second day of March 1658. This Depont. being sworne & examd. saith, That to the
        best of his knowlege there was never any Indenture made from MARGARETT
BASHAWE to WM. ALLENSON, & further sayth not
Jurat Coram me SAMLL. SMYTH   RICHD: R WHITE his marke
Test RI: FLYNT. Cl. Cur. Northumberland
 22 March 1658 This Depo: was recorded

p.   WALTER WEEKES aged 43 yeares or thereabouts sworne & examined saith that
19   (   ) his knowledge hee cannot remember or ever did see a (   ) from MARGARETT
        BASHAWE to WM. ALLENSON & further this Depont. sayth not
 22 March 1658 Cur et Record   WALTER WEEKES

p.   To all &c., Whereas &c., Now Know yee that I the sd. Sr. WILLIAM BERKELEY,
19   Knight &c., give & grant unto HENRY RAYNER Two hundred & forty acres of
        land in the County of Northumberland, Begining at a quarter (   ) upon PATO-
MACK RIVER side, soe running West 120 poles to the Creekes mouth called MOSLEYS
CREEKE, from the Creekes mouth aforesd. to the point next to HENRY MOSLEYs Land at
the Branch p:ting this Land from MOSELEY abovesd., Southwest from the sd. Point up
(   ) from the Land of HENRY MOSLEY to a (   ) West 100 pole from the sd. Quarter to (   )
trees giv(   ) this Land from the (   ) the first marked tree by (   ) acres of land being due
from EDWARD COPPAGE for (   ) mentioned under this Pattent (   )
 23th day of December 16(   )

HENRY RAYNER's Assignemt. of halfe this Pattent to WM: HOPKINS
KNOWE ALL MEN that I HENRY ( ) assigne over the right of ( ) and all appurtenances
to ( ) his assignes for ever ( ) 1655
Witnes EDWARD PARKER
22th March 1658. MARY RAYNER the ( ) RAYNER, And is ( )

MARY RAYNER's Assignemt. of halfe the Pattent of her Husband, HENRY RAYNER to
her Children; the other halfe being assigned to WM. HOPKINS.
KNOWE ALL MEN by these pr:sents that I MARY RAYNER, Administratrix of HENRY
RAYNER deced., ( ) right & interest of halfe ( ) WM: CANE fi( ) yeares after my ( ) WM.
CANE then unto SUSANNA CANE ( ) Witnes my hand this 22th of March 1658
Witnes: PETER PRESLY   MARY RAYNER
22th March 1658. This Assignemt. was acknowledged in Cort. by the abovesd. MARY
RAYNER and recorded

Whereas MARY RAYNER the Wife & Relict of HENRY RAYNER, deced., hath acknowledged the Assignemt. of the one halfe of a Pattent of 240 acres of Land & the houseing
upon ye Land menconed in the said Patt:, unto WM. HOPKINS as by Endorsemt. or
Assignemt. in the back side of the sd. Patt: from under the hand of the sd. HENRY RAY-
NER bearing date the 21th of December 1655 at large may and doth appeare; NOW KNOWE
all men by these pr:sents yt: I the sd. WM. HOPKINS doe oblige my selfe that if in case I
am determined to make sale of my part of the sd. Land & Houseing that then the sd
MARY RAYNER shall have the first refusall thereof & the value of One hoggsd. of tobco.
abated her in the price of what another will give; & in case of the death of the sd. MARY
RAYNER the same to be granted & allowed to her heire or heires; Witnes my hand this
22th of March 1658; More I doe acknowledge to be properly the dwelling house of Five &
twenty foote due to MARY RAYNER her heires &c.
Witnes THO: BROUGHTON,   WM: HOPKINS, his marke
22th March 1658 This Writeing was acknowledged in Court by the sd. WM: HOPKINS
and is recorded

p.   These pr:sents are to testifie to all whom it may concerne that I MARY RAYNER
20   Widow, being of a mind to match my self to Mr. THOMAS BROUGHTON in the
           Honble: Estate of Marryage for severall consideracons moveing mee thereto
have resolved to preserve the property & power of all my Estate moveable or unmove-
able unto my own possession to sell alienate or dispose of it at my pleasure & as I shall
thinke gud, the wch: condicon the sd. Mr. BROUGHTON doth by these p:sents yeild &
consent unto; & doth agree & consent to & wth: the sd. MARY RAYNER to have these
p:sents recorded in the Bookes of the Court; As Witnes our hands this 22th of March 1658
Witnes JOHN H( ),   the marke of MARY RAYNER
   ( ) HOPKINS, sig.   THO: BROUGHTON
22th March 1658. This Writeing was acknowledged in Court by the sd. MARY RAYNER
and THOMAS BROUGHTON and is recorded

p.   KNOWE ALL MEN by these pr:sents that I JOHN CLARKE doe hereby assigne all
20   my title & interest of the Bill of Sale unto MARTINE COLE his heires, Exrs. Admrs.
           or assignes. In Witnes whereof I have hereunto set my hand this two & twenti-
eth of March 1658
Test JOHN CONTANCEAN,   JOHN CLARKE
      ye marke of WM: BOND

5 March 1658. The Assignemt. was acknowledged in Court by JNO: CLARKE and is recorded

( ) for this Land here assigned is recorded in ( ) Records in folio 129; Novembr: 21th 1657 ( ) MARTINE COLE to the sd. JNO: CLARKE

p   ( ) Whereas &c., Nowe Knowe yee that I the sd. SAMUELL MATHEWES Esqr.
20   give & grant unto THOMAS BROUGHTON ( ) of Land scituate & being in the ( )
           of Northumberland abbutting Northwest upon MATOPONY ( ) upon the land of
JANE PERREY, Widdowe. S: E: ( ) upon the Maine Woods, the sd. Landbeing formerly
( )NICHOLAS SEBRELL by Pattent dated the 30th of ( ) & was deserted for want of
seating and is ( ) sd. THOMAS BROUGHTON by Order from the ( ) Councell bearing date
with these pr:sents ( ) transportacon of two p:sons into this Collony ( ) the Records
menconed under this Pattent &c. Dated the first of Decembr: 1657
                    SAMUELL MATHEWES   W: CLAIBORNE, Secr.
  ( ) that I THOMAS BROUGHTON doe assigne ( ) title & interest of this Pattent within
( )unto ABRAHAM JOYCE his heires ( ) the better p:formance of the same, I THO: ( ) my
heires to defend ( ) claimes of any p:sons ( ) Witness my hand this 23th March ( )
Test PHILLIP CARPENTER,   THOMAS BROUGHTON
        JOHN CONTANCEAN
  ( ) This Assignement was acknowledged in Court by THOMAS BROUGHTON & is recorded

  ( ) mee ABRAHAM JOYCE my heires or assignes to pay or cause to be paid unto THO-
MAS BROUGHTON hie heires or assignes the full & just sume of One thousand two hundred & fifty pounds of good sound merchantable tobco & caske: according to act upon
demand or other commodities to that value; As Witnes my hand this 23th of March 1658
Test PHILLIP CARPENTER   the marke of ABRAHAM JOYCE
        JOHN CONTANCEAN
  23th March 1658 This Bill was acknowledged in Court by the sd. ABRAHAM JOYCE and
is recorded

THIS BILL bindeth me ABRAHAM JOYCE my heires & assignes to pay or cause to be paid
unto FRANCIS CARPENTER his heires or assignes the full & just sume of One thousand
pounds of good sound merchantable tobco: & caske according to Act, due to be paid at or
upon the tenth day of November next ensueing the date hereof, in p:formance of the
same I have hereunto sett my hand this 23th March 1658
Test JOHN CONTANCEAN,   ye marke of ABRA: JOYCE
        PHILLIP CARPENTER
  23th March 1658 This Bill was acknowledged in Court by the sd. ABRAHAM JOYCE and
is recorded

p.   BE IT KNOWNE to all men by these pr:sents that I EDWARD SIMMONS of WAP-
20   PING WELL ( ) of Steben Heath otherwise STEPNEY in the County of MIDDLESEX
            doe hereby assigne & appoint my trusty & well beloved Sonne, GEORGE SIMMONS
of the same place, Pish: & County, Marriner, my true & lawfull Deputy or Attorney for
me & in my place & to my use to demand sue for and recover all sums of money debts
dues tobacco merchandize & other demands whatsoever wch: shall appeare to be oweing
unto me by or from any p:sons in Virginia or else where whether they be by Bond, Bill,
Book, Accompt or by any other wayes or meanes giveing unto my sd. Attorney my full
power touching the pr:misses for me & in my name to receive arrest and to recover ( )
In Witnes whereof ( ) twelfth day of ( ) according to the ( ) six hundred fifty ( ),

Sealed subscribed & ( )
    HENRY SMITH, AUSTON WILLIA( )
30th March 1659 ( ) Recorded

p.   KNOWE ALL MEN by these pr:sents that I THOMAS SHEPPARD for consideracon
20   in hand received have sold unto ROBT. SMITH one heifer with a calfe ( ) being
      of a black colour & white under the ( ) & one black heifer of a yeare old, being
both marked with a crop on the left eare & a swallow forke on the right, which heifers
with their future increase I have sold from mee my heires or assignes unto ROBT.
SMITH his heires or assignes for ever; And doe warrant the sale to be good & lawfull As
Witnes my hand this 21th day of March 1658
Teste HEN: VINCENT,   ye marke of THO: SHEPPARD
      the marke of JNO: AIRES
 20th May 1659 This Bill of Sale was acknowledged in Court by the sd. THOMAS SHEP-
PARD & recorded

p.   KNOWE ALL MEN by these pr:sents that I JNO: HULL for divers good & valuable
21   consideracons mee theretunto moveing have sold & made sale and doe by these
      pr:sents sell one black Cowe knowne by the name of Nancy haveing a little
white under her flanke, shee being marked wth: her left eare cropt & two slitts in the
same & swallow forke in the right eare & a nick outt under the same, wch: Cowe with
her future increase I the sd. JNO: HULL doe for my selfe my heires sell to THOMAS
HAYLE & THOMAS SHEPPARD & to their heires & assignes for ever, warranting the sd.
Sale agst. all p:sons that shall thereto make any claime; In Witnes whereof I have here-
unto sett my hand and seale this ( ) day of March 1652
Signed & delivered in presence of
     ROBT. NEWMAN, his marke   JOHN HULL
     RICHARD ILAND
I THO: SHEPPARD doe assigne over all my right & title of this Bill of Sale unto JOHN
AIRES or his assignes, As Witnes my hand this 21th day of March 1658
Test HEN: VINCENT,   the marke of THO: SHEPPARD
     ROBERT SMITH
 ( ) May 1659. This Assignemt. was acknowledged in Court by the sd. THOMAS SHEP-
PARD & recorded wth: the Bill of Sale

p.   THIS INDENTURE made the 22 of Aprill in the yeare of our Lord 1659 Betwixt
21   ROGER WATERS of the ( ) Northumberland, Planter, of the one pty: and
      RICHARD ILEFFE of the same County aforesaid; Witnesseth that the sd. ROGER
WATERS for diverse consideracons him thereunto moveing to ( ) valuable consideracons received before signeing doth hereby assigne over from said ROGER WATERS his
heires or assignes unto sd. RICHARD ILEFFE his heires & assignes ( ) Three hundred
acres of land seated ( ) sd. County of Northumberland ( ) GREAT WICOCOMOCO & bounding ( ) GEORGE NICHOLLS & the land of Mr. ( ), the Woods as may appeare more at ( )
upon Records. Now Knowe yee that ( ) hereby warranting the same, there ( ) to the sd.
RICHARD ILEFFE his heires and assignes for ever from all p:sons that can may or will
lay claime or title to the same, the sd. ROGER WATERS ( ) signeth over to the sd.
RICHARD ILEFFE his heires and assignes all priviledges & rights belonging to the Land
in as full & ample manner as it was given by Pattent to the said WATERS; In Witnes
whereof the said ROGER WATERS hath hereunto set his hand & seale the day & yeare
above written

Signed Sealed & Delivered in the presence of us

    HENRY WATTS,   the marke of ROGER WATERS the Seale
    THOMAS WEB
  20th May 1659. This Sale of Land was acknowleged in Court by the abovesd. ROGER
WATERS & recorded

p.   KNOWE ALL MEN by these pr:sents that I GERVASE DODSON for divers good con-
21   sideracons mee thereunto moveing did the last yeare give unto JNO: HULETT,
        Sonne of JOHN HULETT of WICOCOMOCO, one black pyde cowe calfe of my marke,
vizt., cropt on the right eare & two slitts in the cropp; & cropt on ye left eare & a peice
cutt from the under side & another peice cutt from the upper side of the sd. left eare
which Calfe is now a yearling which I the sd. GERVASE DODSON confirme to the sd. JOHN
HUGHLETT JUNR., To have & to hold to the sd. JOHN HULETT JUNR. his heires or assignes
for ever; In Witnes whereof I have hereunto sett my hand and seale ( ) 1659
Witness JOHN HULETT,   GER: DODSON
        the marke of BRIDGET PRICKETT
  20th May 1659. This Deed of Guift was recorded

p.   This ( ) of M( ) 1659. KNOWE ALL MEN by these pr:sents that I ISAAC ALLER-
21   TON doe assigne & make over unto GABRIEL ODGER his heires or assignes all my
        right & interest unto a parcell of land the quantity of 300 acres lying on the
Easterne ( ) MACHOTICK RIVER in County of Northumberland, part of a great Dividend
that I have there ( ) large appeare; the sd. p:cell of land ( ) begining from the
extreame ( ) RICHARD COLE, the sd. land ( )
Testes RICHD: WRIGHT,   ISAAC ALLERTON
       NIC: SPENCER
  20th May 1659. This Assignemt. was acknowledged in Court and recorded
  These p:sents Witnes that I ISAAC ALLERTON ( ) well esteemed Freind, WM: THOMAS to
confirme ( ) doe as in the pr:misses as I ( ) shall doe as my owne act & deed, Witnes my
hand this ( ) of May 1659
Teste RICH: WRIGHT   ISAAC ALLERTON
      NICH: SPENCER
  20th May 1659   This Lre. of Attor: was recorded

p.   I WILL: THOMAS JUNIOR doe authorize my Freind, HENRY CLARKE to confesse
21   a Judgmt. in my behalfe for Three hundred & fifty pounds of tobacco wth:
        caske due to JNO: HULL, As Witnes my hand this 18th of Aprill 1659
Test   Sig: JNO: GRAVES   WILLIAM THOMAS
  20th Maii 1659 This Lre. of Attor. was recorded

p.   Aprill 13d. 1659. Northumberland County
22   Whereas it was ye desire of ELIZABETH NEWMAN, Widdowe of this County deced.,
        that PETER PRESLY JUNIOR & MARTHA & ELIZABETH HAYNIE should have some
p:e: of the Estate belonging unto her, the sd. ELIZA:, and in p:ticular of ye pt. of the sd.
Estate hereafter in these pr:sents expressed; Vizt., Unto the sd. PETER PRESLY one yearling heyfer marked with a crop in ye left eare & slitt downe ye sd. eare as likewise unto
the sd. MARTHA & ELIZA: HAYNIE joyntly one black pide Cow being marked with an
under keele of ye right eare & cropt of ye left; as likewise unto the sd. MARTHA one
f( ) a rugg curtaines & vallences & unto the sd. ( ) gold rugg; NOW KNOWE YEE that wee
the ( ) doe hereby accordingly confirme ye sd. Estates ( ) PETER, MARTHA & ELIZA:

together wth: ( )male increase unto the sd. PETER ( ) till he shall come to ye age of Seventeen yeares & them male & female to belong tohim the sd. PETER and likewise the female increasse of sd. Cowe the ( ) & ELIZA: untill they shall attaine to the age of ( )or shalbe marryed and further we doe make promise yt: the sd. Cattle shall at all times remaine ( ) shall thinke convenient or in case eyther of them shall dept. this life (before the sd. p:ties be at age of the Receipt of the sd. Estate) then the pr:misses shall dispose thereof; And if eyther the sd. PETER, MARTHA & ELIZA; shall dye before the age aforesd. that then that parties estate to come to such as by Law shalbe qualified ( ) thereof; In Witnes of ye pr:misses we have hereunto sett our hands the day & yeare abovesd.

Teste ( ) PRESLY   WM. PRESLY
                                                   JOHN HAYNIE

   ( ) This Writeing was acknowledged in ( ) WM. PRESLY & JNO: HAYNIE and is recorded

p.   KNOWE ALL MEN by these pr:sents that I SAMUELL GARDNER ( ) England,
22   Marriner, doe hereby ( ) my well beloved Freind, Mr. DANIELL ( ) WICOMOCOE
        in the County of Northumberland my true & lawfull Attorney to receive in my
( ) debt due to me from ( ) within the aforesd. place ( ) to act for me and for my use & in my name as fully and amply as if my selfe were p:sonally pr:sent; In Witnes whereof I have here sett my hand & seale this 15th of February 1658
Witnes WM. DOWNING,   SAMUELL GARDNER
       WILLIAM CORNISH
   20th May 1659. This Lre.of Attor: was recorded

p   BE IT KNOWNE unto all men by these pr:sents that I JOHN HAYNIE of the County
22   of Northumberland in Virginia have for diverse ( ) out of the affecon I beare
        unto my two Daughters, MARTHA & ELIZABETH HAYNIE, & likewise unto my
Daughter in Law, SUSANNA WARE, to each of them these cattle following, vizt., unto the sd. MARTHA one black Cowe knowne by the name of Nancey she being over( ) of both eares and holes in both eares; likewise wth: one black two yeare old heyfer ( ) name of Cocke and her, the sd. Heyfers Calfe being ( ) colour & a female, ye sd. Heyfer & Calfe being ( ) with a swallow tayle of both eares; Likewise unto my Daughter, ELIZABETH, I doe give one Cow knowne by the name of Browning, shee being cropt of both eares & slitts cutt in each;·together with one yearling heyfer of a browne colour being swallow tayld. of both eares a small nick cutt under ye right eare; As alsoe unto my Daughter in Law, SUSANNA, one browne Cowe called Korny ( ) of the left eare & cropt & slitt of the right, all which sd. Cattle with their future female increase ( ) I hold within my keeping untill each pty: shalbe ( ) of Sixteen yeares or else married; or otherwayes ( ) p:sons custody as I shall hereafter ( ) in such p:sons disposall to be for ( ) PRESLY or his Brother, Mr. PET( ) eyther of the sd donatee( ) before their abovesd. time ( ) arrived, that then the Ca( ) to remaine at my dis( ) to the ( ) exd. &
Signed and sealed in p:sence of us
       PETER ASHTON,   JOHN HAYNIE   ye Seale
       NICHOLAS MORRIS
   20th Maii 1659. This ( ) acknowledged in Court by the sd. JNO: HAYNIE and is recorded

p.   KNOWE ALL MEN by these pr:sents that I ANNE RICE, Wife of RICHARD RICE,
22   doe make & ordaine my loveing Freind, JAMES CLAUGHTON, my good & lawfull
        Attorney to acknowledge for mee & in my name the Land wch: THOMAS HAR-

DING & JAMES JOHNSON is nowe possessed withall & to acknowledge it unto the said
THOMAS HARDING & JAMES JOHNSON as my good true & lawfull act as Witnes my hand
this 19th of May 1655
Witnes WILKES MAUNDER   ye marke of ANNE RICE
   20th May 1659 This Land was acknowledged in Court by JAMES CLAUGHTON, Attorney
of the sd. ANNE RICE and is recorded. The Pattent for this Land is recorded in folio 13
huius libri

pp.   AN INVENTORY of ye Estate of WM: BACON Gent., deced., taken this 18th day of
23-   December 1658.   Imprimis one feather bed bolsters rugg blankett cotton sheets
24   curtaines & vallances, one catt-tayle bolster & pillowes, one old blankett, brasse
           kettle, iron pott, frying pan, pestle, milk tray, powdering tubb, lookinge glasse,
two old axes & one old hoe; one old case, earthin dishes, yard of trading Cloth, pair of old
shooes, iron hooke, brush, searge doublet, paire of fustian drawers, gray felt cloth,
bootes, 2 yearling calves, one hefer, one bull & one steare, pigg, combe, steel buttons,
bulls hide, wooden chaire;
   A list of Debts due to ye Estate by Specialty: Imprimis. One Bill wherein JOHN CLARKE
stands bounds to SYMIN COX for the paymt. of Five hundred & fifty pounds of tobacco &
caske upon the Tenth of October last past, wch: Bill is (by the sd. COX), assigned over to
the sd. BACON; Item One Bill wherein RICHARD HOLDING standeth bound for the paymt.
of Foure hundred & forty pounds of tobco: & caske, this pr:sent yeare; 440. Item. One
Bill wherein WM: JEFFERS standeth bound for ye paymt. of Two hundred sixty & five
pounds of tobco: & caske this pr:sent yeare; Item. One Bill wherein JOHN WARD stands
bounds for the paymt. of Three hundred & twenty pounds of Tobco: & caske this pr:sent
yeare; Item. One Bill wherein THOMAS LAMBKIN stands bound of the paymt. of Foure
hundred & fifty pounds of tobco: & caske this pr:sent yeare; Item. One Bill wherein WM.
THOMAS stands bound for ye paymt. of One thousand pounds of tobco. & caske in ye year
1659; Item. One Bill wherein WM. JEFFERS stands bound for ye paymt. of Eight hundred
pounds of tobco. & caske in ye yeare 1659; Total: 3825.
   There is also due from RICHARD HOLDING upon Accompt. Six bushells of Indian Corne;
from THOMAS CHEWE 100 lbs. of tobco: and caske; Two barrells of Corne more about a
hogshd. of tobco. yett to (   )   ye marke M.B. M B of MARGARETT BACON
20 May 1658. Jurat in Cur   l.B.
   Goods belonging to ye Estate of Mr. WM: BACON sold at an Out Cry; Imprimis to Mr.
CLAY with a bull Calfe; to RICHARD COLE (   ) black Calfe; To WILLIAM (   ) named Lilly at
(   ); To Mr. CLAY (   ); To WM. BUSHELL (   ); To THOMAS PHILPOTT; To Mr. CLAY one sowe
wth: piggs; a churne, a p:cell of tobacco; To RICHARD COLEMAN one iron pott, one
frying pan & one pestle; To RICHARD HOLDEN a p:cell of pewter, of corne, of old iron
and three fishing hookes, a ladder & a peice of hide; To JNO: POWELL one Bible and
looking glass, a pockett pistoll; To THOMAS DURAND an old case, a little box & three
earthen dishes, a wooden chaire & a horne combe; To JOSEPH CHURNELL (?) half yd.
trading cloth; 3 iron hookes, a chest, an old serge doublett, pr. of drawers; To WM.
THOMAS (   ); To WM. DANI(   ); To JAMES GAYLARD;   Total 1396
(   ) 1659. This Outcry was recorded

p   To all &c., whereas &c., Now knowe yee that I the sd. SAMUELL MATHEWES Esqr.
25   &c., give & grant unto RICHARD FLYNT One hundred & fifty acres of Land scitu-
           ate & being in the County of Northumberland on the North West side of YEACO-
MOCO RIVER bounding Northeasterly upon the head of a Creeke wch: issueth out of ye
sd. River. Northwesterly upon the Land Pattented by THOMAS SHEAPHARD & JAMES

CLAUGHTON, Southerly upon the sd. Creeke & a line of markt. trees running from an Oake tree marked on three sides standing on the Southwest side of a small Creeke or Branch of the aforesd. River & running Southerly into the Maine Woods, this sd. land being due unto the sd. RICHARD FLYNT for the transportacon of three persons into this Colony whose names are all in the Records menconed under this Pattent, &c., Dated this 26th of Septr: 165( ).   SAMUELL MATHEWES
                                          W. CLAIBORNE, Secr.

KNOWE ALL MEN by these prsents that I RICHARD FLYNT for a valuable consideracon reced., (and with ye Consent of my Wife, DOROTHY), doe for me my heires Exrs, and assignes & every of us, assigne over unto WILLIAM COLMAN his heires Exrs, Admrs, & assignes for ever all my right (together with my Wife, DOROTHY's), of this ( ) & the land therein menconed, As Witnes our hands & seales this 26th of November 1658
In presence of us
          ( ) CARTWRIGHT;   RI: FLYNT
          ( ) his marke   DO: FLYNT
  ( ) 1659. This Assignemt. was acknowledged in Court by sd. RICHARD FLYNT & is recorded (with the) Pattent

KNOWE ALL MEN by these prsents yt: I WILLIAM COLMAN for a valuable consideracon received, doe for mee my heirs Exrs. Admrs. & every of us assigne ( ) WARD for ever all my right title ( ) Pattent of Land therein ( ) my hand this 20th of May ( )
          ( ): FRAN: CARPENTER   WILLIAM COLMAN
  ( ) This Assignemt. was acknowledged in Court by WM. COLMAN & is recorded

p.   ROBERT BAINHAM did wth: WM. COLMAN joyntly ( ) FLYNT 300 acres of land
25   lying ( )MOCO as by Assignemt. & Writing from the said FLYNT more at large
        may appeare. KNOWE ALL MEN by these prsents that ROBERT BAINHAM doe for
me my heires Exrs. & Admrs. remise release & forever disclaime all my right title or interet that I or any of my heirs Exrs. or assignes have in & to this sd. Land or every hereafter may lay claime to by or under mine or their Estate interest or title, & alsoe I the sd. ROBT. BAINHAM doe binde my selfe my heires Exrs. &c. to assigne all my right of & in the sd. Land unto ye sd. WILLIAM COLMAN or his assignes & to acknowledge ye Sale in Northumberland County Court in Septembr: or Novembr: next for a valuable con-sideracon already by me received: As Witnes my hand this 12th of July 1658
Witnes JOHN WALKER,   ROBERT BAINHAM his marke
        RICHARD HOLDING his marke
  20th May 1659. This Writeing was acknowledged in Court by the sd. ROBERT BAINHAM & is recorded

p.   KNOWE ALL MEN by these prsents that GEORGE MARKES have for a valuable
25   consideracon sold unto JOHN HOPPER one Cowe of a browne colour & cropt on the
        right eare & a hole in the same eare & under keeld. in the left; And I the sd.
GEORGE MARKES doe confirme the Sale of the above named Cowe from me my heires or assignes for ever unto JNO: HOPPER his heires & assignes for ever; To hold the same from all person or prsons whatsoever, As Witnes my hand the 20 of May 1659
Witnes JOH( )BERT, ABRA: BYRAM sig.   ye marke of GEORGE MARKES
  20th May 1659. This Bill of Sale was acknowledged in Court by the sd. GEORGE MARKES & is recorded
  I JOHN HOPPER doe acquitt & discharge GEORGE MARKES from all former Bills of Sale,
As Witness my hand the 20th of May 1659   JNO: HOPPER his marke
Witnes JOHN OBERT. ABRA: BRYAM

20th May 1659. This Writeing was acknowledged in Court by the sd. HOPPER and is recorded

p.   Mr. HUGH LEE and his Wife their Bill to Mr. MATH: RHODEN

25   This Bill bindeth us HUGH LEE & ( ) severally or together & our heires to pay or cause to be paid unto MATHEW RHODEN his heires Exrs. Admrs. or assignes the just sume & quantity of Fowre hundred & thirty pounds of tobco: and caske according to Act of Assembly ( ) upon the Tenth of November Sixteen hundred & ( ) or his Wife &c. ( ) vth: (Estate bound over) ( ) now live on with our ( ) belonging to our ( ) acknowledge this (vee have both here( ) of July 1659

Signed & Delivered in presence of

     ROBERT SECH

20th July 1659. The sd. HUGH LEE and HANNAH his Wife on her ( )

     I HANNAH LEE doe ( ) Husband, HUGH LEE, my lawfull Attorney for ( ) Court, a Bill wherein vee both stand bound to ( ) RHODEN with ye Plantacon our Stock of Cattle & ( ); In confirmacon whereof I have hereunto subscribed this 13th of July 1659

Witnes ye marke of MARY BRICKFEILD   the marke of HANNAH LEE

     JOHN HAYLES

20th July 1659 This Lre. of Attor: was recorded

p.   KNOWE ALL MEN by these prsents that I ROBT. SECH of the Parrish of CHICA-

25   COAN in the County of Northumberland doth give for his marke of Cattle & hoggs (Vizt.) the left eare cropt & a hole in the same, and the right eare underkeeled

20th July 1659 This marke was recorded

p.   KNOWE ALL MEN by these prsents yt: I GERVASE DODSON for a valuable con-

26   sideracon received wherewth: I acknowledge my selfe to be fully satisfied have sold & by these prsents doe sell unto DOCTR. RICHARD RUSSELL. Five hundred & fifty acres of Land scituate lying & being in ye County of Northumberland at & neare the North side of ye head of GREAT WICOCOMOCO RIVER, begining by the sd. River at GEORGE CLARKEs Land & runing Northerly Six hundred & forty poles, thence Northwesterly, thence Southerly ( ) & forty poles to ye River & soe along the River courses to the sd. CLARKE his Land, including ( )hree Popler in the sd. quantity of Land; the sd. ( )rd & Fifty acres of land being part of a tract of t( ) thousand acres formerly granted to mee the said GERVASE DODSON & renewed by Pattent bearing date the 27th day of Aprill 1658; To have & to hold to him the sd. DOCTR. RICHARD RUSSELL his heires & assignes for ever with all rights & priviledges thereto belonging in as large & ample maner as it is to me granted by the sd. Pattent, yeilding & paying onely the Rent in the said & as the Pattent menconed; In Confirmacon of the prmisses I the sd. GERVASE DODSON have hereunto sett my hand & seale this ( ) of May 1659

     GER: DODSON

( ) with the consent of my Loveing ( ) vee firmly bind our selves our heires ( ) to acknowledge it in Court for a further ( ) witnes our hands & seales as abovesd.

     GER: DODSON his seale

     ISBELL DODSON her mke. ye seale

( ) this Sale of Land was acknowledged ( ) GER: DODSON by Lre. of Attor: & alsoe by her the sd. ISBELL & recorded

KNOWE ALL MEN by these prsents that I GERVASE DODSON appoint my loveing Wife (ISBELL DODSON) my true & lawfull Attorney for me to appeare before the Court of Northumberland to acknowledge the Sale of Five hundred & Fifty acres of land to

DOCTOR RICHARD RUSSELL to implead JNO: WOOD of WICOCOMOCO ( ) assigned to me by
JNO: WOOD of POTOMACK ( ) by Specialty & to implead any other with whome I have a
cause of accon as alsoe to answere any complaint agt. mee, alsoe I authorize my said
Attorney to appeare for mee before ye Comrs. of LANCASTER & implead & prosecute the
sd. JNO: WOOD (sometime of POTOMACK) in an accon of Cause if the Sher: have arrested
him & if occasion require I the said GERVASE DODSON doe hereby authorize my sd. Wife
to make any other Attorney or Attorneys under her; I hereby engageing to confirme
what shee or they shall doe lawfully to be as firme as if I my selfe were prsent to doe
the same; Witnes my hand this 18th of July 1659
Witnes ROBERT BOGGIS.   GER: DODSON
    RICHD. NEALMES his marke
  20th July 1659. This Lre. of Attor: was recorded
I RICHARD RUSSELL doe hereby authorize my loveing Freind, JOHN HUDNALL, to see
the acknowledgemt. of this Bill of Sale from GERVASE DODSON in the County Court as
Witnes my hand this 5th of May 1659
Wit: GER: DODSON,   RICHARD RUSSELL
    JNO: SMITH his marke
  20th July 1659. This Lre. of Attor: was recorded
(The Sale is recorded in ye prsent leafe.)

p.   AN INVENTORY of ye Estate of GEORGE BERRY deced,, Tob: & caske
26   Imprimis: an old sute, two wastcoats & a hatt, an old sute & 2 pr. of drawers; 2
        prs. of shooes, stockings & a cap; an old coat, old stockings, and an old pr. of
shooes, 13 ells of linin, a holland shirt, drawers, 2 caps, a Neck Cloth, 2 bands, a pr. of ( )
& 2 pailes, 9 doz: of pipes, an old chest, an old bed & sea rugg, two Bills of GEORGE
DURANTs, one Cap
  20th July 1659. JNO: BENNETT Admr. of the Estate of the sd. BERRY sworne that this is
( ) Inventory (in open Court)   Test RI: FLYNT, Cl. Cur.
  20th July 1659. This Inventory is recorded

p.   Goods remaineing in ye Estate of JOHN HOWELL, deced.
26   Imprimis: 100 ac( ), feather bed, rugg & blankett, 2 cowes, 3 yearlings, 4
        calves, 1 sun diall, 1 Chest   ELIZABETH HOWELL
  20th July 1659. This Inventory was recorded

p.   July ye 9th 1659. JOHN RAVEN maketh Oath That hee his Depont. (about the
26   first of June last) did heare JOYCE, the Wife of DANLL. HOLLAND, say yt: ye first
        time shee could conveniently meete with MARY the Wife of RALPH KEY that
shee could teare the bastard out of her belly & swore (by Gods Life) that shee would doe
it and further this Depont. sayth that the sd. JOYCE did call the sd. MARY Whore severall
times & further saith not
Sworne before me WM. PRESLY .   the marke of JNO: RAVEN

NICHOLAS BUTLER sweareth the same wth: JNO: RAVEN verbatim,
Before me WM. PRESLY   NICHOLAS BUTLER
  20th July 1659. These two Deposicons were recorded

p.   KNOWE ALL MEN by these prsents that I JOHN EARLE of YEOCOMOCO, Planter, in
27   the County of Northumberland hath bargained and delivered one pcell of Land
        containing One hundred acres lying in YEOCOMOCO NECK joyning upon the

North Branch of the ISLAND CREEKE & joyning to ye marked trees of a Thousand acres of land belonging to ye sd. EARLE for which I ye sd. JNO: EARLE doe acknowledge to have reced., full satisfcon therefore, I JOHN EARLE doth warrant & grant ye sd. Land unto LUKE DYNE his heires Exrs. Admrs. or assignes from all other grantes & or sales & I JOHN EARLE binde my selfe my heires or assignes to warrant the sd. Land unto LUKE DYNE his heires or assignes that hee or they shall peaceable & quietly enjoy sd Land with all priviledges whatsoever; & that I JOHN EARLE doth warrant that the sd. LUKE DYNE his heirs shall peaceable and quietly enjoy the sd. Land without the hinderance of me the sd. JNO: EARLE my heires or assignes or any p:son or p:sons whatsoever that shall lay any claime unto the sd. Land or any things belonging to the sd. Land, As Witnes my hand & seale the 5th day of March 1658
Signed Sealed & delivered in the prsence of

WILKES MAUNDER,   JOHN EARLE, the seale
THOMAS ELDRED

( ) 1659. This Sale of Land was acknowledged in Court by the sd. JNO: EARLE & is recorded

p.   KNOWE ALL MEN by these pr:sents that I JAMES AWSTEN have bargained & sold
27   & doe hereby bargaine & sell ( ) CASTLETON for a valuable consideracon ( )
        small necke of Land lying at ye ( ) ye begining at a mkt. red Oake of ( ) mkt.
trees to a mkt. Gum wch: sd. ( ) tract of land belonging to mee ( )OCOMOCO CREEKE, To
have & to hold unto said ( ) CASTLETON his heires & assignes forever; ( ) all p:sons by
me my Exrs. & Admrs ( ) with liberty for timber for his ( ) the Swampe & Barrens next
adjoyning ( ) where I shall appoint. Witnes my hand this ( ) of July 1659
        ( )OUGH   JAMES AWSTEN   ye Seale
        ( )ARKE
( ) This Sale of Land was acknowledged in Court by the sd. JAMES AWSTEN & is recorded

p.   I the Subscriber doe acquitt exonerate discharge & release JNO: GATCHENS (hee
27   delivering up and chanelling a Bill for a Cow & yearling heyfer) from all
        claimes Debts differences & causes of difference whatseover from the begining
of ye World unto this instant 12th of May. Witnes my hand the day beforesd. Ano: Dom: 1656
Witnes GER: DODSON,   WM. THOMAS
        THOMAS SALISBURY, his marke
    20th July 1659. This Acquit was recorded

p.   KNOWE ALL MEN by these pr:sents that I RICHARD FLYNT for diverse good
27   causes & consideracons mee thereunto moveing have freely & absolutely
        given & confirmed and by these pr:sents doe freely and absolutely give unto
ANNE GAMBLIN, the Daughter of JOHN GAMBLIN, one Heyfer two yeares old or thereabouts of a colour browne with a mealy mouth & marked (Vizt.) Cropt on ye right eare & two slitts with a nick under the crop & the left eare whole; To have and to hold the sd. Heyfer with all her future increase unto the sd. ANNE GAMBLIN & her heires for ever from mee my heires & asignes, excepting onely unto the sd. JNO: GAMBLIN the male increase of the sd. Heyfer during the minority of the sd. ANNE; As Witnes whereof I the sd. RICHARD FLYNT have hereunto sett my hand this 2d. of July Ano: 1659.
                                        RI: FLYNT
    20th July 1659 This Deed was acknowledged in Court by the sd. FLYNT and is recorded

p.   I HENRY CORBYN, Attorney ( ) JNO: WHITTY doe authorize my Freind, HENRY
27   CLARKE to implead imprison to release & out of prison & receive of HUGH LEE of
WICOCOMOCO ( ) belonging to Capt. JNO: WHITTY ( ) CLARKE shall doe lawfully in ye
pr:misses; ( ) & confirme July 5th ( )
Test WILLIAM BALL, R(   )
  20th July 1759

p.   HENRY ROCKE his Lre. of Attor: to ABRAHAM JOYCE
27   Witnes. ROWLAND CART( ) Recorded 20th July 1659

p,   KNOWE ALL MEN by these pr:sents that I ROBERT LAND doe appoint & make
27   JOHN GATEHOUS my true & lawfull Attorney for mee & in my name to demand
          and receive a Bill of Mr. WILLIAM BACONs & to plead the sd. Bill in Court in as
full ample manner as I my selfe were p:sonally p:sent, As Witnes my hand this 16th of
July 1659
Teste JNO: PALMER his marke   ROBERT LAND his marke
  JOSEPH CHURNELL. his marke
  20th July 1659. This Lre. of Attor: was recorded

p   I CAPT. RICHARD WRIGHT, Administrator of ye Estate of Coll: JNO: MOTTROM
28   deced., doe assigne & transferr unto WM: GREENSTEAD a Maid Servant formerly
          belonging unto the Estate of the sd. Coll. MOTTROM, commonly called ELIZABETH
KEY, being nowe Wife unto the sd. GREENSTEED and doe warrant the sd. ELIZABETH & doe
binde my selfe to secure her & the sd. GREENSTEAD from any molestacon or trouble that
shall or may futurely arise from or by any p:son or p:sons that shall pr:tend or claime
any title or interest to any manner of service whatsoever from the said ELIZABETH;
Witnes my hand this 21th of July 1659
Teste WILLIAM THO( )   RICHD. WRIGHT
  JAMES AWSTON
  21th July 1659 This Writeing was acknowledged in Court by the sd. Capt. RICHD:
WRIGHT unto the sd. WM. GREENSTED & is recorded

p.   KNOWE ALL MEN by these pr:sents that I SAMLL. GRIFFIN for diverse consider-
28   acons me thereunto moveing do confirme unto RICHD. MOTTROM, Sonne ( ) &
          JANE MOTTROM, 2 cowes & 2 calves, there ( ) markt. cropt on both eares &
marked overkeele in both eares and cropt on the right eare; To have & to hold unto the
sd. RICHARD MOTTROM & his heires with all their future increase for ever by these
pr:sents; Witnes my hand this ( ) day of July (59)
Witness ( ) GH; JAMES AWSTEN   SAMUELL GRIFFIN
  21th July 1659. This Deed was acknowledged in Court by SAMUELL GRIFFIN and is
recorded

p.   KNOWE ALL MEN by these pr:sents that I JAMES AWSTEN doe ( ) mee thereunto
28   moveing ( ) confirme unto my Daughter, FRAUNCES AWSTEN ( ) cowe calfe
          markt. underkeeled on both eares; To have and to hold unto the said FRAUNCES
with all her future increase for ever by these pr:sents, Witnes my hand this ( ) day of
July 1659   JA: AWSTEN
  21th July 1659. This Deed was acknowledged in Court by JAMES AWSTEN & is recorded

p.   KNOWE ALL MEN by these pr:sents yt. I HUGH FOUCH doe hearby ( ) by these
28   pr:sents give freely to HUGH MAGREGGER the Sonne of JAMES MAGREGGER one
        Heyfer of one yeare old or better; browne coloure, cropt on the right eare & a
hole in each eare & underkeeled on ye left eare called Blossome, the sd. Heyfer (with
her increase) I the sd. HUGH FOUCH doe hereby warrt. to ye sd. HUGH MAGRIGER & his
heires or assignes for ever; In Witnes whereof I have hereunto sett my hand this
Twentyeth of September 1659
Signed & Delivered in the pr:sence of
        DANIEL ROBERTS   the marke of HUGH FOUCH
     20th 7br: 1659. This Deed of Guift was acknowledged in Court by the sd. HUGH FOUCH
and is recorded

p.   Mr. WM: PRESLY his Accompt upon the Estate of Mr. ROBT. NEWMAN deced.,
28   7br: 20th 1659.   Ano: (55). The Estate of ROBERT NEWMAN deced. Dr. Tobco.
        Imprs. To 2 gall. Wine; To wine & sugar at ye funerall, 1 gall: Wine to my Aunt,
To Sher. fees pd. Coll. TRUSSELL; To Sher. fees recovering ye Cowe; To pd. Mrs. MOORE 20
lbs. & JNO: LOVE 20 lbs.; To pd. DA( ) & LEE for Dyett 77 lbs. 2 hoggs. a Servant ( ) & a pr.
of shooes; 8 ells of ( ) to RICHD. CLARKE p order; To CORNISH 50 lbs.; to Capt. PAINTER
for a hatt 130 lbs., To ( ) dowlas, pd. HOLLAND 760 lbs.; to ye NEW ENGLAND M( ) p.
Corne, 300 lbs., to 3 S( ) Starch; 8 bottles 7 drams, 1 pettecoat & wastcoate; 1 pr. Irish
Hose, 1 bushell Salt, a pr. hose to THOM: ( ); paid HOLLAND 800 lbs.; to Coll. ( ); To Mr.
KNIGHT 1032 lbs.; to HOLLAND 1172 lbs., 2 pr. shooes, to Discompt upon Bill; 12 yds. of
Ozenbrig, 1 gall; drams; to yds. Holland, 20 lbs. sugar, 2 yds. of broadcloth; to buttons
silke, ells canvas, 2 bottles of ( ); 3 pr. shooes, pd. Coll. TRUSSELL, 4 lbs, Soape, 100 lbs.
pd. ANDREW for Vinegar 30 lbs; pd. Coll. MOTTROMs Estate; pd. MARY KEY 155 lbs; 2
Coffins 200 lbs: 400 nailes 12 lbs., a Sheete 100 lbs, ye Cowe Cherry lost 600 lbs; a Steere
yt: dyed 500; a Cowe pd. for WHITE, a barren Cowe sold KENT my Aunt sold, a Steare &
coulter my Aunt sold; The land which ought not to have bin appraised; SAMLL.
NICHOLLS his Debt not solvend; SIMON RICHARDSONs the life; Mr. FLYNT for stuffe for a
Pettecoate, and a hoes, p. 3 steeres kild. by MRS. NEWMAN, p. 4 hoggs at 0550; allowed
mee by the Court -3000; Sum totall is 31148
                        Errs. excepted p. WM. PRESLY
     21 7br: 1659. Jurat in Cur & Record

p.   Report to ye Court of Mr. PRESLEY's Accot. upon Mr. NEWMANs Estate
29   Mr. WM. PRESLY ( ) p Contra: Credr. Mr. ROBERT NE( ) by severall Debts paid
        by the sd. PRESLY as pr. Accot., make to appeare - 31148
                        Rest of Ball: 666
     ( ) 21th 1659. Wee whose names are hereunder written being appointed by this Court
doe find the ballance of ( ) above appeareth   PETER KNIGHT
                                                  SAMUELL GRIFFIN

     21st. 7br. 1659. ( ) was recorded

p.   KNOWE ALL MEN by these pr:sents yt: I THOMAS BREWER, ( ) DEVEIDEING
29   CREEKE in County of Northumberland, Planter, have sold and doe by these pr:
        sents sett over & deliver unto THEORDORE ( ) of sd. CREEKE & County, Boate-
wright, a pr:cell of land scituate & being on the South side of DEVIDEING CREEKE, containeing fower ( ) five arces being part of the ( ) JOHN HULL & the sd. BREWER ( )
by the Pattents nowe in possession ( ) To have & to hold the sd. Land unto the sd.
THEODORE his heires or assignes for ever; without trouble or incumbrance of the sd.

THOMAS BREWER my heires with warranty from any p:sons whatsoever; in considera-
con whereof I doe acknowledge to have received full consideracon; In Witness whereof
I the sd. THOMAS BREWER have hereunto sett my hand & seal the 20th day of September
Anno Dom: 1659
Signed Sealed & delivered in the presence of
        JOHN HULL, THO: DENT   the marke of THOMAS BREWER   ye seale
                                           the marke of ELIZ: BREWER   ye seale
    20th September 1659 This Sale of Land was acknowledged in Court by the sd. THOMAS
BREWER and ELIZABETH his Wife and recorded

p.   KNOWE ALL MEN by these pr:sents yt: I JOHN JONES (for a consideracon in hand
29   received) have bargained and sold unto JENKIN PRICE one red pyde Cowe aged
            seaven yeares or thereabouts, cropt on both eares; To have & to hold the sd Cowe
with her future increase from mee my heires & assignes for ever, warranting the sale
hereof from all claimes whatsoever. Witnes my hand the 12th of 7br: 1659
Witnes: THO· BROUGHTON   sign   JNO: JONES
    20th 7br. 1659. This Bill of Sale was recorded

p.   KNOWE ALL MEN by these pr:zents yt: I JUSTINIAN TENNIS for diverse consider-
29   acons as mee hereunto moveing give & confirme to THOMAS DAVIS the Younger
            one browne Cowe cropt in both eares & slitt on both eares; To have & to hold
with her future increase for ever; Witnes my hand ye 10th. day of (   )
Witnes. SIMON COX   the marke of JUSTINIAN TENNIS
    20th 7br: 1659 This Deed of Guift was acknowledged in Court by the sd. TENNIS and is
recorded

p.   KNOWE ALL MEN by these pr:sents yt: I JNO: ESSEX doe for diverse consideracons
29   give & bequeath unto ELIZABETH NEPPER, Daughter of JAMES NEPPER, (   )
            flower de luce (   ) away under the (   ) with her increase for ever; As Witnes my
hand this (   ) 1659
Witnes JOHN BO(   )   JNO: ESSEX
    20th 7br: 1659. This Deed of Guift was acknowledged in Court by the sd. ESSEX and is
recorded

p.   By this pr:sents, I PETER LEFEBUR doe constitute & appoint my loveing Freind,
29   JAMES CLAUGHTON, my lawfull Attorney for this pr:sent Court of Northumber-
            land, Witnes my hand the 10th of Sept: 1659
Teste ROBERT BRADSHAWE,   PETER LEFEBUR
      ELLIS COLMAN
    20th 7br: 1659 This Lre. of Attor. was recorded

p   KNOWE ALL MEN yt: I HUGH LEE doe constitute my loveing Freind, JAMES
30   CLAUGHTON, my lawfull Attorney to crave a Refference in the suit betweene Mr.
            COOPER & my selfe this present Court; as alsoe to peticon for an Appraisemt. for
my goods in the Sherr.s hands and what my Attorney shall doe herein I doe confirme as
if I were pr:sent: Witnes my hand this 14th of September 1659
Witnes JOHN TRUSSELL   HUGH LEE
    20th 7br: 1659 This Lre. of Attorney was recorded

p   I doe hereby appoint & make DANLL. HOLLAND my lawfull Attorney for mee in
30   my name to act in any business for or concerning mee in Northumberland
          County Court ratifying & confirmeing what my sd. Attorney shall lawfully do;
Witnes my hand this 20th of 7br. 1659
Witnes RICHARD FLYNT.   SIMON COX
  20th 7br: 1659 This Lre. of Attor. was recorded

p   KNOWE ALL MEN that I SIMON COX doth bargaine and sale unto JOHN COLE (?)
30   one Maid Servant which hath ( ) yeares to serve or thereabouts & doth warrt.
          ( ) p:son & p:sons whatsoever; as Witnes my hand this 12th of September 1659
Teste JOHN ( )HOUS, RI: FLYNT.   SIMON COX
( ) This Writeing was recorded

p.   ( ) Accot of the Cattle belonging to ( ) WM. REYNOLDS deced., presented by
30   ( ) NICHOLAS OWEN Heyfers and calfes (torn) total 24
                              NICHOLAS OWEN

p   ( ) Accot. of the Cattle belonging to the Estate of WM: MEDCALFE deced., ANNE
30   MEDCALFE her cattle -3; ELIZABETH MEDCALFE hath one 2 yeare old heyfer;
          Whereas I NICHOLAS OWEN am indebted unto the Estate of WM. MEDCALFE the
sume of 1899 lbs. of tobco: I doe hereby acknowledge to pay the Orphans three Cowes
and three yearling Cowe Calves forthwith; Witnes my hand the 10th of Octobr: 1659
                               NICHOLAS OWEN
One Cowe called Browne Besse underkeeled on both eares and the top of the left eare
cutt off, one Cowe called Pretty of the same marke, one called Star overkeeled on the left
eare cropt & 2 slitts in the right eare
  Recorded the 10th of 8br: 1659

p.   The Orphans of THO: CANE their Stock of Cattle
30   A true Accot. of Cattle belonging to the Children of THOMAS KEENE deced., de-
          livered the 10th of Octobr: 1659; WILLIAM KEENE, two cowes one three yeare
old heyfer, two steares about 2 yeares, three calves, one 2 yeare old heyfer -9;
SUSANNA KEENE, one cow, one two yeare old heyfer, 2 yearelings, one calfe, one steere
6 yeares old -6; THOMAS KEENE one cowe, 2 calves, 2 steeres, one heyfer two yeares old
-6, MATHEW KEENE one heyfer, su( ) old a Guift of the subst) -1.
                    p   THO: BROUGHTON
One Steere of THO· KEENEs given for two yeares schooleing
  10th 8br: 1659. Jurat in Curt et Recor:

p.   SAMUELL NICHOLLS his Accot. ( ) to PRUDENCE PELLAM, one black cowe called
30   Jugg, one cowe called Black ( ) right eare slitt with an underkeel ( ) and a
          heyfer of the same ( ) blacke Cowe called Pretty ( ) cowes cropt on the right
eare
  Recorded the 10th of 8br. 1659

p.   HENRY MEDCALFE his Stock of Cattle 10th 8br: 1659
30   JANE MEDCALFE her Stock of Cattle: DENNIS CLAR( );
          10th 8br: 1659. Jurat in Cur et Record:

p.   These are to certify yt: wee WILLIAM WARDER and JNO: STANDLEY have in our
30   custody of GEORGE MEDCALFE's Cattle five females that have had calves, one bull
          calfe of the last yeares fall; two bull calves & a cow calfe of this yeares fall & 400
lbs. of tobco in PHILL: CARPENTERs hands due to the sd. GEORGE MEDCALFE
  10th 8br: 1659. This was recorded

p.   KNOWE ALL MEN by these presents that WILLIAM WILLDEY doth give for his
31   marke of cattle & hoggs (vizt.) Cropt on the right eare & a hole in the left
          29th Octobr: 1659. This marke was recorded

p.   THESE PR:SENTS witnesseth that I THOMAS GASKIN SENIOR of the County of
31   Northumberland doe give assigne and make over unto DIANA MAYES, Daughter
          of HENRY MAYES, of ye same County, one heyfer betweene two and three yeares
old with a mealy mouth, browne couloured, cropt on the left ear and slitt on the right
eare. the sd. DIANA MAYES to have & to hold the sd. Heyfer & all her female increase for
ever with warranty agt. all men: Witnes my hand this 19th day of November 1659
                              THO: GASKIN
( ) This Writeing was acknowledged by the sd. THOMAS GASKIN and is recorded

p.   IN THE NAME OF GOD Amen. Whereas I RICH: BUDD being weake & sick in bodye
31   yett at pr:sent p:fect sence & memory have made this my Last Will and Testament
          in manner & forme as followeth·
  ( ) l give my Soule to God that gave it and my body to the Earth from whence it came
( ) buried.
  ( ) in Law ELIZABETH, I doe give & ( ) Cowes with their increase for ever ( ) Flower
& Young Cherry
  ( ) in the yeare 1661, I doe ( ) each of them one Cow calfe ( ) MAZE, ANNE,
GAMLING, ELLENR: ( ), ( ) Dennis; and to JOHN MULTON ( ) Sprunt
  ( ) my men vizt., JOHN and SIMON ( ) service being faythfully fulfill'd ( ) &
bequeath one cow calfe;
  ltm. To my loveing Wife, ELIZ: I doe give & bequeath all & every the Land goods
chattells moveables & imoveables wch: shall belong or be found due or apperteyning to
my Estate (my Debts & Legacies being paid) And doe constitute & ordaine her my Executrix. desireing my good Freind, Mr. LAWR: DAMERON, to see this my Will & Testamt.
p:formed: This I doe ackowledge to be my Last Will and Testamt. as Wittness my hand
this 22th of Octobr: Ano Dom: 1659
Signed & sealed in the presence of
     THO: DENT, JOHAN MOUTON,   RI: BUDD, ye seale
     the marke of SIMON BOWLEY
  21 Novembr: 1659. This Will was proved in Northumberland County Court to be the Last
Will & Testamt. of RICHARD BUDD deced., by the Oaths of THO: DENT, & JOHN MOUTON, And
execucon thereof committed to ELIZABETH, ye Relict of the sd. RICHARD BUDD, And the
Will is recorded

p.   Country Man Mr. PETER ASHTON:
31   As touching ( ) order concerning Debts in ABRAHAM BYRAM his hands doe
          againe desire you to call the sd. ABRAHAM BYRAM to accot: & to take these debts
out of his hands ( ) allowe him such a consideracon for his time as you may think convenient for ye paines hee have ( ) in my business as alsoe to receive from ABRAHAM
BYRAM that tobco. hee owe to mee & to give discharge for the same or what else you

receive eyther tobco: or ( ) hands further doe desire you as m( ) demand and receive
all such tobco. as you ( ) to me in the County of Northumberland ( ) payment arrest
implead or ( ) discharge ( ) best of yor: skill ( ) rather then stay ( ) for they be
value( ) old heyfer for my tobco: the ( ) of tobco. they owe me ( ) able by occasion
they by rason they ( ) them soe I rest ( ) given
                    Nancemu( ) May 1657   GEORGE ABBOTT
    23th 9br: 1659 ( )

pp.   KNOWE ALL MEN by these pr:sents that I ROBERT CROWDER for diverse con-
31-   sideracons mee hereunto moveing doe freely and absolutely give & confirme
32   unto SARAH BREWER, the Daughter of THOMAS BREWER, one heyfer calfe, six
           months old or thereabouts, of colour redish browne & marked with a crop on the
left eare & a hole in the same & the right eare swallow tayled with a nick over & under
& a hole in the sd. right eare alsoe; To have & to hold ye sd. Calfe with all her increase
unto the sd. SARAH BREWER her heires for ever; from my my heires or any other p:son
whatsoever; the male increase (during the minority of the said SARAH) to belong to the
sd. THOMAS BREWER. In Witnes whereof I ye sd. ROBT. CROWDER have hereunto sett my
hand this 14th of 9br: 1659
Witnes RI. FLYNT. WM: FURBISH sig.   ye mke. of ROBT. CROWDER
   21th 9br: 1659. This Deed of Guift was acknowledged in Court by RICHARD FLYNT,
Attorney of the sd. ROBERT CROWDER, and is recorded

    I ROBERT CROWDER doe hereby appoint RICHARD FLYNT my true Attorney to acknow-
ledge a Deed of a Heyfer Calfe (in Northumberland County Court) conveyed from mee to
SARAH BREWER, the Daughter of THOMAS BREWER. as by a Writeing from under my
hand may at large appeare: bearing date with these pr:sents and what my sd. Attorney
shall lawfull doe I hereby ratify and confirme to be authentick & valid in the Law as if
I my selfe were pr:sent and did the same; Witnes my hand this 14th of 9br: 1659
Witnes. JOHN WIDE.   the marke of ROBERT CROWDER
        the marke of WM: FURBISH
   21th 9br: 1659. This Lre of Attor: was recorded

p.   KNOWE ALL MEN by these pr:sents that I Collonell WILLIAM CLAIBORNE doe by
32   these pr:sents for diverse good causes & out of the affecon I bear ( ) Eldest
           Sonne, WILLIAM CLAIBORNE, give & grant unto the sd. WM. CLAIBORNE JUNIOR
all that tract of land adjoyning to my Divident of WICOCOMOCOE lying neare the mouth
of LITTLE WICOCOMOCO ( )tely in the possession of SAMUELL SMYTH, To have & to hold
the same to him & his heires and assignes for ever; Reserving allwayes to my selfe ( )
regresse on the same for the lookeing ( ) & hoggs; In Witnes whreof I have sett my
hand & seale this twelfth day of ( ) in yeare of our Lord one thousand ( ) fifty nine
Delivered in the pr:sence of us
        ( ) COLCLOUGH,   W: CLAIBORNE ye Seale
        JOHN CLAYBURNE
    ( ) & authorize RICHARD FLYNT to ( ) conveyance of Land above specified ( ) County
Court witnes my hand ( )   W. CLAIBORNE
        ( ) SMYTH, GEO: COLCLOUGH
   21th 9br: 1659. This Conveyance of Land to WILLIAM CLAIBORNE JUNIOR was acknowledged in Northumberland County Court by RICHARD FLYNT being impowered by the
abovesd. Coll. WM. CLAIBORNE & is recorded

p.   JNO: BENNETT's Acct. for Sickness Charges & the Funerall of GEORGE BERRY
32   The Estate of GEORGE BERRY is Dr. to JNO: BENNETT. Tobco: & Ca:
        To Drinke for his funerall -0350; To 1 fatted Calfe then expended -0150; To 1 fatt
hogg then alsoe -0150; To poultry & Sugar -1050; To Mr. WRIGHT for his charges during
his Sickness at ye sd. Mr. WRIGHT his house & his burial there -0800 Total 1550
     21th 9br: 1659. This Accot. was recorded

p.   KNOWE ALL MEN by these pr:sents that I WILLIAM HOLLINGSWORTH, Marriner,
32   of the Towne of SALEM in NEW ENGLAND, doe by these pr:sents constitute &
        authorize my trusty and well beloved Freind, NICHOLAS OWEN, Planter, of
CHERRY NECK in County of Northumberland to be my true & lawfull Attorney for me &
in my name to aske demand receive & to recover all such debts as are owed by Bill or
Bond or any other lawfull accompts which are owed to Mr. WILLIAM BROWNE or my
selfe in tobacco, and I doe further give power unto my sd. Attorney that upon non
paymt. to sue implead & upon paymt. out of prison to release and acquit. as whatseover
my sd. Attorney shall lawfully doe about the sd. pr:misses I shall ratify & confirme &
allsoe of the same as if I were p:sonally pr:sent, hereunto give my hand and seale this
23th of Febr: 1658
Witnes SAMUELL ( ),   WILLIAM HOLLINGSWORTH   ye Seale
    MORDECAI NICHOLLES
     21th 9br. 1659. This Lre. of Attor: was recorded

p.   KNOWE ALL MEN by these pr:sents that I RALPH KEY doe for my selfe my heires
32   ( ) be paid unto WILLIAM CORNISH ( ) sume of Six hundred ( ) due to be paid
        at or before the ( ) ensuing the date hereof as with ( ) of Novembr: 1659; Now
for the better security for ( ) the sd. RALPH KEY ( ) transferr & sall over ( ) browne
cowe with a mealy mouth ( ) colour being marked on ( ) keeld. in bothe eares ( ) &
valued esteemed & ( ) be fully satisfied, ( ) Novembr: 1659
Witnes PETER PRESLY
     21th Novembr: 1659. ( ) by the sd. RALPH ( )

p.   KNOWE ALL MEN by these pr:sents we WILLIAM WARDER and JOHN STANDLEY
32   doe ( ) wee have, moveables ( ) that if WILLIAM WARDER ( ) the Land shalbe
        at WM: WARDERs ( ) pleases but if JOHN STANDLEY ( ) or then the sd. STANDLEY
is to have the ( ) ye sd. WARDER & STANDLEY lives upon to the sd. JOHN STANDLEY his
heires or assignes for ever; & the sd. JNO: STANDLEY is to have halfe the sd. Land during
the sd. WARDER's Life for him & his Servants, moreover the sd. JOHN STANDLEY is not to
take into the house any man to plant for a share or otherwise without the consent of
the sd. WM. WARDER, As Witnes my hand & seale this 9th of Aprill 1659
Teste THOMAS ORLEY,   WM. WARDER, his marke   ye Seale
    ROB: JADWYN   JNO: STANDLEY his marke   ye Seale
     22th 9br: 1659. This Writeing was recorded

p.   I doe hereby authorize & appoint Mr. WM. THOMAS to be my true & lawfull
33   Attorney for mee & in my name to implead & recover & discharge JOHN HUGH-
        LETT. GEORGE MARKES & JOHN BENNETT; Witnes my hand the 21th of Novembr:
1659   SIMON COX, his mke.
     22th 9br: 1659. This Lre. of Attor. was recorded

p.   The severall Cttle belonging to JOHN PLAYER in the possession of HENRY HURST
33   4 cowes, 2 2 yeare old heyfers; 2 yearling heyfers, 1 cow calfe - 9.
      21th 9br: 1659. Recorded

p.   Accot. of ye severall Cattle belonging to ye Children of HEN: MOSELEY
33   (torn)   JOHN TINGEY

p.   KNOWE ALL MEN by these pr:sents that JOHN COLMAN the (   )LMAN of
33   YEOCOMOCO in the County of Northumberland doth give for his marke of Cattle
      (   )lowe forke on the right eare (   ) keeld. in the left eare
  21th 9br: 1659. This Marke is recorded

p.   WM. THOMAS doe assigne & transfer all my right of this Pattent of 1000 acres
33   of Land unto WILLIAM SHIRT his heires or assignes for ever; Witnes my had
      this 19th of February 1659
Sig· EDW: COLES, s. (   ) HUNLEY   WM. THOMAS
  20th Febry: 1659. This Assigemt. was acknowledged in Court by the sd. WM. THOMAS
recorded. The Pattent was originally granted to ROBT. CASTLETON & by him assigned to
Mr. WM. THOMAS & is recorded in the other Booke of Records folio 135.

pp,   IN YE NAME OF GOD Amen. I SAMPSON COOPER late of RIPPIN in the County of
33-   YORKE in England, Alderman, being weake in body but in p:fect memory praised
34   be God doe make & ordaine this to be my last Will & Testamt. as followeth;
      First, I doe bequeath my Soule to God who gave it me and my body to the Earth
from whence it came, desireing to have xpian & decent buriall in the Land of Coll. JOHN
TRUSSELL & in his burying place; Itm. I desire that my loveing Freinds, Major GEORGE
COLCLOUGH and JOHN TRUSSELL both of this County of Northumberland in Virginia to
be Overseers of this my Will and that they (   ) pleased to take care of my Sonne,
SAMUELL COOPER, after my decease, and alsoe of all such goods that doth belong unto me
and that all such debts that they shall find to be due & belong unto me in this Country
of Virginia I desire that they use their utmost endeavours from time to time to receive
into their custody & send it for England (   ) all goods & wares as is at present by me
(   ) sold to the best advantage excepting those Guifts (   ) that I given out of them; Allsoe
it is my (   ) Son. SAMUELL be sent for England this next (   ) & every with him all such
sumes of (   ) received, and when hee, my Sonne (   ) that then hee bind himselfe an
Apprentice (   ) COCKE SILBEMAN at the Signe of (   ) Poultry at LONDON; Allsoe my (   )
COOPER & Mr. JOHN CONYERS of (   ) and with Mr. COCKEs and that (   ) of that tobaccoes
tht (   ) England; allsoe it is my (   ) Sonne SAMUELL shall (   ) these my Overseers (   )
and that HUGH LEE (   ) nor have ought to (   ) Collony nor any part (   );
      First, I give & bequeath unto (   ) acres & ahalfe (   ) place called (   ) PALGRAVE;
      Item. I doe give untomy (   ) medow land at MANDLAN (   ) the CHAPPELL being about (   )
      Item. I give mor(   ) of meddow land that I bought of mr. EDWARD WRIGHT and his
Brother, NICHOLAS, & of MILES SMITH, it being three roode joyning to the former five
acres & a halfe;
      Item. One roode more I give unto my Sonne, JONATHAN, lately in the occupacon of
Alderman WARWICKE, & one roode more I give unto him in the same feild neare thereunto LEONARD PICKESGILL hath the same quantity of ground, one roode lying upon the
South side of mine & his bulleth upon Mr. JEFFERSONs on the West, for this roode & the
former three roodes up the acre for JONATHAN in SWILLING-INGS;
      Item. I give unto JONATHAN, my Sonne, more one little close neare unto Mr. JENNINGS

his house. neare unto a Lane called the PREST-LANE, now in the occupacon of THOMAS DAY which close I bought of FRANCIS PLUMLAND & THOMAS his Sonne

Item. I give unto SAMUELL & JONATHAN, my Sonnes, the House garden & Orchard at ALHAWES GATE in RIPPEN with all the appurtenances thereto belonging, joyntly & severally, desireing God to blesse them and that they may both agree & serve the Land;

Item. I give unto my Wife, BRIDGETT, the full & utmost some of my house & land which can be made of it during her naturall life desireing my Wife & my Children to see all my due debts paid unto every man, which is no great summes

Item. I doe give unto Mr. GEORGE COLCLOUGH my best paire of shues with silver & ( ) fringe.

Item. I doe give unto Colo. JOHN TRUSSELL my best sute of clothes of Spanish Cloth, the Coate ( ) trimed with silke & gold buttons;

Item. I doe give unto Mr. JOHN ROGERS & to Mr. WM: PRESLY, each of them, a paire of Cordevant gloves perfumed;

Item. I doe give unto Mr. DAVID LINDSAY, Minister, a Booke called r( ) Master( ) peice

Item. I doe give to WILLIAM BEDLAM ( ) landlord two shirts which be not bound at the ( ) wrists

Item. I doe give unto his Wife, ELIZABETH, a ( ) pin, (?hisknett) standing in the roome

Item. I doe give unto young WILLIAM ( ) six paires of handstrings, 3 paire of one sort ( ) paire of another; And the like quantity of hand ( ) I give to HANNAH FRANLIN, I doe alsoe give to THOMAS BALDRIDGE one paire of old black Britches ( ) that my two Sonnes, SAMUELL & JONATHAN ( ) Wife, BRIDGETT, be Executors joyntly of this my ( ) and that Mr. NICHOLAS KITCHIN & Mr. ANTHONY ( ) Aldermen be Overseers of my two Sonnes & ( ) Vizt., with my loveing Freind, Mr. COCKE of ( ), and concerning the Wares that he be in ( ) in Mr. BRENT WHITEs custody or in any place ( ) be called in & made sale of to the most ( ) p:duce put forth for the good of my ( ) & that to be equally devided when ( ) and after two yeares that my Sonne, ( ) of my good Freind, Mr. COCKE, ( ) Sonne, a Master,

( ) that now I weare on my finger to ( ), alsoe it is my Will that Major GEO. ( ); ( ) TRUSSELL & my Sonne, SAMUELL ( ) Estate in the Country of Virginia ( ) administra-con they use all lawfull ( ) debts in this Collony & to send ( ) for England with my sonne, SAMUELL ( ) & the rest that shalbe left in ye ( ) home the yeare following as they shall ( ) order from my Wife & Overseers in England, To ratify & aprove of all this my Will I have to the truth put to my hand & seale this 1th day of August Ano: Dom: 1659 Signed sealed & delivered in the pr:sence of us

    WILLIAM BEDLAM,   SAMPSON COOPER, his marke   ye Seale
    THO: HASELLRIDGE his marke
    HANNAH FRANKLIN her marke,
    JOHN TRUSSELL

This 12th of August 1659 was two words interlined by the appointment of SAMPSON COOPER that is to say, lately & my Land Lord, which day above written Mr. SAMPSON COOPER did sett his hand againe to this Will being in better memory then day before & it was againe witnessed by these p:sons

    JOHN TRUSSELL, WILLIAM BEDLAM   SAMPSON COOPER
    the marke of THO: HASELLRIDGE

20th February 1659. This Will was proved in open Court to be the last Will & Testamt. of the sd. SAMPSON COOPER by the oathes of WILLIAM BEDLAM & THOMAS HASELLRIDGE and the Will is recorded

p.   I JOHN RAVEN doe assigne all my right title & interest of this Bill of Sale to
34   WILLIAM CORNISH his heires & assignes for ever; as witnes my hand this 20th
          of February 1659
Witnes GEO: DURANT.   JOHN RAVEN his marke
  Vid. folio 17 huius Libri
  20th Feb: 1659 This Assignemt. was acknowledged in Court by the sd. JNO: RAVEN & is
recorded

          I WILLIAM CORNISH doe assigne all my right title & interest to this Bill of Sale
with the Land thereto belonging to THOMAS ROE & his heires for ever; as Witnes my
hand this 20th of Febru: 1659.
Witnes: GEO: DURANT   WM: CORNISH his marke
  20th Febrr: 1659. This Assignemt. was acknowledged in Court by WM. CORNISH & THO:
ROE & is recorded

p.   Mr. ROBT. PHILLPOTT his Last Will & Testamt.
34   Aprill this 24th 1657. IN THE NAME OF GOD Amen, I ROBERT PHILLPOTT ( ) upon
          my depture for ( ) I comitt my body to ( ) Lord first I appoint my ( ) THOMAS I
give with her, your( ) and the death of my Wife ( ) be equally devided to my Children
( ) KENT & one Shallop called the B( ) THOMAS further I dispose not ( )
Witnes JOHN RUSSELL,
     JOH· POWELL his marke
  20th Febru. 1659 This ( )

p.   JOHN BEERMAN Guift of a Calfe to SARAH SUTTON
34   20th Febru: 1659. This Deed of Guift was acknowledged in Court by the sd.
          BEERMAN and ordered to be recorded

p.   I THOMAS JARRET doe by these prsents freely give unto JNO: LAMKIN & GEORGE
34   LAMKIN, Sonnes of THOMAS LAMKIN, one black cowe wth: some white in the
          flank & a white starr in the forehead marked with a crop on the right ear &
under keeld. on the left knowne by the name of Lady, warrenting the Guift of the sd.
Cowe unto the sd. JOHN & GEORGE LAMKIN with her increase for ever, from me my
heires or assignes unto them the sd. JOHN & GEORGE LAMKIN & their heires; In Witnes
herein I have hereunto sett my hand this 20th of Febru: 1659
Witnes FRANCIS CARPENTER,   the marke of THOMAS JERRAT
     JOHN WALKER
  20th Febru: 1659. This Deed of Guift was acknowledged in Court by the sd. THOMAS
JERRAT & is recorded

p.   KNOWE ALL MEN by these prsents that PHILIP NUTT and WALTER OWEN both
35   of the County of Northumberland doe give for their marke of Cattle & hoggs
          vizt., cropt on the right eare & underkeeld. on the same & cropt on the left eare
& three slitts
  20th Febr: 1659. This marke was recorded

p.   KNOWE ALL MEN by these prsents yt: JAMES AUSTON of LITTLE WICOCOMOCO in
35   the County of Northumberland doth give for his marke of Cattle & hoggs Vizt.,
          cropt on the left eare two slitts in the same and the right eare slitt
  21th Febr: 1659. This Marke was recorded

p.
35
To all &c., Whereas &c., Now Know yee that I the sd. SAMUEL MATHEWS Esqr.
&c. give & grant unto WILLIAM THOMAS Five hundred acres of land scituated in
Northumberland County on the North side of GREAT WICOCOMOCOE vizt., 250 acres
part thereof abutting Westerly ( ) upon SAFFALLS CREEKE, Northerly upon ( ) &
North East upon a Creeke called the ( ) upon the sd. WICOCOMOCOE RIVER and ( )
Southwesterly upon another Devident belonging to the said THOMAS, North Westerly
upon ( ) of ROGER WALTERS North Easterly upon the Path yt. goes to CHICKOCOAN &
devides this land from the lands of HENRY WATTS & THOMAS DORRELL, South Easterly
upon ( ) HENRY SMITH & the land of Mr. WM: ( ), 250 acres by a former Pattent
bearing date ( ) of July 1654 & 250 acres the residue ( ) transportacon of Five p;sons
into this Collony whose names are in the Records menconed under this Pattent, Dated
the 11th of Septembr: 1658
                          SAMUELL MATHEWES   W: CLAIBORNE Secr.
   ( ) assigne all my title & interet of ( ) acres land unto RICHARD GIBLE ( ) for ever as
witnes my hand this ( ) 1659   WM: THOMAS
   ( ) This Assignemt. was acknowledged in Court by WM. THOMAS & recorded

p.
35
Lre. of Attorney. BE IT KNOWNE & manifest unto all People that on the Thir-
tieth day of the moneth of Septembr: one thousand six hundred fifty & nine
before me, FREDERICK IXEM, Notary & Tabellion Publick, admitted & sworne
dwelling in this Citty of LONDON, in the presence of the Witnesses after named, personally appeared NICHOLAS HEYWARD of LONDON, Merchant, unto me Notary well
knowne and hath made & in his place doth put NICHOLAS SPENCER of LONDON aforesd.,
Merchant, and Capt. SAMUELL TILGHMAN, Commander of the Ship called the "GOLDEN
FORTUNE," now bound for Virginia, jointly and eyther of them severally his true &
lawfull Attorneys giveing unto them full power in the name of him & to his use to aske
recover & receive of HENRY RAYNOR of Virginia, Planter, & of GEORGE BERRY, of the
same place, deceased, & of eyther of them their heires goods whatsoever they shalbe
found or if such other p;son as it of right shall appertayne all sumes of money debts &
things whatsoever as the sd. HENRY RAYNER & the sd. GEORGE BERRY doe owe be it by
Bill Specialty Account for Servants to them or eyther of them delivered with all costs
and if they refuse to pay to prosecute ( ) all things whatsoever as shalbe needfull
( ) sdd Constiuant himselfe might doe about the pr;misses ( )
       EDWARD PERKINS   (torn)
Witnesses GEO: IXEM, ( )
 21th Febr: 1659, ( )

p.
35
KNOWE ALL MEN by these pr;sents that I WILLIAM ALLEN have assigned & constituted Mr. GILBERT METCALFE my true & lawfull Attorney to receive of all &
every persons resideing in any pt. of Virginia & MARYLAND in pts. beyond ye
Seas or eyther of them (except the Inhabitants adjacent or neare JAMES RIVER) and all
such sumes of money debts as they doe owe unto me giveing unto my sd. Attorney lawfull authority to act in the pr;misses ratifying & confirmeing all my sd. Attorney shall
lawfully doe; In Witnes whereof I the sd. WM: ALLEN have hereunto set my hand & seale
dated the 7th day of July in the yeare of our Lord God (according to the Accompt used in
England) one thousand six hundred fifty & nine
Sealed & delivered in the presenceof
       JOHN ALSOPE SER: WILLM. BRAXTON,   WM: ALLEN, the Seale
       JOHN ( ); ROW: PLACE,
       WILL: MUNFORD, ROBERT CARTER
 21th Febr: 1659. This Lre of Attor: was recorded

p.   KNOWE ALL MEN by these pr:sents that I GILBERT METCALFE of LONDON, Mercht.
36   & p( ) resideing on PEANKATANCE RIVER in Virginia by a ( ) of a Lre. of
        Attorney & power therein by Mr. WM. ALLEN of LONDON, Mercht., bearing date
the 7th day of July 1659; assigned by these pr:sents constitute Mr. NICHOLAS SPENCER
my true & lawfull Attorney to receive of all p:sons whatsoever inhabiting in any ( ) pt.
of Virginia or MARYLAND to the behoofe of Mr. WM. ALLEN of LONDON, Mercht., all
such sumes, to sue arrest ( ) ratifying & by these pr:sents confirming all my sd.
Attorney shall lawfully doe concerning the receipt of the pr:misses by virtue of these
pr:sents; In Witness whereof I the sd. GILBERT METCALFE have sett my hand & seale
dated the Tenth day of January in the yeare of our Lord (according to the Accompt used
in England) one thousand six hundred fifty nine
Sealed & Delivered in the presenceof
     JOHN SNELLINGE, RICH: YOUNG, JUNR.,   GILBERT METCALFE ye Seale
     EDM· BERKELEY, JOHN CARTER
  21 Febr: 1659 This Lre of Attor: was recorded

p.   KNOWE ALL MEN by these pr:sents that I ISAAC ALLERTON of MACHOATICK in
36   the County of Northumberland, Mercht., doth give for his marke of Cattle &
        hoggs (vizt.) Cropt on the right eare & swallow forked on the left eare
  20th March 1659 This Marke was recorded

p.   KNOWE ALL MEN by these pr:sents that I Lt. Coll. HENRY FLEETE for a valluable
36   consideracon paid by CHRISTOPHER GARLINGTON due for mee my heires grant
        unto the sd. XOPHER GARLINGTON all my right wch: I the said HENRY FLEETE now
hath wch: WILLM. SPICER, late hd in Two Pattents of Land ( ) three hundred acres of
land as by the sd. Pattent more at large appeare; To have & to hold the sd. Three hundred
acres of land with all houses ediffices & buildings belonging & alsoe all other the rights
whatsoever unto the sd. XOPHER GARLINGTON his heires & assignes for ever in as ample
manner as in the Pattents thereof and I the said HENRY FLEETE the said Land warrant &
defend the said Land from us our heires and all p:sons whatsoever; In Witnes whereof I
the said HENRY FLEETE have ( ) this first day of ( )
Sealed & delivered in the presence of
     RICH: PERROTT, EDWARD DALE   HENRY FLEETE
  30th ( ) I HENRY FLEETE doe ( ) now Wife shall surrender her ( ) by her selfe or
her ( ) in the Court of Northumberland ( ) moneth next after the date hereof
Test RICH: PERROTT, EDWARD DALE   HENRY FLEETE
  20th Aprill 1660 JAMES MACGREGER by virtue of a Lre. of Attorney from the above-
mencqned HENRY FLEETE & SARAH his Wife acknowledged the abovesd. Sale of Land in
Northumberland County Court & the sd. Sale was then recorded

  Wee HENRY FLEETE & SARAH FLEETE my Wife, doe hereby authorize & impower JAMES
MACKGREGER in our behalfe to acknowledge a Bill of Sale or Conveyance for a tract of
land of about One hundred & Fifty acres of Land or more as appeare by the sd. Bill of
Sale bought of WM. SPICER and this to be done according to a Law p:vided for the same &
wee doe hereby disclaime all right to any part or p:cell of the same, And for our Attorney JAMES MACKGREGOR doe doeing doe hereby confirme under our hands this 18th of
March 1659
Test GEORGE LANGFORD.   HENRY FLEETE
     JENKIN PRICE his marke   SARAH FLEET her marke
  20th Aprill 1660. This Lre. of Attorney was recorded

p.   To all &c. Whereas &c., Now knowe yee that I the said SAMUELL MATHEWS Esqr.
37   &c., give & grant unto Mr. HUGH LEE 1100 acres of land in POTOMACK FRESHES
        above PUSCATOWAY on the Westward side of the River, bounding Easterly upon
the POTOMACK RIVER, Southerly upon the Land called Mr. CLAIEs Land & running
Northerly alonge the River from CLAY 275 poles WEsterly from the River parallel to
Mr. CLAY 640 poles into the Woods; the sd. Land being due unto the sd. HUGH LEE by &
for the transportacon of 22 p:sons; To have & to hold &c., yeilding &c., Dated ( )th July
1657.   Vera Copia Test   THO: BRERETON
KNOWE ALL MEN by these pr:sents that I HUGH LEE with the consent of my Wife,
SARAH LEE, for the love I beare my Cozen, SAMUELL COOPER, doe freely give & sell over
all my right of the 1100 acres of land within menconed due to me by Pattent; To have &
to hold the sd. Land as his owne proper goods for ever to him the sd. COOPER his heires
or assignes; In Confirmation thereof of the pr:misses wee have hereunto sett our hands
and seales this ( ) of Aprill 1660
                                        HUGH LEE
                                        HANNAH LEE her mke.
    20th Aprill 1660. This Deed was acknowledged in Court by HUGH LEE & RICHARD
FLYNT, Attorney of HANNAH, the Wife of the said HUGH LEE, and is recorded

    I doe freely give my consent to my Husband's ( ) in the Freshes of POTOMACK to my
( ) COOPER and I doe authorize you to ( ) my behalfe & request you to doe soe ( ) very
loveing Freind   HANNAH LEE her marke
    20th Aprill 1660. This Lre. of Attorney was recorded

p.   KNOWE ALL MEN by these pr:sents that I PETER KNIGHT of WICOCOMOCO in con-
37   sideracon of my love & affecon I bear unto HENRY HAWLEY I give unto the said
        HENRY one pyde cowe calfe marked as followeth; cropt & underkeeld. on the
right eare & a swallow tayle on the left eare, the said HENRY to enjoy the sd. Calfe for
ever: with her increase to him & his heires; as Witnes my hand this 20th of Aprill 1660
Test RI: FLYNT, ED: SANDERS   PETER KNIGHT
    20th Aprill 1660 This Writeing was recorded

p.   These are to Testify that I NICHOLAS JOURNEW have given unto ALICE SHAWE,
37   Wife to THOMAS SHAWE, one browne pyde heyfer with all her whole increase
        for ever, the marke of the sd. Heyfer is that shee is cropt on the right eare slitt
and an underkeele under the halfe crop, the which heyfer I desire to be recorded for
her use as Witnes my hand this 20th of Aprill 1660
                                        NICHOLAS JOURNEW, his marke
    20th Aprill 1660 This Deed of Guift was acknowledged in Court by the sd. Mr. NICHO:
JOURNEW and is recorded

pp.   AN INVENTORY of the Estate of JOHN HUDNALL deced., taken as it was p:sented
37-   by MARY, the Widdowe & Relict of the sd. JNO:HUDNALL this 5th day of Decembr:
38   1659. Imprs. His wearing apparell, pewter, brasse, potts, kettles, tin ware, 12
        cowes, 5 steeres, 4 heyfers, 1 steere, 9 calves, 1 mayde Servant; 2 men Servants, 3
yeares to serve or thereabouts, 1 old man Servant & 1 boy, a man Servant to serve upwards of one year; and one woman Servant ( ) upwards to serve by ( ) hath a young
Child, the stock of hogges, 3 guns, 2 boyes hatts, 15 sheates, 7 old shirts, 8 pillowbers, 4
table cloths & ( ), 7 towells, old linnen stockins, 1 feather bed, bolster, pillowe, rugg
blankett curtaines & vallens; 1 old flock bed & appurtenances, the Servants bedding &

furniture, 1 chest & several goods in it; 2 pr. Stilliards, 1 pr. can hookes & 1 paire of
bellowes; wooden ware belonging to the Dayry; 1 old chest with severall things in it,
iron ware, 2 old chests & lumbr: in the Buttery; 1 table, forme & carpett, 1 cupboard,
chaires & stooles; 5th Xbr. 1659. 1 chest, 1 lookeing glass & 2 smoothing irons, some
small lumber in the hall, 1 couch & fishing lines, sugar, salt, Brandy, Wine and 1 old
blankett, Lumbr: in the Kitchin; Corne, more Lumbr:, 1 small Boate, her ( ) & Canowe, 1
Silver Dram; 8s. 6d. in money, 1 old box, 9 hoggsds. of tobacco, tobacco hanging, 2 hides
& ( ) barrell   37031
  Bills (Vizt.) JOHN HOPPER, HUGH BAKER, JOHN HOPPER by Bill 1684 lbs., by ( ) JONES &
JENKIN PRICE, ( ) GIBLE, ( ) BOGGAS by Bill 736 lbs.; by ( )HARD LANDSELL &
MARTINE CRAFFORD remaining; JNO: BENNETT by Accot; WM. DOWNING by Bill
remaining; EDWARD ( )ED & THOMAS SHEILES, ( )CLOUGH by Bill; DANLL. CROSBY's;
( )ARDSON by Bill 350 lbs. ( ) Gocke p Bill remaining; GEO: ( )CKERIN p Bill
remaining; RICH: ILAND p Bill remaining; JOHN LARRETT, ABRA: BYRAM p Bill re-
maining; DAVID CUFFIN p Accot., MATHEW WILLCOCKS p Accot., MRS. BUDD p Accot.,
Bills left in hands of WM: BRESSIE as by a Note appeares from under his Hand, and 20s.
Sterl: sume Total 57461 & 20s. Sterl.,
  This Estate appraised by us   HENRY WATTS   JNO: MOTLEY sig.
                                       GEORGE NICHOLLS sig. WM. DOWNINGE
  Jurat Coram me WILLI: NUTT
  (on side) ( )HAMs man -063 lbs. tobco. ( ) MAGREGER at 30; - 180; ( ) AUSTEN
( ) presented this Inventory to the ( ) to be a true Inventory of all the goods & ( ) to
the Estate of her late Husband, JOHN HUDNALL ( ) said Inventory was then recorded

p.   To all &c., Whereas &c., Now knowe yee that I the sd. SAMUELL MATHEWES Esqr.
38   &c., give & grant unto JAMES MAGREGERY & HUGH FOUCH fower hundred & Fifty
        acres of land scituated in Northumberland County upon the South West side &
towards the head of Lower CHOTANCK CREEKE, begining at a marked Chesnut standing
neare the Creekes side & oposite to another tract of land of the sd. JAMES MAGREGORY &
FOUCHes, & extending into the Woods; South West 320 pole, South East 225 pole, & from
thence Northeast down a head Branch of CHOTANCK CREEKE & along the sd. Creeke
Northwest to ye place where it first began; the said Land being formerly granted by
Pattent unto the said JAMES MAGREGARY & HUGH FOUCH bearing date the 4th day of
July 1653; & by them assigned unto DUNKIN ROY & MICHAEL VANLONGEGAN which sd.
DUNKIN ROY assigned unto the sd. MICHAELL VANLONGEGAN his share & part thereof;
and by the said VANLONGDEGAN assigned unto the sd. JAMES MAGREGORY & HUGH FOUCH
& renewed by order of the Quarter Court bearing date by these pr:sents by ne rights for
transportacon of ( ) persons into this Collony, whose names are in the Records men-
coned under this Pattent; To have & to hold &c., yeilding &c., the 11th day of June 1658
                SAMUELL MATHEWES   W. CLAIBORNE, Secr.
  JAMES MAGREGER & HUGH FOUCH their Assignemt. of the abovesd. Patt. to ALEX:
MACOTTER. Witnes ourhand this 21th ( ) JAMES MAGREGER his marke
                                          HUGH FOUCH his marke
                                          MARIAN MAGREGER her marke
  (On side) Assigned to GEO: PICKERIN & CHARLES HOYLE fol: 48)
  21th May 1660. This Assignemt. by the above named JAMES MAGREGER & HUGH FOUCH
and the ( )

p.   KNOWE ALL MEN by these pr:sents that I ROGER CLATWORTH doe bind my selfe
38   my heires ( ) to be paid unto MARTINE COLE ( ) full & just sume ( ) good sound
        merchantable tobacco & caske to conteyne it to be paid this Tenth of ( ) hereof

and for the true performance I doe bind my selfe my heires & doe bind my Crop & ( ) to
MARTINE COLE and his assignes; untill such time ( ) said Debt satisfied unto the sd.
MARTINE COLE or his assignes & for the true p:formance of the same I the sd. ROGER
CLATWORTH have hereunto sett my hand & seale this 18th of January 1659; This tobacco
to be paid in YEOCOMOCO NECK
Test JOHN GATCHENS,   ye mke. of ROGER CLATWORTH   ye Seale
      JOHN KNIGHT
  21: May 1660. This Bill was recorded and ye 5th of 7br: was acknowleged in Court by
Mr. WM. THOMAS, Attorney of the sd. CLATWORTH

p.   KNOWE ALL MEN by these pr:sents that THOMAS STEAD doth give for his marke
38   of Cattle & hoggs (vizt.) the right eare underkeeled & a slitt on the top, and the
          left eare cropt & underkeeld.
  21: May 1660. This marke was recorded

p.   KNOWE ALL MEN by these pr:sents that GEORGE ENGLISH of the DEVIDING
39   CREEKE in the County of Northumberland & Collony of Virginia doth give for
          marke of Cattle and hoggs (vizt.) a crop & ahaole on the right eare, and a slitt in
the left eare
  21: May 1660. This marke was recorded

p   MR. TRUSSELL. I have carried away Mr. COOPER's Trunck according to my
39   order from the Governor & Councell; If anybody can claime ( ) debt that hee
          doth owe them, if they have any Note under his hand I will pay them without
trouble;   Yor: loving freind,   HUGH LEE
  21: May 1660. This Writeing was recorded

p.   To all &c., Whereas &c., Now knowe yee that I the sd. Sr. WILLIAM BERKELEY
39   Knt., give & grant unto NICHOLAS JERNOW Gent., Nine hundred acres of Land
          scituate upon ye South side of PATOMACK RIVER begining at a white oake which
standeth upon a point on the Eastward side of MACHOATICK CREEKE, South ( )st along
PATOMACK RIVER 300 poles to the West side of JERNEWS CREEKE into the Maine Woods
including many branches of the sd. JERNEWS CREEKE, South West 480 pole, Northwest
300 pole & downe MACHOATICK CREEKE to the place where it began, Northeast 480 pole;
the sd. Land being due unto the sd. NICHOLAS JERNEW by & for the transportacon of
Eighteene persons into this Collony all whose names are in Records menconed under
this Pattent; To have & to hold &c., yeilding &c., Given at JAMES CITTY & sealed with the
seale of the Collony the 18th of October 1650
                                   WILLIAM BERKELEY
KNOWE ALL MEN by these pr:sents that I NICHOLAS JERNOW for a valuable consideracon to mee in hand paid by HENRY CORBYN have sold unto the sd. HENRY his heires &
assignes for ever all my Estate claime & demand of ( ) Pattent & land therein specified
with ( ) belonging to him his heires for ever and doe by these pr:sents warrant the
same & every pt. & pr:cell of the pr:misses withall priviledges belonging to the sd.
HENRY CORBYN his heires or assignes for ever; against all men whatsoever always
P:vided that the sd. HENRY CORBYN his heires doe seate or cause to be seated within
three yeares after the INDIANS shall depart the sd. Land; In Witnes whereof I have
hereunto sett my hand & seale this 18th day of February 1659; I doe hereby acknowledge I was not a married man at the sealing & delivery hereof

Sealed & delivered in the presence of
    ELLIS COLMAN,   NICHOLAS JERNEW his marke,   ye Seale
    ROBERT MIDLETON, his marke
22: May 1660. This Assignemt. & Sale was acknowledged in Court by Mr. FRANCIS
CLAY, Attorney of the sd. NICHOLAS JERNOW & ANNE his Wife in both their names & the
said Sale & Pattent are recorded

KNOWE ALL MEN by these pr:sents that wee NICHOLAS JERNEW of YEOCOMOCO in the
County of Northumberland in Virginia, Planter, & ANNE JERNEW, Wife of the said
NICHOLAS JERNEW, have appointed our trusty and welbeloved Freind, GEORGE COL-
CLOUGH of WICOCOMOCO & FRANCIS CLAY of YEOCOMOMICO in the aforesd. County of
Northumberland Gent., or eyther of them our true & lawfull Attorney for us & in both
our names to acknowledge an Assignement of Bill of Sale endorsed uppon a Pattent
granted to me, the sd. NICHOLAS JERNEW, for 900 acres of Land lying at MACHOATICK in
the County aforesd., (which Pattent beareth date the 18th day of Octobr: 1650); & the
Assignemt. or bargaine & sale endorsed as abovesd. beareth date the 18th day of February 1659; unto HENRY CORBYN of the County of LANCASTER in Virginia, Gent., his heires
for ever; in any ( ) within this Collony of Virginia where the sd. CORBYN shall require
I the sd. NICHOLAS JERNEW doe alsoe give unto my Attorney or eyther of them full
power to acknowledge a Bond by mee entered into for ye Security of the sd. Land unto
the aforesd. HENRY CORBYN his heires dated the 18th of Febr: 1659; and wee the said
NICHOLAS & ANNE JERNEW and eyther of us p:ticularly doe hereby declare the said
acknowledgement to be made to be firme & stable and wee doe ratify what our said
Attorneys or eyther of them shall do in the pr:misses in as ample manner as if we ourselves were both us us there; In Witnes whereof wee have hereunto set our hands and
seales this 19th day of ( )
Sealed & delivered in the pr:sence of
    JA· GAYLARD,   NICHOLAS JERNEW ye Seale
    THOMAS PHILLPOTT   ANNE JERNEW, ye Seale
 This was confirmed ( ) JERNEW by the Oath ( ) in Court the 22th ( )
Test RI: FLYNT
 22th May 1660. This Lre. of Attorney was recorded

p.   KNOWE ALL MEN by these pr:sents that WM: GREENSTED of CHICACOAN in the
39   County of NORTHUMBERLAND and Collony of Virginia doe give for his marke of
      Cattle and hoggs (vizt,) a ( )yle on ye right eare, the left eare cropt and a hole
in the ( )
 19th June 1660. This marke was recorded

p.   PETER SMITH pray deliver unto JOHN STOWELL the Cowe which I bought of you
39   and to deliver him a Bill of Sale for her as Witnes my hand this 22th of December
      1657; And this my Note shall discharge you of Eighteene hundred pds: of tobac-
co & caske in pt. of a Bill which you passed to mee. Witnes my hand the day & yeare
above written   JOHN WOOD
 Test RICHARD AYRES; EDWARD WILLIAMS, his marke
 20th July 1660. This Discharge was recorded

p   These pr:sents may certify all those whome it may any wayes concerne that I
40   EDWARD COCESHUD of WICOCOMOCO, Planter, being very weake in body but of
      p:fect mind & memory (blessed bee my God) doe make & declare this my Last Will

& Testament if God please by this sickness or hereafter to call mee out of this life; in maner & forme following:

I give unto my loveing Freind, JOHN SMITH, one Heyfer with a white tayle.

What goods houses or stuffe hath bin bought since my Freind, THOMAS SHILES & I livered together I give my pt. unto him the sd. THOMAS SHILES.

I give unto JOHN HILL's third Child, one cowe calfe;

I the sayd EDWARD COCKSHED doe make my sd. Freind, THOMAS SHILES, the Executor of this my Last Will & Testamt. Witnes my hand this 17th day of the 4th moneth 1660 & my Seale

Witnessed sealed & delivered in presence of us
         EDWARD SANDERS,   PETER HULL   EDWARD COCKSHUD   ye Seale
21th July 1660. This Will was proved in Court by the Oathes of EDWARD SANDERS & PETER HULL to be the Last Will & Testamt. of EDWARD COCKSHUD deced., and with the Will is recorded

p.   ( )ember ye 24th 1659. IN THE NAME OF GOD Amen. I Coll. JOHN TRUSSELL
40   being ( ) of body but p:fect in memory doe make my Last Will & Testamt. as
          followeth. ( ) to God that gave it mee & my body to ( ) be buried decently with
Christian buriall. ( ) MARY TRUSSELL my plantacon that I nowe ( ), Sonne JOHN shaU come to age, and if ( ) come to age then the Land & plantacon ( ) Sonne, WILLIAM.

( ) Daughter, ELIZABETH, one hundred acres of Land ( ) BETTYS NECK;

( ) Sonne, WILLIAM. the Five hundred acres of Land ( ) DODSON survayed for mee in July last and that JAMES CLAUGHTON & ROBERT SECH be Overseers & see this Will full-fild;

Item. It is my will that the Cattle that are left after my debts are paid to be equally devided among my Children

Signed sealed in the p:sence of
         ROBERT SECH, JAMES CLAUGHTON   p me. JOHN TRUSSELL, ye Seale
         MATHEW SHIP's marke;
         ABIGAIL BRIDGES her marke
20th July 1660. This Will was proved in Court to be the Last Will & Testamt. of Coll. JOHN TRUSSELL deced., by the Oathes of MATHEW SHIP & ABIGAIL BRIDGES and the Will recorded

p.   IN THE NAME OF GOD. I JOHN BENNETT being dangerously sick in body but
40   p:fectly whole & sound in Soule & mind doe desire according to Gods appointmt.
          to put my house in order before my departure out of this life. I doe therefore
Will and Ordaine that my Last Will & Testamt. shall be recorded in manner & forme as followeth; (vizt.) First I recommend my Soule into the hands whoe hath created & re-deemed it beliveing stedfastly & trusting confidently (through ye merits of my God in the blood of Jesus Christ) to be received unto his heavenly Kingdome. I doe comitt my body to the Earth whence it had its first begining desireing nothing in this world but ( ) & decent Christian buriall. As for my worldly Estate, I doe by these pr:sents appoint & order that it shall be distributed & devided in manner & forme as followeth;

Imprimis. I will & ordaine that all the Lands belonging unto mee and whereof I am now pr:sently possest shall belong unto my lawfull Sonne, ROBERT CONNE( ) excepting the Hundred acres which did formerly belong to my Wife, the which I will to be re-stored back again to her & her heires; as alsoe I except one hundred acres out of my land in WESTMORELAND County which I bequeath unto my God Sonne, JOHN ( )OTT, Further I doe render up unto my aforesaid Sonne, his ( ) Cowes his yearling heyfer &

cowe calfe which I have had custody for him, as alsoe I give & bequeath unto him (   )
proper goods two yearling steeres; further I give unto (   )OTT my (   )onne, one black
heyfer of three yeares old with all her increase to him & his heires for ever; the sd.
heyfer is at pr:sent in NOMINYE; Further, I give my Sonne, ROBERT, one feather bed &
furniture, bolster; Further I give unto him one wyanscot (   ) gun (   ) that is nowe in
England to be (   ) to him two Sowes & three shotes (   ) one feather bed & a sute of cu(   )
my Sonne, ROBERT, one pestell; Further I leave my Child, ROBERT, (   ) whatsoever to
any p:son (   ) him to be counselled & a (   ) may concerne good breed(   ) continue with
her (   ) and his owne estate or does (   ) ELIZABETH BENNETT my (   ) appointing her
both to (   ) dispose of all the (   ) namely to receive (   ) by mee to any p:son (   ) desire
my sd. loveing (   ) my Sonne, ROBERT, with (   ) and wholesome victualls till (   ) for
himselfe & that now (   ) any nor other accomodacons (   ) her further I will that ANNE
NOTT if shee shall (   ) with her Mothers consent shall not have any Legacy from me;
Farther I desire Mr. NICHOLAS SPENCER that hee would take the oversight & superin-
tendence both of my Sonne, ROBERT, & his Estate, & of all my Wifes Children & their
Estates to see them brought up to vertue, & their goods & lands pr:served to them as
alsoe I desire him if hee shall chance to leave this Country to substitute & appoint some
honest man whom hee may trust to succeed in his charge which requests I trust hee
will p:forme; In Witnes hereof I have signed & sealed these pr:sents this 28 of May
1660
Witnes DA: LYNDSAY, HENRY ROCKE   JOHN BENNETT ye Seale
  20th July 1660. This Will was proved in Cort. by the Oathes of Mr. DAVID LYNDSAY &
HENRY ROCKE to be the Last Will & Testament of JOHN BENNETT deced., and the Will
recorded

p.   IN YE NAME OF GOD Amen. I WILLIAM BACON, Sonne & Heire of WILLIAM &
41   ANNE BACON, Vintener of LONDON, being very weake in body but of p:fect
            memory doe ordaine constitute & appoint this my Last Will & Testament Amen.
  Imprs. I give & bequeath my Soule to God Almighty whoe is the Father that gave it
mee trusting that hee will receive it into his glorious Kingdome;
  Item. I bequeath my body to my Mother Earth to be decently & Christianly buried after
the order of the Christian Church;
  Item. My whole & worldly Estate that is or shall ever hereafter be found any wayes
belonging unto mee, I doe give & bequeath unto my dearly beloved Wife, MARGARETT
BACON, and I doe make her my full Executrix of this my Last Will and Testament; And my
desire is that Mr. JOHN POWELL & Mr. THOMAS PHILLPOTT, shall assist her in it for the
better managing of it, and I will that if I have any goods sent out of England the next
yere that MARGARETT, my Wife, shall by vertue of this my Last Will also recover it &
dispose of it according to her will & pleasure & for the more (   )mty of it I have sett my
hand this 24th of July 16(   )
Witnes W(   ) COLMAN,   WILLIAM BACON
          WILLIAM PIGGOTT
  20th July 1660. This Will was proved in Court by the Oath of WILLIAM COLMAN to be
the Last Will & Testamt. of WILLIAM BACON Gent., deced., And the Will recorded

p.   BE IT KNOWNE unto all men by these pr:sents that we EDWARD WILLIAMS with
41   the consent of my Wife, TEMPERANCE, for a valuable consideracon have sold
            unto WILLIAM FISHER one (   ) acres of land with all ediffices cleare ground &
  (   ) now in the tenure of the sd. EDWARD WILLIAMS being (   ) of Three hundred forty
five acres of Land (   ) in the name of JOHN BRADSHAWE scituate (   ) in Northumber-

land. To have & to hold the sd. One ( ) hundred acres of land with the ediffices unto the sd WILLIAM FISHER his heires Exrs. Admrs. & assignes for ever and said EDWARD WILLIAMS with the consent of his Wife, TEMPERANCE WILLIAMS, doth covenant with WM: FISHER his heirs to defend harmless from all p:sons that shall lay claime thereto; In Witness whereof said EDWARD WILLIAMS and sd. TEMPERANCE have hereunto set their hands & seales the 17th of January 1656

Testes ( ) CARPENTER.   ED: WILLIAMS his marke, ye seale
         THO· BROUGHTON   TEMP: WILLIAMS her mke. ye seale
  20th July 1660. This Sale of Land to WM. FISHER was acknowledged in Court by EDWARD WILLIAMS & is recorded

p   I EDWARD WILLIAMS Attorney of JOHN STOELL. doe hereby assigne over all the
41   right & title of this Pattent unto PERCIVALL HAMMAND, As Witness my hand this
        20th day of July 1660   EDWARD WILLIAMS his marke
Witnes. FRAN. CARPENTER. PETER SMITH
  20th July 1660 This Assignemt. was acknowledged in Court by EDWARD WILLIAMS. Attorney of JNO. STOELL and is recorded. The Patt: was originally granted to JNO. WOOD by him assigned to JNO: STOELL & recorded in the other Booke of Records fol· 121

p   To all &c . Whereas &c . Now Knowe yee that I the sd. SAMUEL MATHEWES Esqr
41   do with the Consent of the Councell of State accordingly give & grant unto Capt.
        RICHARD BUDD two hundred acres of Land in Northumberland County bounding Southeast upon the head of GREAT WICOCOMOCO RIVER, Northeast upon the Maine Branch of the said River, Southwest upon another Branch and Northeast upon the Maine Woods. the sd. Land being formerly granted unto the sd. Capt. RICHARD BUDD by Pattent dated the 9th of March 1653. and nowe renewed by Order of the Governor & Councell bearing date with these pr:sents; as is due by & for the transportacon of fower p:sons into this Collony whose names are in the Records menconed under this Pattent; To have & to hold &c., Dated the 6th of October 1656.
                   SAMUEL MATHEWES   W. CLAIBORNE. Secr.

p   KNOWE ALL MEN by these pr:sents that I THOMAS WILLIAMS with ELIZABETH
41   my Wife doe for a valuable consideracon in hand received, assigne our right of
        this Pattent of Land within menconed and to warrant the said Land from any p:sons whatsoever as granted to us by Pattent & doe engage our selves to acknowledge the said Land in Court unto JOHN HUGHLETT or his assignes, As Witnes our hands this 2( ) of June 1660
Witnes JOHN BENNETT   the marke of THOMAS WILLIAM
       DAVID ILAND   the marke of ELIZ: WILLIAMS
  20th July 1660 This Assignemt. was acknowledged in Court by the sd. THOMAS WILLIAMS and is recorded next under the Pattent

p.   To all &c., Whereas &c. Now Knowe yee that I SAMUEL MATHEWES Esqr. doe with
41   the Consent of the Councell of State accordingly give & grant unto ROBERT
        COLLINS ( ) acres of land scituate in County of Northumberland bounding Northerly ( ) deced.. at certaine Branches ( )MAN & MORRATICOE NECK ( ) of WICO-COMOCO, South into the Maine Woods, the land being due by & for the transportacon of ( ) p:sons into this Collony whose names are in the Records under this Pattent· To have & to hold &c.   SAMUEL MATHEWES   W. CLAIBORNE. Secr.
  KNOWE ALL MEN by these pr:sents that I ROBERT COLLINS for a valuable consideracon

sell & assigne over unto JOHN HUGHLETT his heires or assignes for ever all my right in the abovesd Pattent & Land, and due engage my selfe to acknowledge the same in Court in p:son or by an Attorney at any time upon demand; Witnesse my hand this 19th day of Octobr: 1659

Witnesse: JOHN JONES, his marke.   ROBERT COLLINS
     GER: DODSON

  20th July 1660. This Sale & Assignemt. of Land was acknowledged in Court unto JNO: HUGHLETT by JAMES POPE, the Attorney of ROBERT COLLINS, & is recorded next under the Pattent

  KNOWE ALL MEN by these pr:sents that I ROBERT COLLINS haveing sold & assigned to JOHN HUGHLETT of WICOCOMOCO on thousand acres of land bounding on some land of JOHN CHANDLER at some Branches of the head of WICOCOMOCO as may appeare by the Assignemt. & Pattent: these pr:sents shall therefore appoint and substitute JOHN HAY-NIE or JAMES POPE or JNO: HOPPER any of them my true & lawfull Attorney to acknow-ledge the same in Court according to my engagemt., to acknowledge in p:son or by Attorney and I doe bind my selfe my heires &c., to ratify & confirme the same to be valid as if my selfe had done it in p:son; Witnesse my hand 8br the 19th Anno 1659

Witnesse GER: DODSON   ROBERT COLLINS
    WM. HUNT his marke

  20th July 1660 This Lre. of Attor: was recorded

p   To all &c.. Whereas &c., Now knowe yee that I the sd. SAMUELL MATHEWES Esqr.
42   &c. give & grant unto JOHN SHAWE fower hundred acres of land scituate & being
       in the County of Northumberland on the South side of GREAT WICOCOMOCOE RIVER & at the head of a Creeke which devides the lands of Mr. THOMAS SALISBURY & HENRY HUFFE (vizt.) Three hundred acres pt. thereof bounding North Northeast upon & betwixt ye two main Branches of the sd. Creeke, East Southeast upon the land of THOMAS KIDBY. South Southwest & West Northwest upon the Maine Woods, And one hundred acres the other pt. thereof bounding Northeast upon the abovesd. Land and the Land of THOMAS BAYLES, South Southwest upon ye land which was JOHN FAWSETTs, FREEMAN CONAWAYs &c.. West Northwest upon the land of Mr. ISAAC FOXCROFT & East Southerly upon a line running South Southwest from the Southeastern Corner of sd. BAYLES his land to the sd. FAWSETTs or BREWERs Land, the sd. Land being due unto the sd. JNO: SHAWE as followeth; (vizt.) Three hundred acres pt. hereof being formerly granted unto the sd. JOHN SHAWE by Pattent dated the first ( ) and the residue being One hun-dred acres by ( ) transportacon of two p:sons into this Collony whose names are in the Records menconed under this Pattent; To have & to hold &c., Dated the 17th of June 1658
         SAMUELL MATHEWES   W. CLAIBORNE, Secr.
  ( ) doe assigne & transfer all my right title ( ) this Pattent with all the land & privi-ledges ( ) unto WM. THOMAS his heires or assignes; Witnes my hand this 1th of June 1660   JOHN SHAW
  ( ) this Assignemt. was acknowledged in Court ( ) by RICHARD FLYNT, Attorney of the above ( ) recorded next under the Pattent

  KNOWE ALL MEN by these pr:sents that I JNO: SHAW doe constitute ordaine & appoint my loving Freind ( ) or PETER PRESLY or eyther of them my Attorney irrevocable by mee or any p:son to acknowledge the Assignemt. of a Pattent of Four hundred acres of land lying on ye South side of WICOCOMOCO RIVER & bounden on HENRY HURST, ( ) KEDBY, THOMAS BAYLES & ISAAC FOXCROFT and THOMAS SALISBURY for & in the be-halfe of me the said SHAW unto WM. THOMAS his heires & assignes for ever & whatso-ever my sd. Attorney or eyther of them shall act or doe concerning the pr:misses I doe ratify & confirme to be as authentiq as if that I was p:sonally p:sent, as Witnes my hand this 1th of June 1660

Witnessed by us: Sig. ED: COLES,   JNO: SHAW
       Sig. JNO: NEWTON

20th July 1660. EDWARD COLES & JNO: NEWTON did sweare in Court that this Lre. of Attorney was signed & delivered by the sd. JNO: SHAW as his act & deed
                     Test RI: FLYNT, Cl. Cur. Northumbld.
20th July 1660. This Lre. of Attorney & Depo: were recorded

p.   To all &c., Whereas &c., Now knowe yee that I the sd. SAMUEL MATHEWES Esqr.
42   &c. give & grant unto ROBERT BRADSHAWE three hundred forty five acres of
          Land scituate lying & being in the County of Northumberland abutting North-
east on MATOPANY RIVER, Northerly upon bank YEOCOMOCOE RIVER, North West upon the Land of LAURENCE DAMERON, Southeast upon the land of the sd. ROBT. BRADSHAWE & Southwest upon the Maine Woods, the said Land being formerly granted unto the sd. ROBERT BRADSHAWE by Pattent dated the 20th day of March 1652; To have & to hold &c., dated the 20th of Novembr: 1657
                     SAMUELL MATHEWES   W: CLAIBORNE, Secr.

KNOWE ALL MEN by these pr:sents that I ROBERT BRADSHAWE doe hereby assigne all my right of this Pattent within menconed unto EDWARD WILLIAMS his heires or assignes. In Witnes whereof I have hereunto sett my hand this Twenty one of J( ) 1660
Teste FRAN· CARPENTER.   ROBERT BRADSHAW
      DANIELL ROBERTS
21 July 1660 This Assignemt. of ROBT. BRADSHAWEs was acknowledged in Court by the sd. BRADSHAWE unto EDWARD WILLIAMS & is recorded with the Pattent

KNOWE ALL MEN by these pr:sents that I EDWARD WILLIAMS doe hereby assigne all my right of this within mentioned Pattent unto JAMES CLAUGHTON his heires or assignes, In Witnes whereof I have hereunto sett my hand this 21 of July 1660
Test DANIELL ROBERTS.   the marke of· EDWARD WILLIAMS
      THOMAS ( )
21th July 1660. This Assignemt. was acknowleged in Court by the sd. EDWARD WIL-LIAMS unto JAMES CLAUGHTON and is recorded

p.   To all &c. Whereas &c., Now knowe yee that I RICHARD BENNETT Esqr., give and
42   grant unto HENRY WEEKES Two hundred & Fifty acres ( ) side of GREAT
          WICOCOMOCOE RIVER, Northeast upon VULCANS CREEKE ( ) of the sd. Branch &
( ) Southwest into the Woods; To have & to hold ( ) 1652
KNOWE ALL MEN by these pr:sents that I GERVASE DODSON for a valuable consideracon have assigned unto RICHARD GIBLE his heires or assignes for ever ( ) acres of Land out of this Pattent joyning upon THOMAS SALISBURY & takeing its breadth according to the Pattent, (vizt.) a mile into the Woods, South Southwest from VULCANS CREEKE; Witnes my hand this 20th of ye 5th moneth called July 1660, with all hoseing & fences to be surrendered the middle of October next; Witnes my hand
                     GER: DODSON
Alsoe assinged upon the same tearmes for consideracon reced., in service one hun-dred acres of land, the residue of this Pattent runing accordingly with all appurte-nances unto DAVID ORLAND his heires or assignes for ever; Witnes my hand
                     GER: DODSON
20th July 1660. These Assignemts. to RICH: GIBLE & DAVID ORLAND were acknowledged in Court by JAMES POPE, Attorney of GERVASE DODSON & are recorded under the Pattent

being granted to HENRY WEEKES; Ye Lre. of Attor: is on ye other side
  Assignemt. from WEEKES to Mr. DODSON in folio 5, huius Libri.

p.   KNOWE ALL MEN by these pr:sents that I GERVASE DODSON make JAMES POPE my
43   true & lawfull Attorney to appeare for mee in my name before ye Comrs. of
        Northumberland & acknowledge the sale of One hundred & Fifty acres of land to
RICHARD GIBLE & One hundred acres of Land to DAVID ORLAND as may more fully appeare by the Assignemt. on the Pattent; I giveing my sd. Attorney as full power as I
might have; Witnesse my hand this 20th of the 5th moneth called July 1660
Witness WILLIAM JEFFARS.   GER: DODSON
         JAMES HILL
  20th July 1660. WM: JEFFARS & JAMES HILL did sweare in Court this to be the act & deed
of GERVASE DODSON.
                  Teste RI: FLYNT, Cl. Cur. Northumbld.

p.   KNOWE ALL MEN by these pr:sents that wee ROBERT BRADSHAW & ANNE my
43   Wife & JAMES CLAUGHTON & JONE my Wife of MATTAPONY in the County of
        Northumberland for diverse good causes & valuable consideracons paid, have
sold a certaine p:cell of land or peice of ground ( ) the two swamps or bays adjoyning
being neare the place where yee abovemenconed doe now live & abutting on a Branch
of MATTAPONY RIVER unto THOMAS SHEPHEARD & ROSE his Wife their heires and
assignes which sd. parcell of land is now & hath bin ( ) yeares last past in the possession of the sd. THOMAS & ROSE; To have & to hold the sd. Land with all appurtenances
unto the sd. THOMAS & ROSE SHEPHEARD their heires & assignes from the time of their
( ) & possession thereof and from the day of ye ( ) for ever to possess as their owne
proper Estate, warranting & defending the same to the use of the sd. THOMAS & ROSE
their heires for ever agt. any p:son that make any demand; In Witnesse whereof wee
have set our hands this ( ) day of Decembr: ( )
                  ROBERT BRADSHAW   ANNE BRADSHAW
                  JAMES CLAUGHTON   JOAN CLAUGHTON
  20th July 1660. This Writeing was acknowledged in Court by ROBERT BRADSHAW &
JAMES CLAUGHTON & JOAN his Wife & is recorded
  KNOWE ALL MEN by these pr:sents that I ANNE BRADSHAW doe give my free consent &
doe hereby acknowledge I have consented to & with my Husband, ROBERT BRADSHAW,
to sale of a peice of land sold by my sd. Husband unto THOMAS SHEPHEARD his heires or
assignes, As Witnes my hand this 20th of July 1660
Test ye marke of EDWARD WILLIAMS   ye marke of ANNE BRADSHAW
  20th July 1660. This Writeing was recorded

p.   KNOWE ALL MEN by these pr:sents that CHARLES ASHTON of CHERRY POINT
43   NECKE in the County of Northumberland doth give for his marke of Cattell &
        hoggs (vizt.) swallow forked on both eares & a notch under the right eare
  20th July 1660. This marke was recorded

pp.   AN INVENTORY of ye Estate of Coll. JNO: TRUSSELL deced., appraised by us the
43-   9th of Aprill 1660; by us whose names are hereunto subscribed, Vizt. Tobco/cask
44   Imprs. ABIGAIL BRIDE Servt., haveing a yeare & 3 qtrs. to serve -1000; 4 cowes
        with calves by their sides, 2 young cowe calves without their dams; 3 brown
steeres 3 yeares old a peice, 1 bull of the same age; 3 heyfers of 2 yeares old a peice, 4
yeare old beyfers & 1 yearling steere, a feather bed & bolster, 2 pillowes, 1 sheet, a rug,

2 blankets with curtaines & vallens & a chimney cloth; 2 old flock beds with ordinary covering, 6 pewter dishes, a pewter chamber pott, a flagon, qt. pott of pewter, a pew-ter candlestick, 3 brass kettles & a skillett, 3 iron potts, 11 treys, a boule, 21 pewter spoones, 3 Guns, 1 frying pan, pr. fire tongs, shovell, cutting hoe, hookes, 3 tables, 1 couch, a chair, 2 chests, 1 old chest, 1 old fourme, 2 Bibles, 1 old earthen pan, 2 hatt brushes; 1 lookeing glasse, 1 smoothing iron, 4 payles, 3 sifters; barrells, tubs, rundletts, a p:cell of hoes, axes, knife, 1 old cowe, 1 canowe.
   Sworne before mee JOHN ROGERS
   INVENTORY of Debts due to ye Estate of Coll: JNO: TRUSSELL; Imprs. JOHN HUDSONs Accot.; of JOHN GAMLIN, of JOHN CLARKE & DANIELL (   ); of RICHARD RICE by JO(   ); of THOMAS SHAW by a Bill, of WM. BEDLAM by Bill; of THOMAS HAZELRIG by Bill; of EDWARD WILLIAMS by Bill, of Mr. HUGH LEE p Accot., of VINCENT COX p. Accot., of WM. WALKER deced., his Bill; of THOMAS LAMPKIN by Bill, of Coll. SPEKE deced. by a Note under his hand; By HENRY WICKER by Bill; of JNO: JOHNSON p Accot; of JNO: HULETT 94 lbs. by Order for BRIDGET PRICKETT 100 lbs. in all; JOHN BENNETT p accot; JNO: HOPPER by 2 Bills delivered him; of HENRY HURST by Bill; of THOMAS DARROW by Bill; of COR-NELIUS ROBINSON by Bill, of JUSTINIAN TENNIS p Accot., of THO: BAILES Accot; of NICHO: SQUIRES Accot., of Mr. THO: HOPKINS Accot; reced in pt. by Mr. PETER ASHTON, of Mr. SAMPSON COOPER, ye Accot for funerall charges; 1310 lbs. reced in pt. in Accot. of Mr. COOPERs; 985 lbs. for the rest due from the Estate of sd. Mr. COOPER unto Coll. TRUSSELLs Estate, allowed him by the Comrs. when they made up the Levies to be taken out of the sd Levies for the Colls. trouble about the INDIANS -1500; Sume totall is 3575
   13th July 1660. Appraised by us whose names are hereunto subscribed part of the Estate of Coll. JNO: TRUSSELL deced., being absent when the former (   ) was made that is to say (   ) sowes, hoggs one boare, 7 piggs. appraised at 0850; (   ) yearling heyfer 0250; Total 1100.   WALTER WEEKES
                                 DANIELL ROBERTS
                                 JOHN CONTANCEAN
   20th July 1660. (   ) Relict & Admrx. of Coll. JNO: TRUSSELL deced. upon her Oath this to be a true Inventory of the Estate of the sd. Coll. TRUSSELL which was then recorded

p   KNOWE ALL MEN by these pr:sents that wee JOHN PEIRCE, HANNAH LEE and
44   WILLIAM GREENSTED of County of Northumberland for the love and affecon
      we have and beare unto the two Children of WILLIAM GREENSTED JOHN & WIL-
LIAM, wee doe by these pr:sents (   ) JOHN & WILLIAM each of them a Cowe Calfe (   ) JOHN GREENSTED about two moneths old by the name of Cherry, the marke a hole & a swallow forke crop & hole & a peice taken of (   ) the Calfe belonging to WILLIAM GREENSTED (   ) knowne by the name of Coale and the (   ) the former red Calfe; To have & to hold the said Cowe calves & their future increase for ever; HANNAH LEE, WILLIAM GREENSTED & JOHN PEIRCE doe by these pr:sents give to the above named JOHN & WM: GREENSTED one black heyfer with a white spot or two in the flanke two yeares old & upwards, the marke a crop in the left eare with two slitts in it, and a slitt in the right eare and a small peice cut of on the top of it; To have & to hold the sd. heyfer & her future increase as their pper: goods for ever; onely the first cowe calfe wee doe give to ELIZABETH the Daughter of WILLIAM GREENSTED and the male cattle that shall come of the whole stock shall goe to the Father or Guardian of the sd. Children for his care of the Stock. And if eyther of the Boyes dye before they come to age the Survivor shall enjoy the whole Stock. And if the boyes doe live till they come to age, then to be devided equally betweene them, And we the aforesd. JOHN PEIRCE, HANNAH LEE & WILLIAM GREENSTED JUNIOR doe bind us our heires Exrs. & Admrs. to defend the aforesd. Gift of

two cowe calves & heyfer & their increase from the claimes of any p:son or p:sons whatsoever; In confirmacon wee have caused this Deed of Gift to be made this 16th day of June And have sett our hands & seales
Signed Sealed & Delivered in the pr:sence of us
      THOMAS ADAMS,   JOHN PERSE   ye Seale
      MICHAELL VANLANDIGHAM   ye marke of HAN: LEE ye Seale
                                 WILL: GREENSTED ye Seale

  20th July 1660. This Deed of Gift was acknowledged in Court by the above mencomed JOHN PERSE & WM: GREENSTED & by RICHARD FLYNT, Attorney of the abovesd. HANNAH LEE, and the sd. Deed is recorded

  MR. FLYNT, my respects pr:sented; I received of WILLIAM GREENSTED a Cowe calfe for bringing his Wife twice to Child bed. I have given the sd. Calfe to his Sonne, WILLIAM, and I doe authorize you my loveing Freind to acknowledge it in Court; Yor loveing Freind
Teste JOHN PERSE, HUGH LEE   HANNAH LEE   her marke
  20th July 1660 This Lre. of Attor: was recorded

p.   KNOWE ALL MEN by these pr:sents that I ALEXANDER MACOTTER for a valuable
44   consideracon to mee in hand paid by WALTER MOORE have bargained & sold
       unto the sd. WALTER MOORE ( ) about ye age of two years of colour black ( ) cropt and a hole in each eare; To have & to hold to WALTER MOORE his Exrs. & assignes and I the sd. ALEXANDER MACOTTER my heires & every of us the said heyfer ( ) increase unto the sd. WALTER MOORE will ( ) by these pr:sents; Witnes ( )
Witnessed by SAMLL. SMYTH, RI: FL( )
  20th July 1660. This Sale was recorded

      WALTER MOORE his marke of Cattle & Hoggs. ( )
  20th July 1660. This marke was recorded

p.   These pr:sents witnesseth that WILLIAM BACON for my selfe my heires sell
44   unto THOMAS LAMKIN his heires and assignes a heyfer ( ) being marked ( )
       in the right eare & the left eare whole with all her increase upon payment of Five hundred pounds of tobacco, for which hee hath passed Specialty for dated March 25th 1658; the which heyfer with a calfe by her side hee hath already received; Witnes my hand March 25th 1658
Wit: ROBT. BINAM his marke   WILLIAM BACON
  sig. THO: DUNKINTON
  I FRANCIS CLAY, Administrator of the Estate of WM. BACON deced., doe acknowledge to have reced. the full contents of the tobacco within mencomed of THO: LAMBKIN as witness my hand this 27th of December 1658   FRANCIS CLAY
  27th July 1660. This Accot. of Mr. CLAY together with Mr. BACONs Sale of a Heyfer & Calfe to THOMAS LAMKIN was recorded

p.   To all &c., Whereas &c. Now Knowe yee that I the sd. Sr. WM. BERKELEY Knt., &c.
45   give & grant unto THOMAS MOULTON Two hundred acres of Land scituate & being
       on the head of HALLOWES CREEKE bounding on the Land of JNO: VAUGHAN & running North 320 pole, West 100 pole, South 320 pole, East along the Creeke side 100 pole to the place where it first began; the sd. land being formerly granted unto WM. FREAKE by Pattent dated the 11th of September 1653, & by him assigned unto JOHN BEARD & by the sd. BEARD assigned unto the sd. THOMAS MOULTON and now renewed

by order of the Governor & Councell bearing date with these pr:sents; To have & to hold
&c., Dated the 16th day of May 1660
                      WILLIAM BERKELEY   W. CLAIBORNE, Secr.
    KNOWE ALL MEN by these pr:sents that wee THOMAS MOULTON and JOANE MOULTON doe
hereby assigne all our right & interest of this Pattent of Two hundred acres of Land
unto THOMAS CARNELL his heires or assignes for ever as Wit: our hands this 5th day of
September 1660
          PAUL LITTLEFEILD, his marke   THO: MOULTON
                                                  JOANE MOULTON her marke
    KNOWE ALL MEN by these pr:sents that I JOANE MOULTON doe appoint (   ) Freind,
RICHARD SPAN. to be my lawfull Attorney to assigne my right of this Pattent in Court
unto THOMAS CARNELL his heires or assignes for ever; as Witt: my hand this 5th day of
September 1660; And doe alsoe ratify what my sd. Attorney shall doe to be authentiq as
if I were there p:sent; As Witt: my hand
Witnes: WM. THOMAS.   sig.   JOANE MOULTON
          PAUL LITTLEFEILD his marke
    5th 7br. 1660 This Assignemt. was acknowledged in Northumberland County Court by
the abovesd. THO: MOULTON & by RICHARD SPAN. Attorney of JOANE MOULTON. and is
recorded with the Pattent

p.   KNOWE ALL MEN by these pr:sents that I FRANCIS CLAY of (   ) of County of
45   Northumberland Gent., in consideracon of the sume of Five thousand pounds of
          tobco. in hand paid have granted unto RICHARD EATON & ADAM YARRETT all that
Land on the South side of (   ) RIVER, butting North North East (   ) at the head thereof;
East South East (   ) Coll. JNO: MOTTROM, West North West into the Maine Woods, (   )
Branches of GREAT WICOCOMOCO RIVER containing (   ) hundred acres of Land together
with all rights & appurtenances belonging; To have & to hold to them the said RICHARD
EATON & ADAM YARRETT their heires & assignes for ever; by the Rent referred by the
Pattent in which the sd. Land is granted to mee which Pattent is dated at JAMES CITTY in
June 1658: And I doe hereby warrant the sd. Land unto the said RICHARD EATON &
ADAM YARRETT their heires & assignes to be free from any p:son whatsoever; In Wit-
ness whereof I have hereunto sett my hand & seale this 28th day of July 1660
Sealed & Delivered in the presence of
          JA· GAYLARD.   FRAN: CLAY, ye seale
          ANTHONY LENTON, his marke
    5th 7br: 1660. This Sale of Land was acknowledged in Court by the sd. Mr. CLAY and is
recorded
    KNOWE ALL MEN by these pr:sents that wee RICHARD EATON & ADAM YARRETT for a
good & valuable consideration to us in hand pd., have granted unto FRANCIS CLAY Gent.
Fower hundred acres of land lying at the head of CHICKACONE RIVER, bounding according to a Grant thereof made unto us from the said FRANCIS CLAY this pr:sent day; To
have & to hold to him his heires for ever; and wee warrant the sd. land to him the sd.
FRANCIS CLAY to be free from any claimes of any p:son whatsoever, Provided alwaies &
upon condicon that if the sd. RICHARD EATON & ADAM YARRETT or eyther of them doe
well & truly pay unto the above named FRANCIS CLAY or his assignes, the fyull sume of
Five thousand pounds of tobco: & caske in manner & forme following, (vizt.) 2500 lbs. of
tobco. & caske at or before the Tenth day of October which shall be in the yeare of our
Lord God 1661, and 2500 lbs. of tobco. & caske at or upon the Tenth of October which
shall be in the yeare of our Lord God 1662, of their owne peculiar crop, then this
pr:sent grant to be void & of none effect anything hereof contayned to the contrary

thereof in any wise notwithstanding; In Witnes whereof vee have hereunto sett our
hands and seales this 28th day of July 1660
Sealed & Delivered in the presence of
     JA: GAYLARD,   RICHARD EATON ye seale
     ANTHONY LENTON, his marke   ADAM YARRETT ye seale
  5th 7br: 1660. This Assignemt. was ( ) in Court & is recorded

p.   BEE IT KNOWNE unto all men that I SIMON RICHARDSON for a valuable consider-
43   acon have sold unto THOMAS GERRARD ( ) of Land part of ( ) To begin at the
     bott( ) HERRING CREEKE & ( ) house of the sd. SIMON RICHARDSON ( ) woods
along the HERRING CREEKE; To have & to hold unto the sd. THOMAS GERRARD his heires
& assignes for ever, warranting against all psons by me the sd. SIMON RICHARDSON my
heires by these prsents, Witnes my hand the 20th day of Aprill 1659; All priviledges
granted unto mee, the sd. SIMON RICHARDSON is granted unto the sd. THOMAS GERRARD
his heires & assignes for ever
Witnes: GEO: COLCLOUGH. ISAAC FOXCROFT   SIMON RICHARDSON
  5th September 1660. This Sale of Land was acknowledged in Northumberland County
Court by the above named SIMON RICHARDSON unto THOMAS GERRARD & is recorded

p   To all &c., Whereas &c., Now knowe yee that I the said RICHARD BENNETT Esqr.,
46   &c. give & grant unto GERVASE DODSON Thirteene hundred acres of Land scitu-
     ate in the County of Northumberland now WESTMORELAND and in UPPER
MACHOATICK NECK, bounding Easterly upon a line runing Northerly from the corner
marked tree of a line which devides the land of PALMER HINTON from the Land of
KOPHER BOYCE, to the Miles End of Mr. TOWNSENDs Land; Southerly upon the Land of the
sd BOYCE, Northerly upon the Land of Mr. TOWNSEND & Westerly upon the Maine Woods,
the sd. Land being due unto the sd. GERVASE DODSON by & for the transportacon of
Twenty six psons into this Collony whose names are in the Records menconed under
this Pattent, To have & to hold &c., Yeilding & paying &c., Dated the 13th of October ( )
            RI: BENNETT   W. CLAIBORNE, Secr.
  These prsents witnesseth that I GERVASE DODSON doe engage my selfe my heires &
assignes to warrant & firmly possess JOHN SMYTH of a Pattent of Thirteene hundred
acres of Land specified according to the contents of the within specified Pattent and
shall further insure unto the sd. SMYTH his heires & assignes upon consideracon
already received, As Witnesse my hand this 17th of August 1658
  ( ) of the above specified engagemt., I doe oblige my selfe my heires or assignes to
pforme or pay unto JOHN SMYTH his heires or assignes the sum of Thirty ( ) of tobco.
upon demand; Witnes my hand the date abovesaid
                   GER: DODSON
  5th 7br: 1660. This Sale of Land to the above named JOHN SMYTH was acknowledged in
Northumberland County Court by JAMES POPE, Attorney of the abovesd. GER: DODSON &
ISBELL his Wife and is recorded
  I doe hereby constitute and appoint my loveing Freind, JAMES POPE, my true & lawfull
Attorney to acknowledge the sale of Thirteene hundred acres of land in Court which I
sold to Majr: JOHN SMYTH, and by him sold to HUGH DOWDING, the Land ( ) and what my
sd. Attorney shall soe doe as authentiq & valid as if I my selfe had done it; Witnes my
hand the 8th day of ye 6th moneth called August 1660
Witness JOHN SMITH, his marke   GER: DODSON
     MICHAELL MILLER
I ISABELL, Wife of the sd. GERVASE DODSON, doe likewise authorize the sd. JAMES POPE

to surrender up my right in Court of the sd. Land; Witnes my hand the day & yeare abovesd.
Witnesse THOMAS SHEILD, JAMES HILL   ISABELL DODSON, her marke
5th 7br: 1660. This Lre. of Attor: was recorded & by vertue thereof the Land menconed acknowledged in Court

| p. | AN INVENTORY of the Estate of HENRY TOPPIN deced., taken & appraised by us |
| 46 | whose names are subscribed; 20th August 1660. lbs. tobco: |

Imprs: His plantation contain 103 acres of Land with all appurtenances thereunto belonging: - 5000; A man servant 3 yeares & upwards to serve being in his seasoning; his wearing apparrel, a shirt & a hatt; five cowes & calves whereof fower of the sd. calves being two calves, one heyfer of 2 yeares old, 3 yeareling heyfers & one steere going on of 4 yeares old, 2 sowes, 2 barrowes of 3 yeares old, 3 barrowes of 2 yeares old, 10 shotes, his share of tobacco pitcht. by him for his crop; 4000 hills of Corne, 2 pair of blanketts & 2 ruggs, a small feather bed & bolster & a paire of canvas sheets, 2 guns with 30 lbs. ( ), 7 yards of blew linnen, 6 ells of dowlas, 7 ells of locerum, 9 ells of canvas, 3 lbs. & 1/2 of thred, a p:cell of spice, p:cell of fishing line, 4 knives, 4 paire of shooes. small table cloth; great chest; a table & forme; 6 pewter dishes; 9 spoones, great kettle, 2 iron potts, 2 frying pans, pestle, old falling axes, paire of fire tongs, p:cell of earthen ware, 8 milke treys. 2 meale trays & 3 sifters, 2 payles & a wooden dish, 4 empty caskes, a grindstone, an old Sea-bed & rugg, p:cell of Salt, p:cell of Poultry, p:cell of Lumber: WILLIAM HOPKINS his Bill; JNO: KENTs 3 Bills.   Summe totall 17305
Jurat coram me JOHN ROGERS   JAMES CLAUGHTON   ROBERT SECH
                         ROBERT BRADSHAW   DANIELL ROBERTS
5th 7br. 1660. THOMAS ADAMS, Admr. of HENRY TOPPIN deced., declared on his Oath this to be a true Inventory of ye Estate of the said TOPPIN and the sd. Inventory was recorded

| p. | To all &c. Whereas &c., Now know yee that I the said Sr. WILLIAM BERKELEY |
| 47 | Knt., &c., give & grant unto HUGH LEE Fower hundred acres of Land lying in |

Northumberland County upon the Eastward side of YEACOCOMOCO RIVER being pt. of a Dividend of Land conteyning One thousand acres granted unto WILLIAM NEW-MAN & JOHN MEEKES, by Pattent dated the 6th of May 1651; And bounded on the Northeast on YEOCOCOMOCO RIVER, on the Southeast with the Six hundred acres residue of the aforesd. Pattent into the Woods, Southwest parallel with the first angle and finally Northwest abutting the Land of ANTHONY LENTON to the place where it began being opposite to the mouth of a Swampe on the head of the sd. River; the sd. Land being formerly granted unto JOHN MEEKES & WILLIAM NEWMAN & by them assigned unto the sd. HUGH LEE. To have & to hold &c., Yeilding & paying &c., Dated the 28th of March 1660
               WILLIAM BERKELEY   W. CLAIBORNE, Secr.
KNOWE ALL MEN by these pr:sents that I HUGH LEE for my selfe my heires or assignes transfer unto JOHN LANDMAN, the Sonne of ( ) LANDMAN deced., & to his heires for ever all my right & interest to that Two hundred acres of Land (pt. of this Pattent) adjoyning to the Land of ANTHONY LENTON with all edifices or appurtenances; Witnes my hand the 5th of September 1660   HUGH LEE
5th 7br: 1660 This Assignemt. was acknowledged in Northumberland County Court by the above named HUGH LEE and is recorded with the Pattent

| p. | KNOWE ALL MEN by these pr:sents that I JENKIN PRICE doe for a consideracon |
| 47 | in hand already received sell unto JOHN MOUTON his heires & assignes all my |

right & interest of this Pattent of Land with warranty against any p:son that

shall thereto make claime for confirmacon witnes my hand this 14th day of November
        the marke of THO: KNIGHT   the marke of JENKIN PRICE
5th 7br: 1660. This Assignemt. was acknowledged in Northumberland County Court by
RICHARD FLYNT, Attorney to JENKIN PRICE, and is recorded. The Pattent for the Land
above menconed is recorded in folio 13 huius Libri granted to THO: BREWER

   I JENKIN PRICE doe by these pr:sents authorize RICHARD FLYNT, Clerke of the County
of Northumberland, to acknowledge a tract of Land containing Four hundred acres
which was bought joyntly betweene mee and JNO: MOUTON of one THOMAS BREWER; all
my right & title of the aforesd. Land. I doe hereby impower you the aforesd. RICHARD
FLYNT, to acknowledge from mee my heires or assignes for ever unto JNO: MOUTON his
heires or assignes as by an Assignemt. appeareth; & for confirmacon thereof I doe
hereby sett my hand
Teste WILLIAM HAWKES,   ye marke of JENKIN PRICE
       HENRY FLEETE
5th 7br: 1660. This Lre. of Atto: was recorded

p.   KNOWE ALL MEN by these pr:sents that I JOHN HOPPER doe assigne over unto
47   Mr. EDWARD SANDERS my full right & title of this Bill of Sale to him the sd. SAN-
          DERS & his heires for ever; as Witnesse my hand this 9th day of September 1660
Test PETER HULL;   JNO: HOPPER , his marke
     JOHN BORN, his marke   DOROTHY HOPPER her marke
18th September 1660. This Assignemt. was acknowledged in Northumberland County
Court by the above named JOHN HOPPER & DOROTHY his Wife and is recorded.
  The Bill of Sale here assigned being 100 acres of Land is recorded in the other Booke of
Records in folio 135, and acknowledged in Court by THO: BREWER to JOHN HOPPER (whoe
sold the sd. 100 acres of Land to the sd. HOPPER January the ( ) 1657

p   KNOWE ALL MEN by these pr:sents that I THOMAS WILLIAMS of GREATE WICOCO-
47   MOCO doe hereby make over all my right of these within mentioned p:ticulars
          unto my Daughter in Law, ELIZABETH JERVICE, for her use; one rugg, two blan-
kets, feather bed bolster & pillow, one sute of curtains & vallens, lookeing glass, Silver
Wine cup with a sw( ); and these to possess & enjoy ( ) date hereof for ever; As Witnes my hand this ( ) Aprill Anno Dom: 1660
Test THO: DENT; THOMAS ( )
  More I give one ( ) the hands of the said ( )   THOMAS WILLIAMS
  18th 7br: 1660. This ( ) in Northumberland

p.   ELIZABETH JERVICE her marke (the Daughter of E( )
47   18th 7br. 1660. This marke was recorded

p.   THOMAS HAZELLIPS Assignemt. of a Heyfer to JNO: COMPTON
47   KNOWE ALL MEN by these pr:sents that ( ) in consideracon of a ( ) of a Cowe
          of JOHN COMPTON ( ) given him by GEOR: COLCLOUGH &c., I doe make over one 2
yeare old heyfer cropt on the right eare & a hole in it & cropt on the left eare & under-
keeted; To have & to hold all her female increase for ever; Witnes my hand the first of
Octobr: 1660   sig.   THO: HAZELLIP
  1d. 8br. 1660   This Writeing was recorded

p.   WM: DAVIS, Gaurdian to HENRY MEDCALFE, doth pr:sent in unto this Court a
47   true & just list of the female cattle of the sd. HENRY MEDCALFE wch: are 7 in
          number, (vizt.) 2 goeing on 5 yeares old & 2 moneths, 1 goeing on 7 yeares old, 1

goeing on 4; 2 goeing one yeares old & 1 goeing on a yeare old.

WM: DAVIS his marke

1d. 8br: 1660. Jurat in Cur et Record

p.   In ye Yeare of or: Lord 1660, the 19th of Septembr:
48   I JOHN EARLE being sick yett haveing my pfect memory & understanding &
knowing the certainty of death & the uncertainty when, I therefore desire that
this my Last Will & Testament shall stand in full power. First I doe bequeath my Soule to
God from whence I have received the same & my body to the Earth from whence it was
taken; comeing to the disposeing of my temporall Estate, I doe give to my two Sonnes,
SAMUELL and JOHN, my Plantacon where now I live; Five hundred acres with ye
houseing to my Sonne, SAMUELL, and the other Five hundred acres to my Sonne, JOHN,
with the cattle belonging to them by the severall markes being knowne, I doe give to
my Daughter, MARY EARLE, the cattle which are markt. for her. And I will that my
Sonne, SAMUELL, shall have the lookeing to the sd. Cattell untill his Brother or Sister
shall come to age or marry and that every one of them shall have the benefitt as well of
male cattle as of female;
  I give to my Daughter, MARY, my feather bed & what ( ) a greene rugg;
  I give to my Sonne, SAMUELL, a feather bed & a rugg;
  I give my Sonne, JOHN, a bed halfe stocke & three ( );
  I give to my Wife, ELIZABETH, the Land and ( ) stuffe & all that did belong unto her
before ( ) her with her cattle, alsoe a man Servant she shall receive of JOSEPH HORS-
LEY. Alsoe I ( ) my Wife the three hundred acres of land lately ( ) THO: BROUGHTON
for her & JOHN CAWSEYs ( ) laid out of my Estate & what shall be ( ) shall be equally
devided betweene my ( ) Sonne, SAMUELL, a Bull which is black ( )earing clothes
unto JOHN CAWSEY. ( ) I desire shall be killed for my buriall ( ) my Wife shall see that
all my debts are paid; my Sonne, JOHN shall life with her during her widowhood, shee
promiseing to free my ( ) Morter. desireing that my Sonne, ( ) & live upon my plantacon & that ( ) Stock shall be kept upon the said ( ) hee come to age, leaveing my
Wife Executrix to this my Last Will I have sett my ( )
Witnesses PEETER LEFEBUR,   JOHN EARLE ye Seale
     NICHOLAS JERNEW his marke
14 9br: 1660. This Will was proved in the County Court of Northumberland by the Oath
of NICHOLAS JERNEW, to be the Last Will & Testament of JOHN EARLE deced., and execucon thereof committed to ELIZABETH EARLE; the Widdow & Relict of the sd. JNO: EARLE,
and the Will is recorded

p.   ANNE THORNTON aged 30 yeares or thereabouts sworne & examined sayth that
48   JOSEPH HINE, Boatswaine, of ye good Ship called ye "Recovery of Bristill," lying
in WICOCOMOCO RIVER at anchor, the sd. JOSEPH HINES did then & there aboard
the sd. Ship lye with yor: Depont. and begott her with Childe & further this Depont.
sayth not.   ANNE THORNTON, her mke.
  14th 9br: 1660 Sworne before us, SAMUEL SMYTH,
                    &   GEO: COLCLOUGH
  14th 9br. 1660. This Depo: was recorded

p.   KNOWE ALL MEN by these prsents that I WILLIAM JEFFARS of the County of
48   Northumberland doe out of the reall and true love which I doe beare unto my
Nephew, WILLIAM WALKER JUNR., give one heyfer of two yeares & nine
moneths old colourd. & marked as followeth; a deep Red with a mealy nose; crop on both

eares & two slitts in the crop of the left eare & a hole in the right eare; unto him his
heires or assignes for ever; And that STEPHEN BAILY shall have the keeping of the sd.
Beast during ye minority of ye sd. Child, & that hee, the sd. BAILY, shall have the male
for his care & paines; And when hee comes to age to have the male & female for ever;
And this I doe acknowledge to be my act & deed, as Witnesse my hand this 14th day of
November 1660.   WILLIAM JEFFARS
  14th Novem: 1660. This Deed of Guift was acknowledged in Northumberland County
Court by the above named WILLIAM JEFFARS & is recorded

p.   I ALEXANDER MACCOTTER doe assigne all my right & title of this Pattent & with
48   all right & priviledges belonging unto the same unto GEORGE PICKERIN &
          CHARLES HOYLE their heires or assignes for ever; Witnes my hand this 15th of
November 1660.
Witnes JAMES AWSTON, THOMAS ( )   ALEXANDER MACCOTTER his mke.
       RICHD: PLYNT
  15th 9br. 1660. This Assignement was acknowledged in Northumberland County Court
by ALEXANDER MACCOTTER & is recorded. The Pattent was granted to ( ) assigned by
them to ALEXANDER MACCOTTER ( ) huius Libri 21: N( )

p   Mr. DODSON to Coll. LEE & the Comrs.
48   Freinds, I intended ( ) weakness hindered & ( ) esxpecially to come to the
          Pro( ) of enlargemt., out of ( ) all p:don & freedome ( ) given out in print ( )
then hinder mee ( ) you from one you all ( ) assert that nothing ( ) & Just price, yett
( )nesse then greatnesse ( ) in love & p:fect V( ) FAIRE FEILD for Noble ( ) Master
( ) & doubt not but yor: love ( ) the wor( ) us for his sake (being his charge his
Children, hee the Father to the Common Weale REx pater patrie (besides yor owne vir-
tues will cause you to leade us by yor: good example in that way, whoe are not to be
quite cast off. for if any of us in p:ticular be nothing but as ciphers you know ciphers
make the figures more of vallue, therefore butt a Royall Kings invitacon take place in
all & the rather it being the Command of the King of Kings love one another as hee
loved us there being noe other way to happiness. I have sent my beloved Wife &
Attorney in my stead to seeke those things & gett my claime recorded whoe am a reall
lover of my King & all his people in p:ticular & yr:selves whome I desire God to leade in
his way for your and our happiness   GER: DODSON
  15th 9br: 1660. This was recorded

p.   MR. DODSONs Claime of the Kings Pardon
49   These may certify that I GERVASE DODSON haveing been a Soldier severall
          yeares in Ireland & England for the King & Parliament till the death of the late
King Charles the First, when I left all & came into this Country, & Now God haveing
pleased in mercy to bestowe his hopefull Sonne, Charles the Second, to the Throwne
whoe hath given a free p:don to all & alsoe liberty to tender consciences of within forty
dayes by any Publiq Act they lay hold & claime the same & returne to their obedience, I
the said GERVASE DODSON whoe ever loved the Kings p:son & posterity onely opposed
that which the Parliamt. said ruined him & the Land (Evill Councell) which I could not
p:sume to knowe soe much as they, I doe hereby lay claime to the said pardone & favour
& if I have done sayd or written any thing at any time which might be soe construed
doe hereby desire to fly to the same a ( ) full & absolute indemnity; And engage to be
faithfull to the sd. King Charles the second our ( ) Prince next under Christ Jesus ( )
to enjoy protection & liberty of conscience ( ) my God as the King hath p:mised in his

( ) which I have claime as my right, and I ( ) beloved Wife & Attorney to deliver this in ( ) RICHARD LEE & the Comrs. of Northumberland (to be) recorded & if need be it is set over ( ) done or read publiquely; Witness my hand this 15th of the 9th moneth 1660
                                    GER: DODSON

15th 9br, 1660. This was recorded

p.   ( ) testifieth to all those to whome ( ) Knowe yee that I RICHARD BROWNE ( )
49   married with the Relict of WM: WARDER ( ) NECK, doe herein bind my selfe
          ( ) Wife now called ANNE BROWNE formerly ( ) heires or assignes firmely ( )
in the penall summ of One thousand pounds of merchantable & well condiconed tobco;
from this day forward & since the ( ) WARDER to all true intents by the ( ) of Justice
towards the inst. delivered ( ) of the deced., WARDER, ye sd. Will never to be ( ) of by
any demand of eyther mine or my ( ) as abovesd. but that by us it shall ever be holden
both powerfull & lawfull accorfding to order of Court already past within this County of
Northumberland for JOHN STANLEY to give sell or dispose at his owne discreson according to his owne Will or Assignemt. during the tearme of his life & alsoe his heires or
assignes to command ye same as in case ye sd. STANLEY were liveing & present; In Witness to all wee the abovesd. RICHARD BROWNE & ANNE BROWNE, lately ANNE WARDER,
have hereunto sett our hands & seales this 2d. day of Novembr: 1660
Sealed & delivered in the sight of
          HENRY ROCKE,   RICH: BROWNE, ye Seale
          ROBERT HEWES   ANNE BROWNE, her mke., ye Seale
    17th December 1660. This Writeing was recorded

pp.   IN THE NAME OF GOD, Amen. I LAURENCE DAMERON being weake in body yett
49-   thanks be to God in good pfect memory doe make & ordaine this my Last Will &
50   Testament in manner & forme following;
          Imprs. I bequeath my Soule to God my Creater & my body to the Earth;
   It. I give & bequeath unto my Sonne, BARTH: DAMERON, one halfe of Five hundred
acres of land scituated in GREATE WICOCOMOCO which I bought of Mr. PETER KNIGHT; the
said land to be enjoyed peaceably by the sd. BARTHOLOMEW his heires for ever; & to be
delivered him at ye death of his Mother, with one Ceder Bedstead, one longe table with
forme & benches to it & one couch all which stands in the Greate Roome
   It. I give unto my Sonne, GEORGE DAMERON, the other halfe of the Five hundred acres
of land above specified to him & his heires for ever with one Ceder Bedstead, one small
Cedar table & one Couch, which all stand in the Chamber, to be delivered at the death of
his Mother and then the land & the houses to be equally devided betweene BARTHO:
DAMERON & GEORGE DAMERON;
   It. I give unto BARTHOLOMEW, GEORGE & THOMAS ( ) men Servants that have fower
yeares or more to serve, six barrells of Corne, ( ) sowes and good feather bed with ( )
guns, one good chest, ( ) & one little one, fower ( ) Silver spoones, these to bee ( )
they come to the age of ( );
   It. I give & bequeath ( ) one able man Servant ( ) serve, six cowes ( ) to it, on one
inlad ( ) iron pott, fower ( ) spoones to be deliv( )
   It. I give & bequeath ( ) of the further ( ) halfe of it & ( ) that & the head as ( ) for
them & their ( ) they come to the ( )
   It. My will is that if ( ) come to the age of ( ) then the Legacy ( ) equally devided
amongst the ( ) surviving to male;
   It. I doe give unto my Wife, DOROTHY DAMERON, (my Debts and Legacies being paid,
and my Children being maintained untill they come to the age of Seaventeene yeares)

the whole remainder of my Estate, hereby makeing her my full whole & sole Executrix
& hereby intreating and ordaining Mr. THOMAS HOPKINS and Mr. ABRAHAM BYRAN to
be the Overseers of this my Will and to see it p:formed; unto each of which sd. p:sons I
doe give Twenty shillings Sterling; In Witness whereof I have hereunto sett my hand
and this I acknowledge to be my Last Will and Testament as witness myhand this first
day of May 1660.
Witness: HENRY MAYES,   LAU: DAMERON
        THO: GASKINS
    17th December 1660. This Will was proved in ye County Court of Northumberland to be
the Last Will & Testaml. of LAURENCE DAMERON by the Oathes of THOMAS GASKINS &
HENRY MAYES, & Execucon thereof committed to DOROTHY DAMERON being appoint
Executrix in the Will, and the sd. Will is recorded

p.   THIS INDENTURE made the 15th day of May in the yeare of our Lord 1658 be-
50   twixt MARTINE COLE of the County of Northumberland, Planter, of the one pty.,
        & JONATHAN JADWYN of the County of NANSEMUND of the other pty., Witnesseth
that the sd. MARTINE COLE for diverse consideracons do for a valuable consideracon
received before signeing hereof doth assigne over unto the sd. JONATHAN JADWYN his
heires or assignes Two hundred acres of Land in sd. County of Northumberland on the
South side of PATOMACK RIVER in YEACOMOCO NECKE & beginning upn the sd. River betwixt the lands of JOHN ( ) the one side & JAMES WILLIS deced., on the other ( )
appeare more at large by the Pattent ( ) sd. North: County Court hereby ( ) Two hundred acres of land being the land whereon said MARTINE COLE now liveth; to the sd. Mr.
JONATHAN JADWYN his heires or assignes for ever agt. any p:son that may lay any
claime; In Witnesss whereof ye sd. MARTINE COLE hath hereunto put his hand & seale
the day & yeare above written
Witnesses GER: DODSON,   MARTINE COLE, his mke: ye Seale
        JAMES HAWLEY
    I the within menconed MARTINE COLE doe further oblige and bind my selfe my heires
to give the sd. Mr. JONATHAN JADWYN or his assignes lawfull possession of the sd. Land
& houseing (vizt.) of the Land at or before Christmas next & of the houseing at or before the last of May following, p:vided the sd. JADWYN or his assignes make lawfull
demand thereof; Witness my hand this 15th of May within menconed 1658
Witness GER: DODSON,   MARTINE COLE, his marke
        JAMES HAWLEY
    20th May 1658. This Sale of Land to Mr. JONATHAN JADWYN was acknowledged in Court
by Mr. JAMES HAWLEY, Attorney of the sd. MARTINE COLE & ALICE his Wife & is
recorded in the other Booke of Records
    I JONATHAN JADWYN doe assigne & transferre over all my right & interest of the with-
in menconed Bill of Sale for Two hundred acres of land with all the priviledges thereunto belonging unto ROBERT JADWYN his heires or assignes for ever without any further hinderance or molestacon; as Witness my hand this 5th of August 1658
Witnes: HENRY CLARKE,   JONATHAN JADWYN
        THOMAS WEB
    17th December 1660. This Assigneml. was acknowledged in Court by RICHARD BROWNE,
Attorney of the sd. JADWIN & is recorded next after the Bill of Sale for the sd. Land
    KNOWE ALL MEN by these pr:sents yt. I JONATHAN JADWYN of RAPPAHANNOCK in the
County of LANCASTER doe by these pr:sents appoint my loveing Freind, RICHARD
BROWNE, of the County of Northumberland my true & lawfull Attorney for me to ack-
nowledge a tract of land the which I bought of MARTINE COLE unto ROBERT JADWYN of

the County of Northumberland his heires for ever; whereunto I have sett my hand &
seale this twenty one of November ( )
Test PETER MOUNTAGUE;				JONATHAN JADWYN
  WM: DAVISON his mke.,
  GEO: MEDCALFE his mke.
 17th Decem: 1660. This Lre, of Attor: was recorded

p. ROBT. JADWYNs Lease of Houses to JONATHAN JADWYN
50 KNOWE ALL MEN by these presents that I ROBT. JADWYN of County of Northumberland ( ) and lett unto JONATHAN JADWYN ( ) DOGG & BEARE for ( ) lying &
being in the ( ) JONATHAN JADWYN to ( ) pounds lawfull money of ( ) the decease of
SISL( )GUE deced., Moreover ( ) or ( ) to have received a ( ) or ( ) Plantacon which
ther( ) moreover ( ) MARTIN COLE lying in ( ) Thirty pounds Sterling in ( )ERT
JADWYN deced., Moreover I the sd. ROBT. JADWYN doe by these prsents bind mee my
heires for the true p:formance above menconed unto JONATHAN JADWYN his heires
Exrs. Admrs. or assignes whereunto I have sett my hand & seale this twenty one of
November one thousand six hundred & sixty
Test PETER MOUNTAGUE,				ROB: JADWYN, ye Seale
  WM: DAVISON, his mke.
  GEO: MEDCALFE his mke.
 17th December 1660. This Writeing was acknowledged in Court by the above named
ROBERT JADWYN & is recorded(See facsimilie on back of Title Page)

(Compiler's Note: From *Cavaliers and Pioneers; Abstracts of Virginia Land Pattents and Grants,
1623-1666, by NELL MARION NUGENT, Originally published in 1934, from Pattent Book No. 4,
EDWARD DIGGES Esqr , Govr.)* p. 381. RICHARD WHITE, Cooper, EVAN DAVIS & SAMUEL
MANN, 1000 acs. in the Freshes of RAPPA. RIV. beg. at a Run of a Creek on the upper side of Land of
ABRAHAM MOONE & head of the land of sd. WHITE & JNO: GILETT, 6 Oct. 1658. p. 233 (332).
Trans: of 20 pers: including WM. TOMPSON, THO: WARRWICK, ROBERT JADWIN, SISLY JADWINN,
ROB: JADWINN SENR., JNO: JADWINN, JONATHAN JADWINN, JEREMY JADWINN &c.,)

p. KNOWE ALL MEN by these prsents that I ELIZABETH CLAIBORNE doe by these
51 prsents depute & authorize my well beloved Freinds, Lt. Coll. SAMUELL SMYTH &
  Mr. RICHARD FLYNT, joyntly & severally, to acknowledge & confirme unto Mr.
HENRY CORBYN his heires & assignes all the right & title by way of Dower or Thirds that
I have or may have in a Pattent of Land scituate in Northumberland County on the
North side of GREAT WICOCOMOCO RIVER called FAIR FEILD containing 1450 acres which
Land my Husband hath sold unto the sd. Mr. HENRY CORBYN, And I doe authorize my sd.
Freinds to make the sd. acknowledgemt. & confirmacon eyther joyntly or severally in
the Court of the sd. County of Northumberland or elsewhere; Witness hereunto my
hand & seale this 30th day of Novembr; 1660
Signed sealed & delivered in the presence of
  WM. BRERETON, ANTHONY ARNELL,		ELIZ: CLAIBORNE, ye Seale
  JOSEPH GRAVES
 17th December 1660. RICHARD FLYNT by vertue of the above ( ) acknowledged all the
right that the above named ELIZABETH CLAIBORNE have or may have unto the above
specified ( ) & confirmed the same in Cour to the ( ) of Mr. HENRY CORBYN his heires
& assignes & is recorded

p.
51   KNOWE ALL MEN by these pr:sents that I JANE BRERETON ye Wife (   ) BRERETON
doe depute & authorize my well beloved Freinds joyntly & severally, vizt., Lt.
Coll. SAMUELL SMYTH & Mr. RICHARD FLYNT to make acknowledgement in the
Court of Northumberland all my right & title by way of Dower or Thirds unto Mr. HENRY
CORBYN his heires or assignes (   ) I have in a Dividt. (   ) WICOCOMOCO called FAIRFEILD
being 1450 acres of land and all my right in the same; In Witness whereunto my hand &
seal this 30th day of Novembr: 1660

JANE BRERETON, ye Seale

17th December 1660. RICHARD FLYNT by virtue of the above mentoned Power acknowledged all the right title & interest eyther by way of Pattent or Dower that the
above named JANE BRERETON have had or may have in & unto the above specified
Pattent & Land & confirm'd the same in Court to the use & behoofe of the abovesd. Mr.
HENRY CORBYN his heirs & assignes and is recorded

p.
51   Whereas I JOSEPH HORSLEY have amongst some other discourse unadvisedly
spoken diverse & scandallous words might disparrage & defame ANNE, the Wife
of JOHN HULL, as by severall oathes appeare; Therefore I the sd. JOSEPH HORS-
LEY doe with all submission acknowledge that I have therein very much wronged the
sd. ANNE HULL & am heartily sorry for such my offence & doe oblige my selfe to pay all
costs of suit to the Sheriff & Clerke; Witnes my hand this 17th of December 1660

JOS: HORSLEY

21th January 1660   This was recorded

p.
51   To all &c., Whereas &c., Now Know yee that I the sd. Sr. WILLIAM BERKELEY
Knt. &c., give & grant unto HUGH LEE Three hundred ninety three acres of Land
scituate in ye County of Northumberland bounding (vizt.) 100: acres pt. thereof
abutting Northerly upon the sd. HUGH LEE; Southerly upon an OLD INDIAN FEILD, Westerly upon the Land of JAMES CLAUGHTON & Easterly upon the Maine Woods; And 228
acres one other pt. thereof abutting Southeast upon the head of a Swamp that cometh
out of KINGS CREEKE, Northeast towards the land of Coll. JNO: MOTTROM, Northwest &
Southwest upon the Maine Woods, and Five acres residue being a very angular figure &
lying at the head of the aforesd. Land upon & betwixt the land of Capt. JOHN ROGERS
called Coll. MOTTROMs Land & Coll. JNO: TRUSSELLs, bounding Northerly upon Capt. JOHN
ROGERS, Easterly upon the abovesd. 100 acres, Southerly and Westerly upon Coll. TRUS-
SELLs & the other 228 acres, Threehundred eighty & eight acres being formerly
granted unto the sd. HUGH LEE by Pattent dated 4th June 1656; And Five acres residue
taken up & joyned together by order of the Governor & Councell dated 24th 7br: 1659;
And allsoe being due by & for the transportacon of eight p:sons into this Collony whose
names are in the Records under this Pattent; To have & to hold &c., Dated this 5th day of
Aprill 1660   WILLIAM BERKELEY   W. CLAIBORNE, Secr.
Mr. HUGH LEE & HANNAH his Wife their Assignemt. of the abovesd. Pattent to Mr.
MATHEW RHODON
Witnes. MILES GOREHAM, JOSEPH ENGLESBY
21th January 1660. Recorded in Northumberland County Court
Mr. LEE's Lre. of Autor: to RICHARD FLYNT for Sale of Three hundred ninety &
three acres of Land in the County Court of Northumberland unto MATHEW RHODEN his
heires & assignes for ever; the sd. Assignemt. or Sale being endorsed on the Pattent for
the sd. Land & is scituated in the sd. County of Northumberland in Virgiia, giveing &
granting unto my sd. Attorney as full power to acknowledge the Land as aforesd. as if I
vere p:sonally p:sent; & did the same and shall and will rtify & confirme it to be good &

valid in Law; Witnes my hand this 2d. of January 1660
Witnes: ANDREW BASHAWE, his mke.   HUGH LEE
      SAMUELL COOPER
   21th January 1660. This Lre. of Attorney was recorded and the Land acknowledged

p.   TO ALL TO WHOME these pr:sents shall come, I MATHEW RHODON of the County
52   of Northumberland in Virginia, Planter, send Greeting in our Lord God ever
        lasting; Whereas by a Condicon under my hand bearing date the 29th day of
January 1648, I did bind my selfe to deliver unto HANNAH LEE, one Deed Writeing for ye
firme holding one hundred acres of Land within the Devident of Six hundred & Fifty
acres of Land surveyed by Mr. WM: MOORE the same yeare as by the Pattent thereupon
granted more at large appeareth; Now Know yee that I the sd. MATHEW RHODON doe
grant and confirme unto HUGH LEE & HANNAH his Wife one hundred acres of Land
scituated & being in the County of Northumberland begining at a marked tree called
THE MONARK TREE & running S: E: 53 pole & a qtr. where a Stake is sett up, thence E:N:E:
294 pole to a marked tree in the barrens; thence North 2/8 Westerly 39 pole to another
marked tree on the plaine, thence S: W: 13 pole & a qtr., to another marked tree from
the point called THE LANDING & from THE LANDING & soe downe the Creeke by the water
side about the Landing & so up to the MONARK TREE; To have & to hold the sd. 100 acres
of land with his due share of mines & mineralls therein contayned with all right waters
& rivers and all p:fits unto the sd.100 acres paying unto the (   )DON his heires or suc-
cessors yearly at the Feast of St. (   ) the fee rent of one Shilling (   ) which payment is
to begin (   ) the Pattent & not before; Witnes my hand & seale this 25th day of (   ) 1653
Signed Sealed & delivered in the presence of us
      JOHN ROGERS,   MATHEW RHODON   ye Seale
      KATHERINE ROCKE, her marke
   I HANNAH LEE & HUGH LEE doe assigne all our right of this Writeing to MATHEW
RHODON & his heires for ever; Witnes our hands this last day of Decembr: 1660
Witnes: MILES GORHAM,   the marke of HANNAH LEE
      JOSEPH HORSLEY   HUGH LEE
   21th January 1660. This Assignemt. was acknowledged in Northumberland County
Court by the above named HANNAH LEE & by RICHD. FLYNT, Attorney of the abovesd.
HUGH LEE, as their lawfull act & deed & is recorded with the Grant of Land above written
   The Lre. of Attor. is recorded in the next leafe following;
   I doe hereby fully impower & authorize RICHARD FLYNT my true & lawfull Attorney
for mee & in my name to acknowledge the Assignemt. above written in Northumberland County Court as my lawfull act & shall & will ratify & confirme the same to be good
& vallid in the Law as if I were p:sonally p:sent, & did the same; Witnes my hand this 4th
of January 1660
Witnes: MILES GORHAM,   HUGH LEE
      SAMUELL FISHER
   21th January 1660. This Lre. of Attor: was recorded & the Assignemt. acknowledged for
the foregoing Lease
   (On margin: Ye Assignemt. is in the pred: leafe made by Mr. LEE & his Wife to Mr.
RHODON)

p.   IN THE NAME OF GOD Amen. I JOHN BAYLES of ye County of Northumberland
52   being sick of body yett of sound & p:fext memory, knoweing the certainty of
        death & the uncertainty of time, doe make this my Last Will & Testament as fol-
loweth; I give my Soule to God and my body to the Earth to be buried in a decent man-

ner, as for my worldly Estate it hath pleased God to endow mee with ( ) of as followeth:

I give & bequeath unto my ( ) BAYLES one yellowish red Heyfer being of ( ) black
Heyfer with a Cowe Calfe ( ) marke with all their increase;

Item. I give to my Daugher. ELIZ( ) called Simple with a Cowe ( ) marked & one yearling Heyfer ( ) Simple likewise with all her increase ( ) & calfe of my owne marke;

Item. It is my will that my ( ) unto my Daugher, RA( ) two Heyfers with calfe ( ) my
Wife give her ( )

Item. For the Two hundred ( ) fower hundred acres ( )son I give to my d( ) Daughter, ANNE BAYLES;

Item. I give to my Sonne ( ) land this my Plantacon ( ) rest adjoyning to it w( ) Will
that hee shall have ( ) make a Crop if hee ( ) ELIZABETH BAYLES shall ( ) their sides
& three So( ) of age of fifteene yeares; ( ) Sonne ( ) portion to be equally devided
among the three Daughters (?) above specified

Item. It is my will that my Daugher. ELIZABETH. shall have a hundred acres of Land
joyning upon the Pond being part of this Pattent; It is my Will to give my Sonne my
Two gunns to be disposed of in Cattell for his use:

Item. I give to my Wife, ELIZABETH BAYLES, all my goods or Estate whatsoever not disposed of my debts being first paid. All this Will to be of force after my decease; As Witnes my hand this Eleventh day of March 1659

Witnes JOHN HULL; SYM· RICHARDSON   JOHN BAYLES his marke
21th January 1660. This Will was proved in the County Court of Northumberland by
the Oathes of JOHN HULL and SIMON RICHARDSON to be the Last Will & Testamt. of JOHN
BAYLES. deced., and the Will is recorded   .

p.   KNOWE ALL MEN by these presents that wee ROBERT SECH and JOHN CONTAN-
53   CEAN haveing a small tract or p'cell of land betweene us consisting of One hun-
         dred acres more or less from a Patint of a greater quantity the which sd. tract of
Land begineth at a Marsh called ye WHITE MARSH at a tree there marked with twelve
notches, being three notches of every side & runneth from the sd. MARSH & Tree soe
markt. upon a straight line to the KINGS CREEKE, South South West & lyeth from the
bounds & marked trees before menconed upwards towards the sd. KINGS CREEKEs head
the which Land being bought by us of JAS: CLAUGHTON! as appeareth by a Bill of Sale
under the sd. CLAUGHTONs hand & seale, with his Wife's, bearing date ye 26th January
1656: the said CLAUGHTON haveing formerly bought it of Mr. JOHN TRUSSELL as alsoe
appeares by Bill of Sale under the sd. Mr. TRUSSELLs hand & seale bearing date ye 20th
January 1652; Now know yee that the aforesd. ROBERT SECH & JOHN CONTANCEAN have
by this p'sent day devided the sd. small tract of Land as by marked trees appeareth
which sd. trees beginneth at Mr. HUGH LEEs corner tree being a twin( ) almost Southeast to a Hickory at the ( ) Swamp lying next to the now dwelling House ( ) the sd.
ROBERT to have that part of Land lyeth from the sd. now marked trees Northeast ( ) sd.
JOHN to have all the other part thereof which ( ) the sd. new marked trees Southwest
with all ( ) orchards & cleared ground ( ) ROBERT doe hereby acknowledge to have
received satisfacon and I the sd. ROBERT doe hereby ( ) my Wife MARY, the deviding of
the ( ) all interest in that devident wch: ( ) sd. JOHN for ever; and I the sd. JOHN ( )
alsoe the sd. devison of the ( ) disclaiming allsoe all interests of ( ) devident which
be-longeth to the sd. ( ). To the true p'formance and in ( ) have hereunto sett our
hands and ( ) of December 1660

                              ROBERT SECH ye Seale
                              ye marke of MARY SECH, ye Seale
                              JOHN CONTANCEAN, ye Seale

21th January 1660. This Writeing was acknowleged in Court by the above named
ROBERT SECH and JOHN CONTANCEAN & by JAMES CLAUGHTON, Attorney of the above said
MARY SECH, and the sd. Writeing is recorded

    KNOWE ALL MEN that I MARY SECH doe hereby authorize & appoint my loveing
Brother, JAMES CLAUGHTON, my Lawfull Attorney to acknowledge a Writeing con-
cerneing a devision of a small tract of Land as appeares by ye sd. Writeing unto which
my hand & seale being thereto bearing date the twelfth of this Instant December to be
acknowledged this succeeding Court; In Witnes whereof I have hereunto sett my hand
& seale this 15th of xbr: 1660
Signed Sealed & delivered in the presence of us
    DANIELL ROBERTS,   the marke of MARY SECH, ye Seale
    the marke of ABIGAIL BRIDGES
  21the January 1660. This Lre. of Attorney was recorded

p.   KNOWE ALL MEN by these pr:sents that I ANNE CLAY, Wife of FRANCIS CLAY, of
53   YEOCOMOCO in the County of Northumberland in Virginia, Gent., have appointed
        & ordeyned JAMES GAYLARD my true & lawfull Attorney for mee in my name &
place to acknowledge all my right to a certain p:cell of Land lying upon South side of
CHICCACONE RIVER conteyning by estamacon fower hundred acres unto RICHARD
EATON & ADAM YARRETT their heirs for ever in Northumberland County Court ratifying and confirming what my sd. Attorney shall act in the pr:misses in as ample manner to all intents & purposes as if I my selfe were p:sonally p:sent; & did the same; In
Witnesse whereof I have hereunto sett my hand & seale this 13th day of November 1660
Witnesse: RICHARD MADDOCKE   ANN CLAY   ye Seale
    LUCE SCUELL
  21th January 1660. This Acknowledgmt. was made by Mr. JAMES GAYLARD, Attorney of
the abovemenconed ANN CLAY in Northumberland County Court & is recorded

p.   IN THE NAME OF GOD Amen I ROBERT BRADSHAWE sick & weake in body but
53   p:fect in memory doe make this my last Will & Testamt. as followeth:
      Impr. I bequeath my Soule to God ( ) my Redeemer liveth & my ( ) with
Christian buriall;
  Item. I give to my Wife, ANNE BRADSHAW ( ) Estate when my Debts are paid ( )
Dater. ANNE BRADSHAWE ( ) not with Childe of a ( )
  Item. It is my will that if ( ) that hee lives to b( ) him two cowes of ( ) stocke & that
hee have ( ) that shee have ( ) yeares of age from ( )
  Item. It is my will that ( ) December the 8th 1660
Witnes JAMES CLAUGHTON,   ROBERT BRADSHAWE ye Seale
    THO: BROUGHTON
  21th January 1660. This Will was proved in the Northumberland County Court to be the
Last Will & Testament of ROBERT BRADSHAWE deced. by the Oathes of JAMES CLAUGHTON
& THOMAS BROUGHTON and the Will is recorded

pp.   KNOWE ALL MEN by these pr:sents that I THOMAS HOPKINS of the DEVIDEING
53-   CREEKE in the County of Northumberland & Collony of Virginia for a valuable
54   consideracon reced., have sold unto HENRY BENTLEY one Cowe & Heyfer marked
      (vizt.) the cowe is slitt in the middle of the right eare & the top of the under
peice taken away & a peice taken of the upper part of the rut of the eare: the left eare is
cropt & a hole slitt out which sd. Cowe was formerly claimed by one WILLIAM ALLEN,
the Heyfer is of my owne marke (vizt.) cropt & slitt on the left eare & under keeled on

ye right of colour darke red with a blackish mouth, white on the udder & a white patch under the right flanke. To have & to hold the sd. Cowe & Heyfer together with all former & future increase unto him the sd. HENRY BENTLEY his heires for ever; & doe for mee my heires warrant the sd. cattell & increase agt. any p:sons that shall thereto make any claime; In Witness whereof I the sd. THOMAS HOPKINS have hereunto set my hand & seale this 28th of January 1660

Witnes: RICHD: FLYNT.   THO: HOPKINS
    PHILL: NUTT, his marke
21th January 1660. This Sale was recorded

p.   KNOWE ALL MEN by these pr:sents that HENRY BENTLEY of the DEVIDEING
54   CREEKE in Northumberland County doth give for his marke of cattell & hoggs
    (vizt.) the right eare slitt in the middle & the top of the upper ( ) of & the left eare cropt & slitt
( ) 1660. This Marke was recorded

p.   WM: THOMAS ( ) Pattent.
54   I WM. THOMAS doe assigne all my right title and ( ) of this within menconed
    Pattent unto RICHD: ( ) as witnes my hand this 23th of February ( )
                         WM. THOMAS
26th February 1660. This Assignemt. was acknowledged by the abovenamed WM: THO-MAS unto RICHARD ( ) recorded. ( ) originally granted to JNO: SHAW & by ( ) the abovesd. WM. THOMAS & is recorded ( )

p.   ( ) for ye County of Northumberland the ( )ber 1658
54   Present   PETER KNIGHT.   Capt. RICH: BUDD
               ( ) MORRIS   Mr., THO: HOPKINS   Comrs.
               ( ) HAWLEY   Mr. WM: NUTT
22: Die. Whereas JOHN HOPPER standeth indebted unto SYMON RICHARDSON the summe of One thousand & ten pounds of tobacco & caske by Bill, the Court doth therefore order that ye sd. HOPPER shall within ten dayes make paymt. of the sd. Debt unto the said SYMON RICHARDSON with Court charges als. Execucon. Provided the Debt be paid within the time limitted then noe costs to be allowed notwithstanding this Order;
               Vera Copia   Test RI: FLYNT. Cl Cur. Nld.
I SYMON RICHARDSON doe acknowledge to have received this order satisfacton of the above menconed. Witnes my hand this 26th of Febr: 1660
Witnes RI: FLYNT. THO: DENT.   SYMON RICHARDSON
26th Febr: 1660. This Order & Discharge were recorded

p.   I JOHN TINGEY & ANNE TINGEY doeth assigne over all our right of the within
54   menconed Pattent unto WILKES MAUNDER, his Exrs. Admrs. or assignes as witnes
    our hands & seales this 23d. day of January 1660
Test PETER LEFEBUR.   JOHN TINGEY ye Seale
    ye marke of NICH: JERNEW   ye marke of ANNE TINGEY ye Seale
This Patt: was originally granted to JOHN HULL, by him assigned to THOMAS HAILES by the sd. HAILES assigned to JNO: TINGEY & the Patt. is recorded in the other booke folio 32.
This Assignemt. was acknowleged in Court by JOHN TINGEY & HENRY MOSELEY. Attor-ney of ANNE TINGEY. unto WILKES MAUNDER &c., and is recorded above
KNOWE ALL MEN by these pr:sents that I ANNE TINGEY doe ordaine & constitute my

Sonne. HENRY MOSELEY, to be my lawfull Attorney to acknowledge my right & title of a Pattent ( ) Land lying & being in YEOACOMOCO ( ) as Witnes my hand & seale this 23th of February ( )

Signed sealed & delivered in the pr:sence of us
        ye mke. of NICH: JERNEW   ANNE TINGEY   ye Seale
        ye mke. of JNO: BUTLER
    This Writeing was attested in Northumberland County Court for ANNE TINGEY by the Oathes of NICHOLAS JERNEW & JON BUTLER 26th Febr. Sworne ( )

p.   To all &c. Whereas &c. Now Knowe yee that I :EDWARD DIGGES, Esqr. &c., give &
54   grant unto THOMAS ADAMS 300 acres of land in the County of Northumberland
          binding Westerly upon ( ) the Land of EDWARD ( ) land of WILLIAM WARDER
( ) the sd. Land being due unto the said THOMAS ADAMS by & for ye transportacon of Six p:sons into this Collony whose names are in the Records menconed under this Pattent; To have & to hold &c., Dated the last day of Novembr: 1656
    KNOWE ALL MEN by these pr:sents that I THOMAS ADAMS of CHERRY POINT, Planter, have assigned & made over & by these pr:sents doe make over all my right of this Pattent & the Land therein conteyned unto the within menconed CHARLES ASHTON his heires & assignes fore ver, Witnesses my hand & seale this 26th of Febr: 1660
Witnes: EDWD. SALMON,   THOMAS ADAMS,   ye Seale
        THOMAS PHILLPOTT
    26th Febry: 1660 This Assignemt. was ackowledged in Court by the abovesd. THOMAS ADAMS & is recorded with the Pattent

p.   IN THE NAME OF GOD Amen. I ROBT. SMITH being sicke & weake but in p:fect
55   sense & memory God be praised, in the first place I bequeath my Soule unto God
          that gave it mee and my body to the Earth; next I give unto my Sonne,. JOHN
SMITH. the Devident of Land I now live on holy & soly to enjoy after the death of his Mother in Lauy, And my Wife, ANNE SMITH, to remaine upon the Plantacon now seated during her life time: Alsoe I give unto my Sonne, JOHN, a Gun & a Sowe, being already possessed therewith freely to enjoy & the above menconed Land unto him & his eyres for ever; Alsoe I give unto my Sonne. WILHAM SMITH his eyres One hundred akers of Land lying by the INDIAN TONE; alsoe I give unto my Sonne, WILHAM, my great gunne & the pip mold with the furniture belonging unto them; Alsoe I bequeaf unto my Wife, ANN SMYTH, one Maid Servant ( ) one draught oxen, alsoe I give unto ( ) my three youngest Children the half of my Estate as Kattell & hoogs & howsel goods ( ) me the other halfe of my Estate & houshold ( ) to my Sonnes, JOHN & WILHAM, equally to be ( ) betweene them towe when they come of age ( ) more my Will is that my Sonne, WILHAM ( ) remaine & worke for his Mother untill hee is ( ) fourteene yeares of aige, alsoe my Will is that ( )AIRES shall have as much Land as ( ) a Servant or two shall make ( ) soe to doe. Furthermore ( ) JOHN AIRES & WINSAINT COKES ( ) Overseers unto this my Will, as ( ) this present day being ye seaventh ( ) 1660
( )   ROBERT SMITH
    26th Febr: 1660. This Will was proved in Cort. by the Oathes of ( ) JOHN TUCKER & ordered by the ( ) SMITH be sworne before two Comrs. ( ) thereof & the Will is recorded

p   ENOWE ALL MEN by these pr:sents to whome shall come I DOROTHY DAMERAN
55   doe appoint my trusty & welbeloved Freind, ABRAHAM BYRAM, of the County of
          Northumberland, Planter, my true & lawfuill Attorney for mee & in my name to

demand & in case of non paymt. to arrest all p:sons to receive or make conveyance of
Land or that standeth indebted by Bill to mee, the sd. DOROTHY DAMERON. Further I give
my sd. Attorney power to compound all such debts and whatsoever my sd. Attorney shall
act or doe in the same I the sd. DOROTHY DAMERON doe by these pr:sents firmly bind my
selfe my heires to ratify and confirme the same as if I were p:sonall pr:sent, as Witnes
my hand & seale this 14th of December 1660
Sealed & Delivered in the presence of us
  JOHN WISE,   the marke of DOROTHY DAMERON ye Seale
  HENRY BENTLEY
 26th Febr: 1660. This Lre. of Attor: was recorded

p. TO ALL XPIAN PEOPLE to whome this p:sent Writeing shall come, I ELIZABETH
55 BENNETT of MATOPONIGH in Virginia, Widdow, the Relict of JOHN BENNETT, late
   of the same place, Gent., deceased sendeth Greeting in our Lord God everlasting:
Knowe yee that I the sd. ELIZABETH BENNETT as well in consideracon of the naturall
love & affection I beare towards my Children & of the Motherly care wch: I have of
their advancement as for divers other good causes have given unto my said Children
their Exrs. Admrs. & assignes the sd. Lands, cattell, goods & tobco. hereafter menconed
in manner & forme following: vizt., that is to say: (   ) GEORGE KNOTT one hundred acres
of Land (   ) lying in YEOACOMOCO RIVER adjoining (   ) land formerly given him by
GEORGE KNOTT (   ) when hee shall accomplish the full age of e(   )eares, and unto JOHN
KNOTT my Sonne, one Cowe (   ) called by the name of Guift to my (   ) feather bed be-
longint to his o(   ) fa(   ) And unto my Daughter, ANN(   )able tobco. & caske at her
(   ) my consent: And I doe (   ) all & every the sd. Land (   ) given unto Mr. NICHOLAS
(   ) onely use & behoofe of (   ) without the lett trouble (   ) or p:sons whatsoever
haveing (   ) any thing in these p:sents (   ) any wise notwithstanding: (   ) ELIZABETH
BENNETT have her (   ) 25th day of February (   )
  CHARLES ASHTON.   ELIZABETH BENNETT ye Seale
  ROBT. P(   )
 26th February 1660. This Writeing was acknowledged in Court by the sd. ELIZABETH
BENNETT & is recorded

p. I ANNE SMITH, the Widdow & Relict of ROBERT SMITH deced., doe acknowledge to
55 have given my free consent & by these presents doe give my free consent &
   confirme unto THOMAS ROE his heires & assignes for ever one p:cell of Land
lying in CHOTANCK CREEKE against JOHN HULL sold by the said SMITH unto WILLIAM
CORNISH & by him assigned unto the sd. ROE, & doe hereby firmly release all my right
& title of Dower thereunto belonging as Witnes my hand this 26th of Febr: 1660
Witnes: RI: FLYNT, WALTER MOORE   ANN SMITH her marke
 26th February 1660. This Writeing was acknowledged in Court unto THOMAS ROE by
the sd. ANNE SMITH & is recorded

p. KNOWE ALL MEN by these pr:sents that I RICHARD NEALMES for & in consdiera=
56 con that JOHN EARLE hath seated & planted upon a Devidend of Land belonging
   to mee & due to mee by Pattent bounding South Easterly upon YOACOMOCO RIVER,
Southwesterly upon the Land of WM: WALKER, Northwesterly & Northeasterly upon the
Maine Woods, for & in the sd. consideracon I the sd. RICHARD NEALMES doe by these
pr:sents give & grant unto the sd. JOHN EARLE one part or Neck of the sd. Land where
the sd. EARLE hath seated, be it more or less, bounding as followeth; vizt., Southeasterly
upon the sd YEACOMOCO RIVER, Southwesterly upon a Maine Creeke by mee called

NEALMES HIS CREEKE, Northeasterly upon a line of markt trees being the bounds of my land in that side & running Northwesterly from the River by a Branch & to the sd. Trees it comes foule of a small Swampe or Branch of the sd. Maine Creeke, & soe downe the sd. Branch & Creeke to the River & downe alone by the River to the first mentioned Branch that runns to the sd. markt. trees; To have & to hold the sd. Neck of Land to him the sd. JOHN EARLE his heires or assignes for ever in as full ( ) as it is by Pattent to mee granted paying his ( ) the quitt rents menconed in the Pattent in full confirmacon whereof I the said RICHARD NEALMES have sett my hand & seale this twenty first of January 1657

      ( ); JOHN BENNETT   the marke of RICHARD NEALMES
  26th Febr: 1660. This Grant was recorded

p.   ( ) BAY. May ye 13th 1659. IN THE NAME OF GOD Amen. I ROREY MACOTTER of
56   CHERRY POINT in County of Northumberland being well in health thanks be to
      God doe by this my Last ( ) of my worldly goods & Estate as foll: ( ) Soule into the hands of Almighty God ye ( ) body to the ground from whence it was taken: ( ) the first place I give unto FRANCIS ( ) with fower head of Cattell toward ( ) the satisfing of some other debts wch· ( ) give unto FRANCIS CARPENTER one iron pott, ( ) household stuffe & I likewise give unto ( ) one pyde Heyfer of towe yeares old ( ) PERCIVALL HAMMON one of the best of my breeding Sowes, & I doe moreover give unto FRANCIS SIMMONS 4 head of hoggs with all the rest of my goods that I shall leave behind soe desirring that this my last Will and Testamt. may be p:formed after my decease & biding the world farewell I conclude
Witnes· FRANCIS CARPENTER,   ye marke of RORRE MACOTTER
      PHILLIP CARPENTER
  FRANCIS CARPENTER in open Court did sweare that this Will above written is the Last Will & Testamt. of ROREY MACOTTER deced.
6d. 7br: 1660. Jurat in Cur   FRA: CARPENTER
  26 Febr: 1660. PHILLIP CARPENTER did sweare in Court ye same with FRANCIS CAR-PENTER that his is the Last Will & Testmt. of ROREY MACOTTER deced., & by their oathes the Will was proved & is recorded

p.   KNOWE ALL MEN by these pr:sents that I JAMES HAWLEY for & in consideracon
56   of my love & affection I doe give unto my Grand Child ELIZABETH KNIGHT one
      Cowe Calfe cropt on both eares a stalpe underneath the left eare & overkeeled under the right eare & a slitt, the sd. ELIZABETH KNIGHT to enjoy the sd. Cowe Calfe with her increase to her & her heires for ever; Witnes my hand this 15th day of February 1660
Test EDWARD HAWLEY, his marke   JAMES HAWLEY
  26th February 1660. This Deed of Guift was acknowledged in Court by ABRAHAM BRYAM, Attorney of the sd. JAMES HAWLEY & is recorded
  KNOWE ALL MEN by these pr:sents that I JAMES HAWLEY doe make my loveing Freind, ABRAHAM BYRAM, my true & lawfull Attorney to acknowledge this Bill of Sale in Court; Witnes my hand this 5th of February 1660
Witnes RICHARD ROBARDS   JAMES HAWLEY
  26th Febr: 1660. This Lre. of Attor: was recorded

p.   KNOWE ALL MEN by these pr:sents that I RICHARD SUTTON of LITTLE WICOCO-
56   MOCO in the County of Northumberland doth give for his marke of Cattel & hoggs
      cropt & ahole in each eare
  21th March 1660. This marke was recorded

p.   KNOWE ALL MEN by these pr:sents that I PETER KNIGHT for a valluable con-
56   sideracon have sold unto JOHN NICHOLLS his heires & assignes Eight hundred
        (   ) side of WICOCOMOCO RIVER (   ) bounding Northerly (   ) woods, a double
length (   ) Mr. ROBERT KING now (   ) that Mr. JAMES HAWLEY (   ) Swamp called by the
name (   ) abovesd., Land the (   ) & assignes for ever (   ) to the sd. NICHOLLS his heires
& assignes for ever; Witnes my hand & seale the 28th day of (   )
Witnes THO: WILLIAMS,   PETER KNIGHT
        EDWARD HAWLEY, his marke
If this Bill of Sale be not firme another to be made & I will signe it.
                                                      PETER KNIGHT
I give my consent to this abovesd. Sale of Land
                                            ANNE KNIGHT her mrke:
    6th June 1661   This Sale of Land was acknowledged in Northumberland County Court
by the above named PETER KNIGHT & the sd. Sale is recorded

p.   To all &c., Whereas &c., Now Knowe yee that I the sd. WM: BERKELEY &c. give
57   & grant unto JAMES HURD Five hundred acres of Land scituated on the South
        side of POTOMACK RIVER begining at the mouth of a small Creeke called HURDS
CREEKE neare to MACHOATICK CREEKE running North by West over or nigh PATOMACK
Maine RIVER; 250 poles to a marked Oake standing by the River side & extending into
the Woods. West & by South 320 poles, from thence South by East to the aforesd. Creeke,
250 poles & downe the Creeke to the place where it began including one small Branch
East & by North 320 poles; the sd. Land being due unto the sd. JAMES HURD by & for the
transportacon of Ten persons into this Collony all whose names are in the Records
menconed under this Pattent &c., Dated the 18th of October 1650
                         WILLIAM BERKELEY
    KNOWE ALL MEN by these pr:sents that I JAMES HURD have bargained and made over
unto ROBERT JONES his heires & assignes all my right unto this pr:sent Pattent & the
Land therein menconed for good and valuable consideracon secured to be paid to mee
the said JAMES HURD; Witnes my hand & seale the last day (   ) one thousand six hundred
& sixty
    I ANNE HURD doe freely consent unto the sale of the abovesaid Pattent of my sd. Hus-
band, JAMES HURD, Witnes my hand the day & yeare abovemenconed
                                            JAMES HURD   ye Seale
                                            ANNE HURD   ye Seale
    6th June 1661. This Sale & Assignement was acknowledged in Northumberland County
Court by EDWARD (   ) Attorney of the abovemenconed JAMES HURD & the Pattent &
Assignemt. is recorded.
    KNOWE ALL MEN that wee JAMES HURD & ANNE HURD by these pr:sents give our full
power & authority to (   )MSTON for us & in our names to acknowledge a Bill of Sale for
Five hundred acres of Land on PATOMACK RIVER sold by us to ROBERT JONES (   ) North-
umberland County Court; Witnes our hands this 30th day of Octobr: 1660
Witnes: JOHN HARWELL,   JAMES HURD
         JOHN RUSSELL   ye marke of ANNE HURD
    6th June 1661. This Lre. of Attor: was recorded

p.   BE IT KNOWNE unto all men by these pr:sents yt: I PETER KNIGHT of WICOCOMO-
57   CO in consideracon of my love & affecon I beare unto MARY HAWLEY, I give
        unto the sd. MARY one Cowe Calfe marked as followeth; cropt & slitt on the left
eare & under keeled on the right eare, the sd. MARY to enjoy the sd. Calfe wth: her in-

crease to her & her heires for ever, As Witnes my hand ye 6th of June 1661
Witness JOHN LANE,   PETER KNIGHT
        EDWARD HAWLEY his marke
  5th June 1661. This Writeing was acknowledged in Court by the above Mr. KNIGHT & is
recorded

p.   To all &c., Whereas &c., Now Knowe yee that I the said RICH: BENNETT Esqr., &c.
57   doe in the names of the Keepers of the Liberties of Englans by authority of
        Parliament wth: the consent of the Counsell of State give & grant unto THOMAS
MALLERD Three hundred acres of Land in ye County of Northumberland abutting upon
WICOCOMICO RIVER, Easterly upon a Creeke that devides this land and the land of THO:
SAFFALL, Northwesterly & Westerly upon the Maine Woods, ye said Land being due unto
ye sd. MALLERD by & for ye transportation of Six persons into this Collony whose names
are mentioned under this Pattent; Dated the 8th of June 1653
                        RICHARD BENNETT   WM. CLAIBORNE, Secr.
  KNOWE ALL MEN by these prsents that I JOHN BARDON & SUSANNA my Wife doe
assigne over all our right of this Pattent from us our heires or assignes unto JOHN
BRADLY & HENRY BRADLY to them & their heires for ever in as full & ample manner to
all true intents as they shall be required to acknowledge the same in Court; As Witnes
our hands this eighteenth day of February 1660
Witnes EDWARD WILLIAMS & ROBERT STEVENS their Ma( )
                                        JOHN BARDON &
                                        SUSANNA BARDON
  6th June 1661. This Assignemt. ( ) Northumberland County Court by EDWARD WIL-
LIAMS ( ) menconed JOHN BARDON & SUSANNA ( ) is recorded wth: ye Pattent
  KNOWE ALL MEN by these prsents that we JOHN BARDON L& SUSANNA my Wife do
appoynt our well beloved Freind, EDWARD WILLIAMS, our Lawfull Attorney to acknow-
ledge for us the Assignemt. of a Pattent that wee were heare ( ) day of February 1660
Witnes HENRY BRADLY

p.   The Estate of Mr. WM. BACON is charged Debts. By Mr. FRANCIS CLAY, Admr.
57   To a Judgmt. obteyned ( ) to soe much paid ( ) over order which hee ( ) to
        expences in getting ( ) selling the Estate ( ) to soe much paid; Capt. ( ) to
JAMES CLAUGHTON; To WM.: COLEMAN by order; To JOHN WARD by order; To Court
charges; To expences about the Estate;
  p. Credits. To goods sould at the Outcry; For severall Bills amounting to 3385 lbs. of ould
debt. which beinge regulated there remaines to be accompted for 00440;
summe total 10375. Dts. 10510   Cr. 10374   Total -00135.
  Wee have prised this Accompt & doe find the same to bee
                        JAMES GAYLARD   JOHN SAFFIN
  The 6th June 1661. This Accompt was recorded

p.   To all &c., Whereas &c., Now Knowe yee that I the sd. SAMUELL MATHEWES
58   Esqr., &c. give & grant unto JAMES CLAUGHTON Five hundred acres of Land
        scituate & beinge in PATOMOCK FRESHES in the Southward side of ye first Creeke
above PASCATAWAY, Begining at a markt. Pochicorey & extending by a Swampe &
finally up the River to the first menconed Creeke, ye sd. Land beinge due unto him ye
sd. JAMES CLAUGHTON by & for the transportation of Ten persons into this Collony
whose names are in the Records menconed under this Pattent; Dated the 5th June 1658
                        SAMUELL MATHEWES   WM. CLAIBORNE, Secr.

June 6th 1661. Memorand: I JAMES CLAUGHTON wth:in menconed doe the day & yeare abovemenconed assigne & sett over unto ANNE BRADSHAW, Daughter of ROBERT BRAD- SHAW, late of MATTA PONII in the County of Northumberland deceased Two hundred & fifty acres of land being the one moyety or halfe of Five hundred acres pts. specified, as Witnes my hand
Wittness WM. PRICE,   JAMES CLAUGHTON
        ROBERT SECH
   6th June 1661. This Assignemt. was acknowledged in Northumberland County Court by JAMES CLAUGHTON & recorded vth: ye Pattent

p.   To all &c., Whereas &c., Now Know yee that I ye sd. SAMUELL MATTHEWS Esqr.
58   give & grant unto RICHARD FLYNT Three hundred & ( ) acres of Land scituate
          & beinge in the County of Northumberland & bounding North by East ( ) THO- MAS RAINER, South by West to LITTLE WICOCOMOCO ( ) & a Branch of the sd. Creeke de- videing this Land from the land of RICHARD THOMPSONs, West by North upon a parcell ( ) surveyed for SAMUELL SMYTH & the said ( ) Land & East by South upon a Neck of Land belonging to sd. SAMUELL SMYTH, ye sd. Land beinge granted unto JOHN HAYNIE bearing date ye thirtie( ) October ( ) & by sd. HAYNEY assigned unto the sd. RICHARD FLYNT; To have & to hold &c., Dated the 7th day of September 1658
                    SAMUELL MATHEWES   WM. CLAIBORNE, Secr.
   KNOWE ALL MEN by these prsents that I RICHARD FLYNT with my Wife, for a valluable consideracon received doe for our heires set over unto Lt. Coll. SAMUELL SMYTH his heires & assignes for ever all our right of Pattent & the land menconed & to acknow- ledge in Northumberland County Court upon demand ( ) or by Attourney, As Wittness our hands & seales ye ( ) of March 1660.
                         RI: FLYNT   ye Seale
                         DOROTHY FLYNT   ye Seale
   6th June 1661. This Assignemt. was acknowledged in Court by Mr. RICHARD FLYNT & DOROTHY his Wife unto ye sd. Lt. Coll. SMYTH &c., & was recorded wth: ye Pattent

p.   KNOWE ALL MEN by these prsents that I ALLEXSANDER CAMILL doe assigne
58   over unto EDWARD WILLIAMS this within menconed from mee my heires or
          assignes unto him his heires or assignes in as full & ample manner to all true intents & meanings as the Law doth require, As Wittness my hand this 19th day of February 1660 & my Wife, doth acknowledge the same
Test   JOHN BARDON,   ye marke of ALLEXSANDER CAMILL
       JOHN BRADLEY   & ELIZABETH CAMILL
   June the 6th 1661. This Assignemt. was acknowledged in Northumberland County Court by HENRY BRADLEY, Attourney of the above menconed ALLEXSANDER CAMILL & ELIZABETH his Wife & is recorded
   KNOWE ALL MEN by these prsents that wee ALLEXSANDER CAMILL & ELIZABETH my Wife doe appoynt our well beloved Freind, HENERY BRADLEY our true & lawfull Attour- ney to acknowledge the Assignement of Five hundred acres of land as if wee were per- sonally present; as Wittness our hands this 19th day of February 1660
Teste JNO: BARDON,   ye marke of ALLEXSANDER CAMILL
      JOHN BRADLEY   & ELIZABETH CAMILL

p.   IN THE NAME OF GOD Amen. The Last Will & Testament of GERVASE DODSON, late
58   of GREATE WICOCOMOCO in the County of Northumberland in the Collony of Vir- ginia. Whereas it hath pleased Allmighty God to visit mee wth: sicknesse in such

measure as that I am neere reduced to the poynt of death, yet beinge of sound mine & memorie, I doe therefore make & ordaine this my Last Will & Testament in manner & former as followeth;

Imprs. I bequeath my Soule to Allmighty God, not doubtinge but that he will bee pleased to receive it into ye Armes of his Mercy & as for my earthly body, I doubt not but yt: my Wife & Freinds will see it received to a decent and Christian like buryall & for my temporall Estate I dispose thereof as followeth;

Item. I doe make & appoynt ( ) Wife ( ) & absolute Executrix ( ) satisfied contracts performed ( ) of former gifts delivered or ( ) whole Estate wheresoever ( ) p:sonall;

Item. The Two hundred acres of ( ) BOGGAS, I doe hereby sur( ) heires or assignes for ever & doe ( ) ratification of the same Pro( ) allwaies by him soe as formerly hee pass( );

Item. I give unto JNO: SMYTH ( ) one hundred acres of land ( ) BOGGAS or HENERY WICKER ( )

Item. I give to THOMAS ( ) Cow at JOHN EDWARDS ( )

In Witness whereof ( ) but first doe alsoe ( ) acres of land lyinge ( ) LEEs Esqr., Two hundred ( ) thereto GEORGE NIC( ); HENERY BOGGAS & all wch: sd. Land lyeth ( ) wth: his Two hundred ( ) soe every partie to receive there severall ( ) as they are recited & named hereby ratifying ( ) too all & every p:son & p:sons foremenconed & there heires & assignes forever. Dated the 7th day of January 1660

Signed sealed & delivered in presence of us

         ye marke of GEORGE NICHOLLS   GER: DODSON, ye Seale
         ROBERT BOGGIS,
         JOHN HAYNEY

( ) 1661. This Will was proved in the County Court of Northumberland to bee the Last Will & Testamt. of GERVASE DODSON by the Oathes of Mr. JOHN HAYNEY & GEORGE NICHOLLS and execution thereof is committed to ISABELL, the Relict & Executrix of the said GERVASE DODSON & is recorded

p   To all &c. Whereas &c., Now Know yee that I the sd. SAMUELL MATHEWES Esqr.
59   give & grant unto FRANCIS CARPENTER One thousand acres of Land beinge in POTTOMACKE FRESHES & extending Northwesterly to the mouth of the SECOND CREEKE above PISCATAWAY, thence W: by S: up the sd. Creeke into the Woods only parralell to ye River; & E: by S: along the land of Mr. RANDOLPH, to the first station; including the quantity of Land beinge unto him the said FRANCIS CARPENTER for the transportation of Twenty persons into this Collony whose names are in ye Records menconed under this Pattent; Dated ye 5th of June 1658
         SAMUELL MATHEWES   WM. CLAIBORNE, Secr.

I FRANCIS CARPENTER doe assigne all my right of ye above menconed Pattent & the Land therein contained unto WILKES MAUNDERS his Executors Administrators & assignes & doe warrt. ye sd. Pattent & the Land cleare from all other Pattents & doe warrt. the sd Land to the said MAUNDERS & to his heires forever from any p:sons whatsoever. As Witnes my hand & seale this 15th day of November 1660
Teste ( )   FRANCIS CARPENTER   ye Seale

This Assignemt. was acknowledged the 22th of July 1661 by the said FRANCIS CARPENTER to the said WILKES MAUNDERS in Northumberland County Court & is recorded wth: ye Pattent

TO ALL CHRISTIAN PEOPLE to whome these prsents shall come, I FRANCIS CARPENTER of Virginia hath sold unto WILKES MAUNDERS of Virginia One thousand acres of Land beinge upon the West side of PISCATAWAY in Freshes of POTTOMACK RIVER which Land

was granted unto sd. FRANCIS CARPENTER by Pattent for the wch: Land I have received full satisfaction from WILKES MAUNDERS; Alsoe I doe bind my selfe my heires firmly by these pr:sents to ye sd. MAUNDERS his heires or assignes to warrt. ye sd. Land at all times for ever hereafter free & clear of all incumbrances; In Wittness whereof I here-unto set my hand & seale the two & twentyeth day of ( )
( ) ( )OBSON & JNO: HUGHLET his marke   FRANCIS CARPENTER   ye Seale
This Sale of Land was acknowledged same day by the sd. FRANCIS CARPENTER to the sd. WILKES MAUNDERS in Northumberland County Court & is recorded

p.   KNOWE ALL MEN by these pr:sents that I WILLIAM DAVIS doe hereby acknow-
59   ledge to have received of RICHARD BROWNE & HENERY ROACH Executors of the
        Last Will of JOHN STANDLY one Cow Calfe fore to the use of my Daughter, ANNE
DAVIS, being given to my sd. Daughter by the sd. JOHN STANLEY, as appeareth by the
Last Will & Testament of the aforesaid JOHN STANLEY deceased, I say reced. for the use of
my Daughter; Witnes my hand this 5th of July 1661
Teste PEETER LEFEBUR.   ye marke of WM: DAVIS
      DANIELL ROBERTS
   22th July 1661. This Acquittance was recorded

p.   I JOHN HUGHLET doe assigne all my right of this Pattent over wth: the privi-
59   ledges therein menconed to FRANCIS ROBERTS his heires, Admrs. or assignes for
        ever: As Wittness my hand this 22th of July 1661
Teste THOMAS HOBSON   JOHN HUGHLETs marke
   This Assignemt. was acknowledged the same day in the County Court of Northumberland by ye sd. JNO: HUGHLET to ye sd. FRANCIS ROBERTS & is recorded

p.   KNOWE ALL MEN by these pr:sents that I JOHN TUCKER, Attourney of WM.
59   THOMAS, doe hereby assigne all the right of Eight hundred seaventy five acres
        of Land scituate on the back line of JOHN SHEPHARD unto THO: BROUGHTON his
heires & assignes & doe ingage that WM. THOMAS & his Wife shall acknowledge the
right of the same in Court to him his heires &c., Wittness my hand ye 29th of December
1660
Test THO: PHILPOT   JOHN TUCKER
      JOHN WALKER
   22th of Julii 1661   This Writeing was acknowledged in Court & is recorded;
Acknowledged to MARY, ye Relict of THOS: BROUGHTON deceast.

p.   KNOWE ALL MEN by these pr:sents that I NICHOLAS MORRIS of ye County of
59   Northumberland have assigned and transferred all my right to ( ) & twelve
        acres of land scituate in County of Northumberland & upon ye ( )ICOMICO
RIVER unto THOMAS GASCOINE SENR., & HENRY MAYES, their heires & assignes, the said
Land I have delivered the ( ) the one originally granted to Mr. ( ) from JAMES POPE &
further ( ) & the land therein menconed ( ) binde my selfe my heires ( ) hand the
24th of M( )
Teste JOHN HAYNIE,   NICHOLAS MORRIS
      SAMUELL GOCKE
   22th July 1661. This Writeing was acknowledged in Court & recorded

p.   An Inventory of the Estate of RALPH KEY deced.,
59   Imprs. 2 ould couches, one small musket, one little iron kettle, one rugg, one
        sheet, one heifer of a yeare & halfe, sute of cloathes, paire of knives, one combe,

one saile needle   Total 642   WM: CORNISH   marke
                                                   MARY CORNISH   marke

The 6th June 1661. WM: CORNISH & MARY his Wife declared on their Oathes this to bee
a true & just inventory of the Estate of RALPH KEY, deceased.

July ye 1th 1661. The p:ticular goods above written appraised by us ye Subscribers
beinge brought to us by WM: CORNISH & his Wife as the Estate of RALPH KEY

SAMUELL NICHOLLS   JNO: RAVENs marke

22th July 1661. This Inventory & Appraisemt. was recorded

p.   A True & Just Inventory & Appraisemt. of the Estate of THOMAS BROUGHTON
60   deceased, taken & appraised by us whose names are hereunto subscribed being
            the appraisers; A Pattent of Three hundred acres of Land appraised at 01600; a
Cloath sute, an ould searge sute & black hat; a p:cell of ould cloathes & an old white hat,
an ould feather bed & furniture belonging thereto; two shirts, a paire of drawers &
waisecoate of linen & a neckcloath, a Surveyers Chaine, a brasse rule, a dyall, an iron
pot, two ould kettles, an ould iron morter, an ould case wth: six bottles wth: some ould
iron ware; three ould bookes & a hat brush;

By Bills: THOMAS MARTIN, JNO: RAVEN, ROBERT SMITH, RICHARD COLEMAN, THOMAS
JONES, HENERY (   ); JAMES CLAUGHTON, WM: GREENSTED by Bill; GEORGE ALDERIDGE,
(   ) COLEMAN, (   ) WANDER, (   ) ERLE; Coll. SAMUELL SMYTH; THOMAS ATWELL of
NOMINII by Bill; (   ) AYRES by Bill; (   ) CARPENTER of NOMINII by two Bills; (   ) SMYTH
by Bill; (   ) CARTWRIGHT by Bill;   Summe totall 10684
Taken by us (   ) 1661.   JOHN TINGEY, NICHOLAS OWEN, FRANCIS SIMMONS marke
22th July 1661. This Inventory was recorded

p.   An Inventory & Appraisemt. of the Estate of ROBT. SMITH deceased taken &
60   appraised by us whose names are hereunto subscribed this eighth July 1661
            (   ) Cowe & Calfe; (3) black cows & younge calfe & steere & a bull, one heifer,
three calves, two pied steeres, thirteene hoggs & a pigg, a flock bed & sheete, a paire of
keyrsy breeches, foure chests, a small table & a carpet, four cases, two boxes & two
chaires, three ould guns, two ould couches, a paire of bellowes, a mayde servant two
yeares & a halfe to serve, a barrell of tarr, pales, runlets, trayes & other wooden ware,
brushes & a parcell of ould bookes, JOHN AYRES Debt to ye Estate; HENRY ROACH Debt to
ye Estate by Bill.   Summe total; 8475.
        JAMES CLAUGHTON   ROBERT (   )   DANIELL (   )
22th July 1661. This Inventory was recorded

p.   JAMES POPE Pattent for Land
60   To all &c. Whereas &c., Now Know yee I SAMUELL MATHEWES Esqr. give & grant
            unto JAMES POPE (   )red & twelve acres of land in County of Northumberland on
(   ) RIVER, boundinge North East (   ) opposite to the lands of RICHARD (   ) West North
West on a Creeke, (   ) PEETER KNIGHTs Land formerly (   ) (   ) of DAVID CUFFIN (   )
the River comonly called (   ) the sd. Land being formerly (   ) MORRIS by Pattent (   )
now granted to ye said JAMES POPE (   ) Councell bearing date (   )
        SAMUELL MATHEWES   WM. CLAIBORNE Secr.
KNOWE ALL MEN by these pr:sents I JAMES POPE transfer one (   ) to NICHOLAS MORRIS
Witnes my hand this 23th of December 1659.
Teste JOHN HAYNIE, ED: SANDERS,   JAMES POPE
22th July 1661. This Assignemt. was acknowledged in Court by JAMES POPE unto
NICHOLAS MORRIS & is recorded wth: the Pattent

p.   KNOWE ALL MEN by these pr:sents that I ISABELL DODSON of WICOCOMICO,
60   Widdow in the County of Northumberland my heires or assignes doth give &
        grant to be given unto ROBERT ROBINSON Sonne of CORNELIUS ROBINSON his
heires & assignes One hundred acres of Land butting at the head of Mr. CONSTANCE &
Coll. MOTTROMs Land, which is part of a Pattent that was betweene GERVASE DODSON &
Coll. TRUSSELL, of a Thousand acres of land according to the Pattent and further in case
sd. ROBERT ROBINSON doth die that then the said Land shall fall to his Mother or her
Children (?) the said Land shall ( ) & that ye sd. SAMUELL MAHEN shall ( ) sd. Land by
the last of October 1661; As Wittness my hand this 10th Aprill 1661
Test   HENERY BENTLEY.   ISABELL DODSON marke
        JOHN WODDEYs marke
  KNOWE ALL MEN by these pr:sents that I ISABELL DODSON, Widdow of WICOCOMICO in
County of Northumberland my heires or assignes doe sell & make over from mee my
heires & assignes halfe a tract of land of Three hundred acres scituate on Northwest
side of HENRY WICKERs Land unto SAMUELL MAYHEN his heires & assignes for to have
and to hold for ever accordinge to Pattent wth:out any molestation or trouble, Further I
ye sd. ISABELL DODSON doth binde my selfe or my assignes to acknowledge ye sd. Land
in Court, As Wittness my hand this 20th Aprill 1661
  22th July 1661. This Sale was acknowledged in Court by JAMES POPE, Attour: of
ISABELL DODSON & recorded
        KNOWE ALL MEN by these pr:sents that I ISABELL DODSON doe make my loveing
Freind, JAMES POPE, my lawfull Attourney in my name to recover all such debts as is
due to mee & to take all such courses in Law for recovery of ye sd. Debts, Further I doe
give my sd. Attourney my full power to acknowledge all sailes in Court & to sell or make
sale of any p:cell of land for me & in my name & whatsoever by sd. Attour: shall doe
therein ( ) as full force & vertue as if I were p:sonally present as Wittness my hand &
seale 4th June 1661.   ISABELL DODSON marke
22th July 1661. This Lre. of Attourney was recorded

pp.   TO ALL PEOPLE to whome this pr:sent writeing shall come, I URSULA THOMPSON
60-   of KIQUOKTON in Virginia, Widd:, ( ) RICHARD THOMPSON of the same place,
61   Gent., send Greeting in our Lord God everlasting; Know yee that I the sd.
        URSULA THOMPSON as well in consideration of the naturall love & affection I
beare towards my Children & of the Motherly care vch: I hve of there prefermt., &
advancement, as for divers other good causes mee theretunto moveing, have given &
assigned these cattle hereafter menconed in manner & forme following; Unto my
Sonne, RICHARD THOMPSON, one young bald face mare, two cowes called by the name of
Simple, the other by the name of Mouse, Unto my Daughter, SARAH THOMPSON, one bald
face mare, two cowes, one called by the name of Stock and the other by the name of
Starr; as alsoe to my Daughter, ELIZABETH, one stoned colt & two cowes one called by the
name of Pye & the other by the name of Mopus; To have & to hold the sd. mares & cattle
unto them the sd. RICHARD, SARAH & ELIZABETH there Executors & assignes, to hold for
ever by these pr:sents; ( ) it may bee lawfull for the sd. URSULA THOMPSON at all times
to have the use of the male increasse & p:fitts of the sd. Mares & Cattle, my said Sonne
shall att the age of one & twenty yeares, my sd. Daughters shall bee married wth:out
any lawfull trouble of the said RICHARD, SARAH & ELIZABETH or any p:sons under
them, In Wittness whereof, I the sd. URSULA THOMPSON have hereunto set my hand &
seale this 25th day of March 1649
Signed sealed & delivered in the pr:sence of
        the marke of WM: PERRY,   URSULA THOMPSON, ye Seale
        HENERY POOLE

23th July 1661. This Deed of Gift was recorded

p.   Mr. POOLE's Certificate.
61   These are to certifie that I ye (   ) signed sealed & delivered (   ) THOMPSON in
        the pr:sence of (   ) marriage with him & is recorded
ELIZABETH CITTY Wittness· (   ). Teste HEN: (   )
 23th July 1661. This Certificate was recorded

 The Deposicon of WM. PERRY
 WILLIAM PERRY aged (   ) doth as foll: That the (   ) sealed & delivered (   ) in the
pr:sence of Mr. (   ) him the sd. MOTTRAM (   ) 15th 1660, Sworne in Court THO.
RRERETON
 23th July 1661. This Deposicon was recorded

 The Deposicon of HENRY POOLE this 27th of September 1658. saith that on the 24th
day of May (   ) pr:sent at the signeing sealeing of a (   ) from Mrs. URSULA THOMPSON
to her Children wherein shee gave to her Sonne, RICHARD, one Mare & two cowes, to
her Daughter. SARAH THOMPSON, one mare & two cowes, & to her Daughter, ELIZABETH.
one stoned colt & two cowes, and saith that the sd. Deed was then signed & sealed, Mr.
JOHN MOTTROM beinge pr:sent which sd. Deed is recorded in the Court Booke for the
County of ELIZABETH CITTY & further saith not
        JERVASE DODSON.   HENRY POOLE
        HEN: HONE
 23th July 1661. This Deposition was recorded

p.   FRANCIS CLAY. Gent., aged about 34 yeares sworne & examd: this first of October
62   1660 saith. That in the yeare 1649, when hee this Depont. came into this Country,
        this Depont. did not know of any mares which did belonge to or were in ye pos-
session of Coll. JOHN MOTTROM deced., other than one bay mare which did belonge or
was reputed to belonge unto SARAH THOMPSON & one younge mare which hee did sell
unto RICE MADDOCKE, that afterwards there was another grey mare brought up from
KIQUOTAN which was known by ye name of RICHARD THOMPSONs Mare; that there was
another mare & foale & two horses brought up at the same time, which mare & foale
died within a short time after there coming to shoare & the said Horse were thus disposed of (vizt.) one of them was sould to ABRAHAM MOONE & the other to Mr. THOMAS
BUSHROD, laied claime to & fetcht away from CHICKACONE and this Depont. doth not
known of any other horses or mares then the above menconed & there p:duce & were
in the possession of the sd. Coll. WILLIAM SMITH the sd yeare 1649.
                                FRANCIS CLAY

WILLIAM GRINSTED aged 29 yeares or thereabouts sworne & examined the day & yeare
above menconed saith that all the mares which were at CHICKACONE in the actuall possession of Coll. JOHN MOTTRAM deced., did belonge or were reputed to belonge to the
Children of Mr. RICHARD THOMPSON deced., (   ) Mare & Colt which did belong eto (   )
SPEAKE and this Depont: is the (   ) believe that the sd. mares did belonge to the Children
for that hee hath heard yee MOTTRAM call them by the names of the (   ) mares & further saith not   WM: GRINSTEDs marke
 (   ) sworne & examined saith the very same (   ) menconed WM. GRINSTED
                                        JOHN PEIRSE
 (   ) erall examinacons & deposicons (   ) full Court this first of October 1660
 (   ) July 1661. They were alsoe recorded

ELIZABETH GRINSTED aged about 28; yeares sworne & examd. this first of October 1660 saith: That shee this Depont. by order from her Master, Coll. JOHN MOTTROM, deced., hath severall times marked certaine cowes & calves in a different marke from his owne which calves hee did acknowledge to bee the proper estate of the Orphans of Mr. RICHARD THOMPSON deced., & hath severall times bin angry wth: this Depont. for beinge soe carefull over those calves & p:tended that shee did neglect his owne & further saith not   the marke of ELIZABETH GRINSTED

WALTER OWEN sworne & examd. the day & yeare above menconed saith the very same as ELIZABETH GRINSTED and further the sd. WALTER OWEN saith that there were noe horses or mares at CHICKACON after hee came there but which did belonge to the Children of Mr. RICHD. THOMPSON deced., except a gray mare & colt which did belonge to Coll. THOMAS SPEKE & further saith not   WALTER OWEN his marke

THOMAS HAZELIP sworne & examd. saith the same with WALTER OWEN & ELIZABETH GRINSTEAD & further saith not   THOMAS HAZELIP his marke
These severall Deposicons & examinacons were taken in Court this first of October 1660
23th July 1661 They were alsoe recorded

PEETER PRESLEY maketh oath that a whitish Mare wch: was called Coll: MOTTRAMs before he married ye Relict of Mr. RICHARD THOMPSON, died in Mr. N( )ANS NECK, but whether shee died before the sd. Coll. married or not this Depont. cannot remember
                                        PETER PRESLEY
23th July 1661. This Depo: sworne ( )

RICHARD BROWNE sworne & examined sayth that hee this Depont lived ( ) MOTTRAM in the time of his ( ) hee intermarried wth. the sd. ( ) doth not remember that he ( ) had other horses or mares ( ) that did belonge ( ) Depont., resided wth: ( ) that hee lived at ( ) till about the August ( ) Relict of ye sd. ( )
Sworne in Court ye 23th July 1661. Alsoe recorded

p.   BEE IT KNOWNE unto all men that I ROBERT SECH acknowledge to have ( ) in
62   Law, ANNE TRUSSELL, Daughter unto ( ) TRUSSELL deced., one heifer together
        with a ( ) from the day of the date hereof for ever; ( ) or claimes of either
mine the abovesd. SECH or my heires or assignes; In Wittness to all above written, I have hereunto set my hand this 23th day of July 1661
Test RICH: BROWNE,   ROBERT SECH
      JAMES HAWLEY
Acknowledged by ROBERT SECH the 23d. July 1661 in Court and recorded

An Account of the Cattle of ELIZABETH TRUSSELL, Orphant, as follows, two cowes, one yearelin heifer & one cowe calfe. This is a true & just account of ye cattle belonging to the sd. Orphant
23th July 1661. This was recorded

p.   An Accompt of the Estate of HANNAH POULTER, Orphant. in the Custody of
62   ROBERT CROWTHERS 23th July 1661. One cowe, two bull calves, two yearelin
        steeres, one two yeares ould steere, one heifer of one yeare old; Two hundred
pounds of tobacco beinge ye p.duce of a two yeare ould steere; one flock bed & bolster, two feather pillowes, one blankett, one pott, one pestle, one haire sifter, milke trayes,

three ould hoes, one ould axe, one earthen butter pott, a butter tub
                                            ROBERT CROWTHERS marke
    23th July 1661. Sworne in Court & recorded

p.   MARY LANDMAN. To the one two yeare ould heifer
63   JAMES CLAUGHTON
          29th July 1661. Sworne in Court & recorded

p.   A just & true Accompt of WM: REYNALLS & WM: MEDCALFEs, Orphans of JAMES
63   REYNALLS. has nine cowes, three two yeare ould heifers, one yeare ould heifer,
          three cowe calves, three yearelin heifers dead;
   (   ) REYNALLS has five cowes two two yeare ould, one yearelin heifer. one cow calfe
deat.
   (   )RINE MEDCALFE has one cowe & one yearelin heifer dead;
   There is one cowe. one three yeare ould heifer and cow calfe wch: belongeth to ELIZA-
BETH MEDCALFE (   ) is dead
   (   ) one heifer being in my hands   NICHOLAS OWEN
   (   ) sworne in Court & recorded
   (   ) of the Cattle which doe p:perly belonge to (   )ERY MEDCALFE, Orphan, are here
menconed (   ) the Guardian of the sd Orphan as (   ) five cowes & one heifer of two (   )
which are livinge 2 there are lost (   ) one cowe calfe & (   ) of ye said Orphan
                              ye marke of WM. DAVIS
    23th July 1661. Sworne in Court & recorded

p.   An Accompt of ye Orphan of THOMAS KEENE. Cattle - (   ) hath 5 cowes, 4 calves
63   & (   ) heifers. (   ) steeres. THOMAS KEENE hath one cowe & a heifer & a heifer
          calfe & 3 steeres, MATHEW KEENE hath one cowe & a yearlin steere
                         the marke of MARY BROUGHTON
    23th July 1661. Sworne in Court & recorded

p.   MARTHA GRESHAM, the Daughter of JNO: GRESHAM, beinge in the Custody of
63   JOHN WADDY hath foure cowes & foure calves
                                 the marke of JNO: WADDY
    23th July 1661. This Sworne in Court & recorded

p   To all &c., Whereas &c.. Now Know yee that I the sd. WM: BERKELEY doe give &
63   grant unto ROBERT BRADSHAWE Foure hundred acres of Land beinge in ye
          County of Northumberland abutting Northwest & North East on MATTAPANY
RIVER, South East upon the Land of JOHN BENNET, South West & North West upon the
maine Woods, the sd. Land beinge due unto the sd. ROBERT BRADSHAWE for the transportation of Eight persons into this Collony all whose names are in Records menconed
under this Pattent &c., Dated the 18th of 8ber: 1651.
                         WILLIAM BERKELEY
KNOWE ALL MEN by these pr:sents that wee JAMES JOHNSON & ANNE my Wife,. do hereby assigne over unto JAMES CLAUGHTON his heires the one halfe of the Land wth: in
menconed in this Pattent. beinge two hundred acres of Land, the halfe of Foure hundred acres: In Wittness whereof wee have hereunto sett our hands this 24th of August
1651
Teste DANIELL ROBERTS,   the marke of JAMES JOHNSON
       THOS· HARDING marke   the marke of ANNE JOHNSON
       HENRY LINTONs marke

9th September 1661. This Assignemt. was acknowledged in Court by JAMES JOHNSON & THO- HARDING ( ) & is recorded wth: the Pattent

Wittnesseth that ANNE JOHNSON ( ) to be my ( ) THOMAS HARDING to be my lawfull Attourney to acknowledge Pattent of Land to JAMES CLAUGHTON ( ) as full power as if I my selfe were present; Witnes my hand this 7th of September 1661

Test WM. CORNISH. his marke.   the marke of ANNE JOHNSON
     NICHOLAS OWEN

9th September 1661. This Lre. of Attourney was recorded

p.   THOMAS HARDING his Assignemt. of a Pattent to JAMES JOHNSON
63   in the presence of us DANIEL ROBERTS, JAMES CLAUGHTON
            9th September 1661. This Assignement was acknowledged by THOMAS HARDINGE
& is recorded

The Pattent of this Land was ( ) to RICHARD RICE by him assigned to the sd. ( ) JAMES JOHNSON & is recorded in folio ( ) (13) huius libri

KNOWE ALL MEN by these prsents that I JAMES JOHNSON wth: ye consent of my Wife. ANNE. doe hereby sell unto THOMAS HARDING the quantity of One hundred & fifty acres of Land scituate in the County of Northumberland wee both dwell, the sd. land beginninge at a Chestnut tree marked foure & from that tree runing upon a line of marked trees into ye woods, South South West & beinge on ye Eastward side of a Pattent of Foure hundred acres formerly belonginge to RICHARD RICE, being part thereof, I the sd. JOHNSON for my selfe my heires doe hereby warrt. the sd. Land unto the sd. HARDING his heires &c., from ye claime of any persons whatsoever for ever; In Wittness whereof wee have each put out hands & seales this ninth of September 1661

Signed sealed & delivered in the prsence of us
        JOHN CONTANCEAN.   ye marke of JAMES JOHNSON   ye Seale
        DANIELL ROBERTS

9th September 1661. This Sale of Land was acknowledged in Court by the said JAMES JOHNSON & is recorded

p.   ENOWE ALL MEN that I JAMES CLAUGHTON doe hereby sell unto THOMAS HAR-
63   DINGE one hundred acres of land be it more or less out of a Pattent of Foure hun-
            dred acres bearinge date ye 18th of Octoberr 1651; granted unto ROBERT BRAD-
SHAW deced., ye sd. hundred acres of land beginninge at a fence formerly belonging to EDWARD WILLIAMS & upon a Swamp called the BEAVER DAM SWAMP & soe runninge South & North West accordinge to ye aforesd. Pattent, the sd. Land being in Northumberland County. I the sd. JAMES CLAUGHTON doe hereby for my selfe my heires do make ye sd. land good unto ye said THOMAS HARDINGE as far forth as the sd. Pattent to ye sd. HARDINGE beinge to pay to the Rent Gatherers when due & soe due for One hundred acres of Land; In Wittness to this Bill of Sale, I have hereunto set my hand this Twenty fourth day of August 1661
        ( ) SECH,   JAMES CLAUGHTON
        ( ) ROBERTS

9th of September 1661. This Bill of Sale was acknowledged in Court by ye sd. JAMES CLAUGHTON & recorded

p.   NOW ENOWE YEE that I ye said SAMUELL MATHEWES Esqr. give & grant unto
64   Coll. JOHN TRUSSELL & GERVASE DODSON One thousand acres of Land in the Coun-
            ty of Northumberland on the East side of CHICKACONE ( ) upon the Lands of
( )TANCEAN & Coll. MOTTROM deced., ( ) corner tree by Mr. CHANDLERs. the land being

due unto the said JOHN TRUSSELL & GERVASE DODSON for the transportacon of Twenty persons into this Collony whose names are in ye Records menconed under this Pattent; To have and to hold &c., Dated ye 19th day of ( ) 1658.

SAMUELL MATHEWES   WM: CLAIBORNE Secr.

KNOWE ALL MEN by these pr:sents that I JAMES POPE, Attourney to ye Widdow. ISABELL DODSON. doe for her, her heires & assignes assigne & transfer unto RICHARD PEIRCE & his heires for ever all my right of the wth:in menconed Pattent; Wittness my hand the 9th of September 1661

Wittness JOHN HAYNIE,   JAMES POPE
         PEETER HULL

The 9th of September 1661; This Assignemt. was acknowledged in Northumberland County Court by the abovesd. JAMES POPE unto RICHARD PEIRCE &c. & is recorded next under the Pattent

p.   IN THE NAME OF GOD, Amen. To all Christian People to whome these presents
64   may concerne. Know yee that I JOHN STANLY beinge at this pr:sent sick in body
         but yet perfect in memory doe herein declare this pr:sent writinge to bee my
Last Will & Testament as followeth;

First. I doe here give & bequeath my Soule unto God my Creator hopeinge through Jesus Christ to receive pardon & forgiveness for all my sins, Next, I doe comitt my body to the earth from whence it came & there to bee decently burryed hopeinge that at the last day both Soule & Body shall receive everlastinge joy & felicity; And as for all my worldly Estate, I give & bequeath as followeth.;

Imprimis. To THOMAS STRAWDER, Sonne of WILLIAM STRAWDER, I doe herein give one Cowe Calfe; It: One cowe calfe unto ANNE DAVIS; those two calves to be delivered wth:in one yeare & one day after my decease; alsoe one cow calfe more in the same kinde I doe herein give unto RICHARD BROWNE, Sonne unto the Writer of this my sd. Will: Alsoe unto WIDDOW WINLEY one Barrill of Corne forthwith upon my decease; Alsoe to WIDDOW HICMAN ( ) Barrill of Corne; Alsoe I doe herein give unto ye Writer of this my Will one Hogshead of tobb: & caske.

Item. I doe here( ) give unto my loveing Freind, Mr. HENERY ROCK, Sonne ( ) sented tobb: ( ) lands or the produce ( ) follows the bed I now ( ) belonginge; moreover ( ) besides my bed, not nominated ( )SEALM, RALPH KEENEs ( ) equall devision toge- ther ( ) for the true perfor( ) Testament I the said ( ) HENERY ROCKE and ( ) power full Executrixes ( ) clearely performed; In Wit( ) hereunto set my hand ( ) past be- tween me ( ) Witness to ( ) November 1660

Sealed & Delivered in the presence of
         ROBERT HEWES,   JOHN STANLEY
         THOMAS ORLEY. WM. STRAWDER sig.

17th December 1660. This Will was proved in Northumberland County Court by the Oath of ROBERT HEWES & further proof thereof made by THOMAS ORLEY on the 3d. July 1661; before Capt. JNO: ROGERS & execution of the sd. Will is committed unto Mr. HENRY ROCKE & RICHARD BROWNE, this 9th of September 1661 & recorded

p.   To all &c., Whereas &c., Now Know yee that I the sd. EDWARD DIGGES Esqr. give
65   & grant unto RICHARD HOLDEN One hundred acres of Land scituate in the County
         of Northumberland & bounding Easterly upon POTOMACKE RIVER, Southerly
upon YEACOMICO RIVER, Westerly upon a Creeke which devides this land from the land of THOMAS HAYLES sold to ROBERT FORD; Northerly upon another tract of land belonging to the sd. RICHARD HOLDEN, the sd. Land being due unto the said RICHARD

HOLDEN by & for a Pattent granted to WILLIAM BEDLAM dated ye 29th of November 1652
& the assigne of the sd. BEDLAM assigned over to ye sd. RICHARD HOLDEN & recorded in
the County Court; To have & to hold &c., Dated the last of November 1656
                    EDWARD DIGGES   W: CLAIBORNE Secr.
I RICHARD HOLDEN doe assigne this Pattent & all my title & interest in the same to JOHN
CARTER & HENERY HEARD & their heyrs & assignes for ever; I doe for my selfe my my
heires confirme the same agt. any p:sons whatsoever; Dated the 9th of September 1661
Wittness JOHN HAYNEY   RICHARD HOLDEN, signe
        JOHN MERREDITH
9th September 1661. This Assignemt. was acknowledged in Court by RICHD. HOLDEN to
the sd. JOHN CARTER & HENERY HEARD in Northumberland Court & is recorded
(On margin: MARY HOLDENs ( ) this Land is recorded in folio 70 huius libri)

p.   KNOWE ALL MEN by these pr:sents that I EDWARD SANDERS doe assigne unto
65   JOHN HOPPER all my right ( )instrated unto JOHN HOPPER his heyres ( ) over as
         Wittness my hand ye 9th day of September 1661
                                                EDWARD SANDERS
    9th September 1661. This Assignement was acknowledged in Court by EDWARD
SANDERS unto ye sd. JNO: HOPPER & is recorded
    ( ) was assigned by the sd. HOPPER ( ) in folio 47 ( )
    KNOWE ALL MEN by these pr:sents that I JOHN HOPPER of ye County of Northumberland
Planter, for a valuable consideracon have sould unto Mr. EDWARD SANDERS, of above
mentioned County of Northumberland, Chirurgion ( ) hundred acres of land scituate in
the County of Northumberland on ye Southside of GREAT WICOCOMOCO RIVER begininge
buttinge & boundinge upon ye lands of CHRISTOPHER GARLINGTON & upon ye lands
which was Capt. RICHARD BUDs. I the said JOHN HOPPER doe binde me my selfe my
heyres or assignes to warrt. the Sale of the sd. Land from all former Grants or Pattents
whatsoever yt: is in this Country or under this Governmt., that shall lay any claime or
title or interest in the same to the sd. Mr. EDWARD SANDERS his heyres or assignes for
ever; As Wittness my hand this 9th day of September 1661
Sealed in the pr:sence of us
        RICHARD PEIRCE. PEETER HULL   JOHN HOPPERs marke, ye Seale
        ABRAHAM BIRAMs marke
    9th Septmeber 1661. This Sale of Land was acknowledged in Court by the sd. HOPPER to
the sd. SANDERS & is recorded

p.   KNOWE ALL MEN by these pr:sents that I ISABELL DODSON, Widdow, have
65   assigned & doe by these pr:sents make sale of unto JOHN HAYNIE & his heyres
         and assignes all my right to Foure hundred acres of Land beinge in the County
of Northumberland & upon the head of GREATE WICOCOMICO RIVER, beinge soe much of
the Pattent whereon HENERY WHICKAR now liveth & the uppermost Foure hundred
acres lyinge upon the Damm's & WHICKARs BRANCH, runninge a mile Northerly into
the Woods, wch: sd. Land I doe hereby binde my selfe to acknowledge unto the sd. HAY-
NIE or his heyres or assignes upon demand to all which the above pr:misses I have
hereto set my hand & doe binde my selfe & my heyres ye 24th of August 1661
Wittness JOHN HUGHLETs sign   ISABELL DODSONs sign
        THO: SALLISBURYs sign
    The 9th of September 1661. This Dale of Land was acknowledged in Court by JAMES
POPE, Attourney of ye sd. ISABEL DODSON, unto the sd. JOHN HAYNIE & is recorded

Loveinge Freind, JAMES POPE. These may serve to desire & likewise doe authorize you
to acknowledge the sale of Foure hundred acres of Land lyinge at the head of GREATE
WICOCOMOCO RIVER in County of Northumberland from me my heyres & assignes to
JOHN HAYNIE & his heyres & assignes for ever (   ) August 24th: 1661, & (   ) as if it were
my owne unto (   ) of which I binde (   ) September 1661
Wittness JEFFERY GOCKE   ISABELL DODSON sign
        JOHN BENNET
    9th September 1661. This Assignement was acknowledged in Court & recorded

p.   THOMAS HOPKINS Deed of Gift of a mare foale to JOHANNA MEREDITH (Daughter
65   of JOHN MEREDITH), this first of February (   )
        Wittness JOHAN GIBBON,   THEODORE BAKER,
            JOHN MERREDITH
This Writeinge was acknowledged in Court (   ) September 1661 by RICHARD FLYNT,
Attor: of THEODORE BAKER, the Attour. of the sd. THO: HOPKINS & is recorded
    KNOWE ALL MEN by these prsents that I THEODOR BAKER the true & lawfull Attourney
of Mr. THOMAS HOPKINS have constituted & ordeyned & by these prsents doe appointe
Mr. RICHARD FLYNT my true & lawfull Attourney for me & on my behalfe of the aforesd
Mr. THOMAS HOPKINS to acknowledge a Writeinge in the Court of Northumberland
County by which hee the sd. HOPKINS hath given a mare foale unto JOHANNA MERRE-
DITH, the Daugher of JOHN MERREDITH & alsoe to record the sd. Writinge in the County
Court aforesd., ratifyinge whatsoever my said Attour: shall act in the prmisses in as
ample manner to all intents & purposes as if I my selfe were prsonally prsent & did the
same; Wittness my hand & seale this 7th day of September 1661
Testes HENERY BENTLEY,   THEODORE BAKER ye Seale
        JOHN MERREDITH
    9th September 1991. This Lre. of Attour: was recorded

p.   BEE IT KNOWNE to all men by these prsents whome this may concerne that I
66   WILLIAM HOPKINS doe freely give unto JOHN GARNER halfe my land at YOACO-
        MICO and to his heires, Executors Admrs. or assignes for ever; beinge Foure
hundred acres in all and Whereas I WILLIAM HOPKINS doe straytly binde the sd. JOHN
GARNER to seale the same by the first of March next insueinge of this prsent yeare &
for sealinge ye same land I WILLIAM HOPKINS doe freely give unto JOHN GARNER the
halfe of my Pattent & Land therein conteyned, As Wittness my hand & seale the 21th of
October 1661
Wittness: WM: PRESLY,   WM. HOPKINGS, his marke & ye Seale
        (   ) RICHARDSON, WILLIAM HILL
    21th October 1661. This Grant of Land was acknowledged in Court by Mr. WM. HOPKINS
to ye sd. JNO: GARNER & is recorded

p.   I JOHN WARDE doe assigne over all my right & title of this within menconed
66   Pattent to THOMAS BEAGLE his heyres & assignes for ever as wittness my hand
        this 21th of October 1661   JOHN WARDs marke
    (   ) This Assignement was acknowledged in Court (   ) to ye sd. THO: BEAGLE & is
recorded
    Mr. COLCLOUGH. From (   ) ye sd. JNO: WARD as in folio (24) huius libri.
    (   ) by these prsents that I MAGDELIN WARD doe ordeyne my welbeloved Freind, THO-
MAS PHILLIPS my lawfull Attourney to acknowledge all my right of this Pattent from me
my heyres to THOMAS BEAGLE his heyres & assignes for ever; In Wittness my hand

this 21th of October 1661
     ( )NEW HILL   MAGDALIN WARD
     ( ) BONAM
21th October 1661. This Acknowledgemt. was acknowledged in Court by THO: PHILLIPS,
ye Attourney of the said MAGDALIN WARD to ye sd. THO: BEAGLE & is recorded

p.   KNOWE ALL MEN by these pr:sents yt: wee CHARLES HOYLE & ELIZABETH my
66   Wife doe assigne all our right to this sd. Pattent & the Land therein conteyned
       wth: all priviledges thereunto belonginge unto GEORGE PICKERIN his heyres &
assignes for ever, as Wittness our hands this 21th October 1661
Wittness   EDWARD ROGERS   CHARLES HOYLE
                                    ELIZ: HOYLE
  21th 8ber 1661. This Assignemt. was acknowledged in Court by THOMAS SOLYE, Attourney of CHARLES HOYLE to GEORGE PICKERIN & is recorded
  The Pattent for this Land was originally granted to JAMES MAGRIGER & HUGH FOUCH,
by them assigned to ALLEXANDER MACCOTTER, & by him assigned to GEORGE PICKERIN &
CHARLES HOYLE as in folio (48) huius libri.
  KNOWE ALL MEN by these pr:sents yt: I CHARLES HOYLE doe hereby appointe Mr.
THOMAS SOYLE for mee & in my name to bee my true & lawfull Attourney to acknowledge all my right & interest to GEORGE PICKERIN & his assignes to a Pattent dated the
11th of June 1658; As Wittness my hand ye 21st of October 1661
Test PETER ASHTON,   CHA: HOYLE
     EDWARD ROGERS
  21th 8ber: 1661. This Letter of Attour: was recorded

p.   Whereas RICHARD HOLDEN transferred & assigned over a Pattent for Six hun-
66   dred acres of land unto us, JOHN BENNETT & VINCENT COX, & acknowledged the
       same in the County Court of Northumberland the 20th of January 1656 as by the
Court Records more at large appeareth; And whereas it is not by the said Assignemt. expressed each mans bounds or portion but remaineth jointly betweene us, NOW KNOW
ALL men by these pr:sents that wee the said JOHN BENNETT & VINCENT COX doe binde our
selves our heyres & every of us that the Survivor shall not have the whole but that it
shall bee lawfull for the heyre of the first ( ) to have & hold possess & enjoy the same
proportion as the deceds. due notwithstanding ( ) or prsecription to the contray; In
Wittness ( ) sd. JNO: BENNET & VINCENT COX have set their hands & seales this 7th day of
February ( )
Sealed and delivered in the pr:sence of us
     PETER ASHTON,   JOHN BENNETT
     RI: FLYNT   VINCENT COX
  21th October 1661. VINCENT COX ( ) of the Land above specified ( ) & heyre of JOHN
BENNETT

p.   A Declaration of MARY HUGHS Freedome
66   Wee whose named ( ) that MARY HUGHS ( ) or either of us can ( ) our hands
     this ( )
  21th 8ber: 1661. This ( ) was recorded

GEORGE DAYE his Sale of MARY HUGHES ( ) to ROBERT BRADSHAW
  KNOWE ALL MEN by these pr:sents that I GEORGE DAYE ( ) hereby make over ( ) I
have ( ) BRADSHAW or his assignes all ( ) I have of or in MARY HUGHES for ( ) I

have ever had in MARY HUGHES for ( ) I have reced. already in hand. In Wittness ( )
I have hereunto set my hand this ( ) of August 1660.
Signed & delivered in presence of
    JOHN CONTANCEAN,   GEORGE DAYE
    DANIELL ROBERTS
    21th 8ber: 1661. This Sale was recorded

p.   September ye 26th 1661. An Inventory of the Estate of WM. LITTLE appraised
67   by JOHN GARNER, FRANCIS SIMONS, ABRAHAM JOYCE & NICHOLAS OWEN.
    Imprs. 2 iron potts, 1 brasse kettle & fryinge pan, 2 puter dishes, 2 pott crookes,
1 paire of pot hookes, 1 paire of fire tongues, 2 ould flock beds & 1 featherbed wth: the
appurtenances; weareinge apparrell belonginge to ye deced. & his Wife is one yard of
broad cloath, paire shoes & 2 Duch hatts, 1 case wth: a parcell of thread & buttons, ould
knives & a parcell of bookes, 4 ould howes, a pestle, a reap hooke, 2 ould axes; a p:cell of
sale, ye remainder of a barrel; 1 chaire, 2 stooles, 4 trayes, earthen dishes, 1 payle, 3
ould spoones, 12 lbs. of nayles, 1 sowe & 4 shotes, a chest, 1 cow & 2 old tubs, cow, 1
heifer & 1 bulchin   Total 2740
          NICHOLAS OWEN   FRANCIS SIMONS
          JOHN GARNER   ABRAHAM JOYCE
( ) Mr. LITTLE's Estate ( ) of a Bill from FRANCIS SIMONS
( ) This Inventory was recorded

p.   TO ALL PEOPLE to whome these pr:sents shall come, I FRANCIS CLAY of YEACO-
67   MICO in ye County of Northumberland in Virginia, Gent., and ANNE CLAY ye
    Wife of FRANCIS CLAY, send Greetinge in our Lord God everlasting; Whereas
JOHN TEMPLE late of ( ) sd. Gent., deced., under his hand & seale bearing date twentyeth
of October in the yeare of our Lord one thousand six hundred Fifty & seaven give &
bequeath unto mee, the said ANNE CLAY, all his lands & tenements, goods & chattells
(amongst which the lands hereafter menconed are pt.), Now Know yee that wee ye sd.
FRANCIS & ANNE CLAY for divers good causes us thereunto moveing have sould unto
GEORGE COLCLOUGH of LITTLE WICOCOMOCO in the abovesd. County of Northumberland,
Gent., all that messuage & tenemt. & one thousand acres of Land scituate in the County
of Northumberland aforesd., on the West Northwest side & at the head of YEACOMICO
RIVER & bounded as followeth, (vizt.) Two hundred acres pt. thereof South East upon the
head of the said River, Northeast on the Lands of ROGER PULLEN deced., the two opposite sides of the Maine Woods & Foure hundred & fifty acres other pt. thereof South East
on the Maine Branch of the head of YEACOMICO RIVER, North East on the said Two hundred acres, the two opposite sides on the Maine Woods & three hundred & fifty acres the
residue South East upon this Land, North East & for breadth upon the Land of JOHN
SHACKLY, North West & South West upon the Maine Woods which Land was granted formerly to Mr. PEETER KNIGHT by Pattent beareinge date the thirteenth day of October in
the yeare of our Lord God one thousand six hundred Fifty & three & by him conveyed to
the abovesd. JOHN TEMPLE the eighth day of September in the yeare of our Lord God one
thousand six hundred Fifty & six & by the sd. TEMPLE devised to mee, the sd. ANNE CLAY,
as above recited; To have & to hold the sd. messuage & tenemt. & one thousand acres of
land wth all its rights unto him the said GEORGE COLCLOUGH his heyres & assignes for
ever and wee the sd. FRANCIS CLAY & ANNE CLAY do grant to warrant the land to bee
free & cleare from any manner of claime from us or our heyres or any other p:sons
under us; In Wittness wee have hereunto set our hands and seales this sixth day of
December one thousand six hundred ( ) yeare of ye Reigne of our Sovereigne Lord
Charles the second of England, Scotland ( ) Defender of ye faith &c.

Sealed & delivered in ye pr:sence of us
     JAMES GAYLARD,   FRANCIS CLAY
     GA: KENNADY   ANNE CLAY
    20th January 1661. This (   ) in Court by the sd. (   ) of ye sd. ANNE CLAY (   ) is recorded
KNOWE ALL MEN by these pr:sents that I ANNE CLAY, ye Wife of FRANCIS CLAY of
YEACOMICO RIVER in County of Northumberland in Virginia Gent., have appointed
JAMES GAYLARD to bee my true & lawfull Attourney for me & in my name to acknow-
ledge one Deed of Bargaine & Sale wherein I the sd. ANNE, together wth: my sd. Husband
FRANCIS CLAY, have sould one thousand acres of land unto GEORGE COLCLOUGH of
LITTLE WICOCOMICO in the said County of Northumberland, Gent., beareinge date wth:
these pr:sents in the County Court of Northumberland aforesd., unto him the sd. GEORGE
COLCLOUGH his heyres & assignes for ever; ratifyinge & confirmeinge what my sd.
Attourney shall act in the pr:misses in as ample manner as if I my selfe were p:sonally
p:sent & did the same: Wittness my hand & seale this sixth day of December in the yeare
of our Lord God 1661
Wittness: GA: KENNADY.   ANNE CLAY ye Seale
       ROBERT HITCHCOCKE
    20th January 1661. This Letter of Attourney was recorded

p.   TO ALL XPIAN PEOPLE to whome these pr:sents shall come, GEORGE COLCLOUGH
68   of LITTLE WICOMICO in the County of Northumberland in Virginia, Gent.,
        sendeth greetinge in our Lord God everlasting; Know yee that I the sd. GEORGE
COLCLOUGH for and in consideration of a Deed of Bargaine & Sale bearinge date wth:
these pr:sents wherein FRANCIS CLAY of YEACOMICO RIVER in the aforesaid County of
Northumberland, Gent., & ANNE his Wife, have sold unto mee the sd. GEORGE COLCLOUGH,
one thousand acres of land scituate in the sd. County of Northumberland & bounded as
followeth (vizt.) Two hundred acres thereof pt. South East on the head of YEACOMICO
RIVER, North East on the lands of ROGER PULLEN deced., the two opposite sides on ye
Maine Woods, & Foure hundred & fifty acres other pt. thereof Southeast on the Maine
Branch of the head of the said River; North East on the sd. two hundred acres; the two
opposite sides on the Maine Woods; & three hundred & fifty acres, the residue, South
East upon this Land North East & for the breadth upon the Land of JOHN SHACKLY,
North East & South West upon ye Maine Woods, have granted unto the sd. FRANCIS CLAY
the sd. messuage or tenemt. and one thousand acres of land with all its rights to him the
said FRANCIS CLAY his heyres for ever free from any manner of claime by mee my
heyres or any other p:sons; In Wittness whereof I have hereunto set my hand & seale
this Sixth day of December in the yeare of our Lord God one thousand six hundred &
sixty one, in the thirteenth yeare of the reigne of our Sovereigne Lord Charles the
second by the grace of God of England Scotland & Ireland &c.,
      (   )   GEORGE COLCLOUGH, ye Seale
    20th January 1661. This Sale of Land was acknowleged in Court by ye sd. GEORGE COL-
CLOUGH to the said FRANCIS CLAY & is recorded

p.   These pr:sents wittnes that I doe impower Mr. JAMES GAYLARD as my Attour-
68   ney to answer any accons or lease shall bee agt. mee or to bringe any accon or
        suite for mee & in my name & to my use as hee shall see necessary and p:ticular-
ly to sue a writt of eviction agst. THOMAS BREWER for the Plantation which he now lives
on beinge properly due to mee; and generally to doe all things necessary in the
pr:misses as if I were p:sonally p:sent.
Wittness my hand & seale ye 20th of January 1661

Wittness. THOMAS SULLEY, GEORGE INGLIS,   RICH: LEE ye Seale
     JOHN CURTIS,   HENERY BENTLEY
20th January 1661. This Lre. of Attour. was recorded

p.   To all &c., Whereas &c. Now Know yee that I the said SAMUELL MATHEWES &c,
68   give & grant unto THOMAS KEDBY 200 acres of Land scituate in the County of
        Northumberland betwixt two Branches of SCOTTS CREEKE buttinge Easterly &
Northerly upon the land JAMES MAGREGORY lives on & the land hee sold to a DUTCH-
MAN, Westerly & Southerly upon the Maine Woods & the land of Coll. CLAIBORNE,
beetwixt the lands of Mr. JOHN HAYNIE, JOHN HUGHLET & the sd. DUTCHMAN; the sd.
land beinge due unto the sd. THOMAS KEDBY by & for the transportacon of fower psons
into this Collony whose names are in the Records menconed under this Pattent &c.,
Dated the 29th of 9br: 1658
                SAMUELL MATHEWES   W: CLAIBORNE, Secr.
  I WILLIAM PRESLY, Attourney of THOMAS KEDBY, have assigned & made over (by ver-
tue of the power to mee given by the sd. KEDBY under his hand & seale dated the 13th of
May 1658) assigne & make over unto MORE PRICE his Exrs., Admrs. & assignes this Pat-
tent together with the lands therein specified; Wittness my hand & seale this 20th of
January 1661
Sealed & delivered in ye prsence of
     FRANCIS CLAY, JAMES GAYLARD   WM: PRESLY   ye Seale
  20th January 1661. This Assignement was acknowledged in Northumberland County
Court ( ) & is recorded wth: the Pattent
  TO ALL TO WHOME these prsents shall come, Know yee that I THOMAS KEDBY have made
Mr. WM: PRESLY my Attourney for mee & in my name to ( ) Bills wth:in ye limits of
America ( ) any person ( ) granting unto him ample power & authority to doe ( )
pr:misses or to intermedle barter & ( ) p:cell of my Estate wheresoever being wth:in
the aforesd. limits of America as if I were psonally psent; And likewise at his pleasure
to make one Attourney or more in stead & what my sd. Attour: shall doe in the pr:misses
I, the sd. THOMAS KEDBY, doe ratifie & confirme; As Wittness my hand & seale the 13th
day of May 1658
Signed sealed & delivered in the pr:sence of us
     JOHN RAVENs sign.,   THOMAS KEDBY, ye Seale
     JONATHAN PARKER
The 20th January 1661. This Letter of Attour: was recorded

p.   I RICHARD GIBBELL doe assigne all my right & title of this Pattent with all
69   the rights thereto belonginge unto JOHN WOOD his heyres & assignes for ever;
        & further I doe ingage my selfe that I & my Wife shall acknowledge the Sale of
the sd. Land (either in p:son or by our Attour.) in the County Court when the sd. WOOD
shall require it; As Wittness my hand this 17th March 1660
Wittness: THO: HOBSON,   RICH: GIBBALL his marke
     THO: SAFFALLs marke
20th January 1661. This Assignemt. was acknowledged in Court by THOMAS HOBSON,
Attour. of RICHARD GIBBALL & ANNE his Wife unto ye sd. JOHN WOOD & is recorded
  The Pattent was originally granted to HENERY WICKER & part thereof assigned by GER-
VASE DODSON to the sd. RICHARD GIBBALL as in folio (42).
  KNOWE ALL MEN by these prsents that wee RICHARD & ANNE GIBBALL doe hereby
appoynt our loveinge Freind, THOMAS HOBSON, our true & lawfull Attourney in our
name to acknowledge in the County Court of Northumberland the Sale of a seale of Land

souId by us to JOHN WOOD and what our said Attour: shall act in the premisses we doe
hereby confirme in as ample manner as it wee were pr:sent; Wittness our hands this
10th of January 1661
( )   RICHARD GIBBALL sign
                                                       ANNE GIBBALL sign
    20th January 1661. This Letter of Attour: was recorded

p.   KNOWE ALL MEN by these pr:sents that I ISABELL DODSON (for a valluable con-
69   sideracon) have sould unto ROBERT JONES his heyres & assignes all my right to
          Five hundred acres of Land now in the possession of the sd. ROBERT JONES ( )
BAY in the County of Northumberland, being part of a Pattent of One thousand acres
granted unto GERVASE DODSON, my late deceased Husband, and ( ) CONAWAY deceased;
To have & to hold the sd. Land with all priviledges unto the sd. ROBERT JONES his heyres
& assignes cleare from all clayme of mee or any p:sons claiminge under mee; & I doe
likewise give full power & authority to Mr. THOMAS HOBSON for mee & in my name to
acknowledge this in Northumberland Court as my absolute & perfect act; Wittness my
hand & seale this 24th day of August 1661
Wittness: GEO: WALE,   ISABELL DODSONs marke   ye Seale
          THO: KNIGHT
    20th January 1661. This Writinge was acknowledged in Court by Mr. THOMAS HOBSON
Attourney of the said ISABELL DODSON, to ye sd. ROBERT JONES & is recorded

p.   KNOW ALL MEN by these pr:sents that I PHILLIP CARPENTER of MATAPANY in
69   the County of Northumberland & Collony of Virginia, Planter, have sold unto
          RICHARD FLYNT Fowre hundred and Eighty acres of Land scituate upon MATA-
PANY aforesd. beinge the tract of land whereon I now live as the Pattent for the same
upon the Records in the Secretaries Office at JAMES CITTY bearinge date the 29th of
August 1657 (?) more at large may appeare; To have & to hold unto him the sd. RICHARD
FLYNT his heyres & assignes for ever; And I the sd. PHILLIP CARPENTER my heyres the
sd. Land with all its rights will warrant unto ye sd. FLYNT against all people that shall
make claime and doe binde my selfe to deliver the sd. FLYNT or his assignes a Pattent by
the 20th of January next wth: such ( ) by the Court as the sd. FLYNT shall require; In
Wittness whereof ( )
Sealed & delivered in the pr:sence of
     FRANCIS CARPENTER, RICHARD BROWNE   PHILLIP CARPENTER
     HENERY BENTLEY, sign   JAMES MAGRIGER
    21th January 1661. This Writeing was acknowleged in Court by the sd. PHILLIP
CARPENTER to RICHARD FLYNT & is recorded

p   INVENTORY of the Estate of HENERY HAYLER deced.,
69   Imprs. old pewter, one old gun unfixed; one paire of pott racks, 3 old payles,
          4 milke trayes, tub, one old barrill, one old siftinge ( ); 1 fryinge pan, 2 old
howes, 1 keyrsy coate, 1 paire searge breeches, one old hat, 1 old chest, a deske, an old
couch, 3 barrells of Corne at 70 lbs. p barrill, 1 old brass kettle full of holes, 1 old little
brass kettle, 1 childres chaire, the meate, 3 old fishinge lines; 1 old hammer, 1 meale
sifter, 1 homony sifter, 1 cow, 1 heifer, 1 calfe   Total: 1535
    21th January 1661. This Inventory was recorded

p.   THESE PR:SENTS Wittness that wee WILLIAM JEFFARS and ELIZABETH JEFFARS
70   hath sold unto SAMUELL BONAM one black heifer cropt on the left eare & slitt
          and a hole in the right, for which heifer wee the foresaid doe acknowledge to

have received full satisfaction & doe warrt, the sd. heifer to ye sd. BONAM or his
assignes from all claimes of any p:sons whatsoever; As Wittness our hands the 8th 9ber:
1661

THOMAS DUNCKATON his marke   WM: JEFFERS   his marke
                                               ELIZABETH JEFFERS   her marke

21th January 1661. This Bill of Sale was recorded

p.   IN THE NAME OF GOD, Amen. I PHILLIP NUTT beinge very sick & weake in body
70   but in perfect sence & memory, doe make & declare this to bee my Last Will &
          Testamt., First, I recommend my Soule into the hands of Allmighty God hopinge
through the merrits of Jesus Christ to receive free & absolute pardon for all my sinnes;
Next, I comitt my body to ye Earth from whence it came there to bee decently buryed
wth: Christian buryall, And as touchinge my worldly Estate, I doe order dispose &
appoint as followeth, (vizt.)
Imprs. That my loveinge Freind, RICHARD FLYNT, take into his custody & possession
all my Estate of what nature or quallity soe far it bee or in whose custody soever it remaine imediately after my decease;
   (   ) sd. RICHARD FLYNT discharge & pay all such just Debts I owe unto any p:son soe
farr forth as my Estate allowe; And it is my will & desire that SYMON (   )SON bee satisfied & paid for his care trouble & (   ) about mee in my sicknesse;
   (   ) I nominate & appoynt the sd. RICHARD FLYNT, (   ) Executor of this my Last Will
and Testament. In Wittness whereof that this is my Last Will I have hereunto set my
hand & seale this (   ) September 1661.
                                           PHILLIP NUTTs marke   ye Seale
   21th January 1661. This Will was proved in Court by the (   ) before by the Oath of WM:
OSBOURNE (   ) is comitted to RICHARD FLYNT (   )

p.   KNOW ALL MEN by these pr:sents that THOMAS BEAGLE of YEACOMOCO doth give
70   for his marke of Cattell & Hoggs (vizt.) cropt & a slitt on the right eare, sllitt &
          halfe cropt underkeeled on the left eare
   21th January 1661. This marke was recorded

p.   KNOW ALL MEN by these pr:sents that I ANNE HOYER of BARBIN in the County
70   of ESSEX, Widdow, have made GAWEN KENADY of Virginia, Mercht., my true &
          lawfull Attorney to my use to recover by all lawfull wayes & meanes whatsoever
from THOMAS SHRILL of WICKACOMICO RIVER in Virginia, Planter, all such tobacco &
caske & other merchandize whatseover bequeathed to mee, the sd. ANNE HOYER, by the
Last Will & Testament of my Sonne, EDWARD COCKSHED of WICKACOMICO aforesd.,
Planter, deceased, And upon recovery of the pr:misses or any part thereof acquittances
to make & deliver & if need be for the pr:misses to appeare the p:son of mee the Con-
stituant to represent in all Courts & before all Judges & Ministers of the Law & give
arrest and moreover fullfull every act about the pr:misses as fully as I my selfe might
doe if p:sonally p:sent; In Wittness whereof I have hereunto set my hand this 30th day
of July (   ) & in the 13th yeare of our Sovereigne Lord Charles the second
Sealed & delivered in the pr:sence of us
   JOHN BOWCHER,   THOMAS COLLINS
   21st January 1661. This Lre. of Attourney was recorded

p.   KNOW ALL MEN by these pr:sents that I MARY HOLDEN, the Wife of RICHARD
70   HOLDEN, doe give my free consdnt to the Sale of One hundred & twelve acres of
          Land lying at YEACOCOMICO POINT, sold by my sd. Husband unto JOHN CARTER &

HENRY HURD, and doe disclaime any interest that I now or hereafter may have by way
of Dower or Thirds and alsoe doe hereby appoint JOSEPH CHURNELL as my lawfull
Attourney to acknowledge this Writeing in Northumberland County Court; Witnes my
hand & seale this 19th of January 1661
Sealed & delivered in the pr:sence of
    RI: FLYNT,   the marke of MARY /M HOLDEN
    EDWARD ℰ TEDMUNS his marke
  19th March 1661. This Writeing was acknowledged in Court by the above menconed
JOSEPH CHURNELL & is recorded

p.   KNOW ALL MEN by these pr:sents that I JENKIN MORGAN doe assigne all my
71   right of this Pattent from mee my heires or assignes unto THOMAS MOULTON
       and THOMAS TREIPE, their or eyther of their heires or assignes for ever; As
Wittness my hand this 24th of February 1661
Signed & delivered in the pr:sence of us
    SAMUELL TAYLER,   JENKIN /M MORGAN
    THO: STANDLEY /\ his marke   his marke
  19th March 1661. This Assignement was acknowledged in Court unto THOMAS MOUL-
TON & THOMAS TREIPE by JOHN HOLLOWAY, Attourney of the abovesd. JENKIN MORGAN &
is recorded
  The Pattent above assigned was originally granted to EDWARD COLES & by him assigned
to the aboves. JENKIN MORGAN August 1657; & is recorded in the other Booke of Records
in folio 122; 300 acres.
  These pr:sents witnesseth that I REBECKAH MORGAN doe assigne unto THOMAS MOUL-
TON all my right of this Pattent within written in the same actuall condicon according
to my Husbands assignement written & made over unto the sd. THOMAS MOULTON &
THOMAS TREIPE; In Witnes to all I have set my hand this 20th day of March 1661
      ( ) BROWNE,   the marke of REBEKAH ℝ MORGAN
      ( ) BURRELL
  20th March 1661. This Assignemt. was acknowledged in Court by THOMAS STANDLEY,
Attorney of the abovesaid REBECKAH MORGAN & is recorded
  KNOW ALL MEN by these pr:sents that I JENKIN MORGAN appoint my Freind, JOHN
HOLLOWAY, my lawfull Attourney to acknowledge a Pattent of Land in Court to THOMAS
MOULTON & THOMAS TREIPE which I have assigned unto them & what my said Attorney
shall doe I doe ratify & confirme to be as authentiq as if I were personally pr:sant; Wittness my hand this 24th of February 1661
               JENKIN his marke /M MORGAN
  20th March 1661. This Lre. of Attorney was recorded
  I REBECKAH MORGAN doe herein appoint my loveing Freind, THOMAS STANDLEY, to be
my lawfull Attorney for mee to acknowledge an Assignemt. of a Pattent made over by
mee the sd. REBECKAH MORGAN unto THOMAS MOULTON & THOMAS TREIPE accordinge to
my Husbands act and deed to the sd. MOULTON & TREIPE; As Wittness of all I have sett my
hand this 11th day of March 1661
Test RI· BROWNE,   REBECKAH ℝ MORGAN, her marke
    ROBERT BURRELL
  20th March 1661. This Lre. of Attorney was recorded

p   KNOW ALL MEN by these pr:sents that I PETER KNIGHT of WICOCOMOCO for a
71   valluable consideracon have granted unto ROBERT KING of WICOCOMOCO Five
     hundred & twelve acres of Land bounding as foll: Begining at a small Branch

belowe the sd. KINGs cleare ground and runing along the severall courses of the River.
first, North Westerly to a point opposite against CLARKEs Land thirty five chaines, then
South South Westerly along the River thirty chaines; then West Northwesterly forty
chaines to the mouth of COGGes CREEKE, then South Southwesterly upon the Creeke to
MACHOTICK PATH eighty chaines (vizt.) halfe a mile, thence along the severall courses
of the Swamp South South Westerly forty seaven chaines to a marked tree by the Swamp
side, thence East South East by the marked trees, thence Easterly ( ) other winding
courses of ( ) some trees being marked ( ) where wee began & ( ) twelve acres of
Land; I PETER KNIGHT doe warrant the sale of the sd. Land unto ROBERT KING his heires
& assignes for ever As Wittness my ( )

  I ANNE KNIGHT doe ( ) for the sale of the ( ) unto ROBERT KING ( )
Test JAMES HAWLEY,   PETER KNIGHT
      RICHARD ROBARDS
  20th March 1661. This Sale was acknowledged in Northumberland County Court by
RICHARD NEALMES, Attorney of the abovesd. PETER KNIGHT, unto the sd. ROBERT KING,
& is recorded

  KNOW ALL MEN by these presents that I PETER KNIGHT doe make my loveing Freind,
Mr. RICHARD NEALMES, my true & lawfull Attorney to acknowledge a Bill of Sale for
Two hundred acres to Mr. KING, the sd. KING now liveth on, & what my sd. Attorney
shall doe therein shall stand in as full force & vertue as if I were then present; Witnes
my hand the 8th of March 1661
Witnes RICHARD ROBARDS,   PETER KNIGHT
  20th March 1661 This Lre. of Attor: was recorded
  an appraismt of a Heyfer which was of ye Estate of JENKIN PRICE attached by JNO: HOPPER :
p.   February 6th 1661. Praised this day & yeare above written by us JOHN HULETT
72   and ABRAHAM BYRAM, appointed by the Court for that purpose, one heyfer
          valued & prised att three hundred & sixty pounds of tobacco in our best
Judgments; In Witness whereof wee subscribe our hands
                                        ABRAHAM α ℓ BRYAMs marke
                                        JOHN Ŧ Ĥ HULETTs marke
  20th March 1661. This Appraisemt. was recorded

p.   KNOW ALL MEN by these presents that I WILLIAM THOMAS doe by these presents
72   appoint my trusty & welbeloved Freind, JOHN TUCKER, my true & lawfull Attor-
          ney for this next ensueing Court for the County of Northumberland, then &
there to answere such causes as shall be there impleaded agt. mee and I doe likewise
give unto my sd. Attorney full power to arrest implead imprison & out of prison to release in as full manner as if I my selfe were personally present; And I doe further give
unto my said Attorney full power to dispose of such Bills of Sale to be ( ) due unto mee
for the paymt. of ( ) alsoe any other of my Estate for payment of my Debts, all which I
by these presents confirme in as full & ample manner as if I my selfe were psonally
present as doth witness my hand this 27th of November 1661
      ( ) COLEMAN   WILLIAM THOMAS
  20th March 1661. This Lre. of Attor: was recorded.

p.   I THOMAS GERARD doe here by these presents acknowledge to have reced. of
72   THOMAS DARLING full ( ) within menconed Bills, I say reced. ( ) alsoe the sd.
          THOMAS GERARD doe ( ) THOMAS DARLING of all services ( ) whatsoever from
the beginning of the world unto this day January ( )
      ( ) EDMONDS: JOHN HILLIER   THO: GERARD
  20th March 1661. This Discharge was recorded

p.   IN THE NAME OF GOD Amen. I ROBERT LORD of YEACOMOCO in the County of
72   Northumberland being sick & weake yet in p:fect memory, doe make this my
      Last Will & Testamt., in manner & forme following, vizt.

Imprs. I doe give & bequeath my Soule unto God my Creator and my body I comitt to
the Earth from whence it came to be buried with Xpian buriall and for my worldly
Estate, I dispose of it as followeth:

Item. I give all my p:sonall Estate unto my loveing Wife, MARY LORD, ALEXANDER
LORD & JOHN LORD, my two Sonnes, to be equally devided amongst them, onely his two
Sonnes to have the two Gunns which be the longest;

Item. I give all my Land unto my two Sonnes equally to be devided betwixt them & not
one to sell his part but to the other nor morgage it;

Item. My will is that if my Wife, MARY LORD, doe intend to marry then my will is that
p:sonall Estate be devided before shee marry by three honest Neighbors;

Item. I give unto my Servant, SARAH PERGATER at the day of her Freedome one Cowe
within the age of five yeares & one breeding Sowe;

Item. I doe engage my Wife, MARY LORD, not to employ any Cooper upon the Land nor
to sell any Timber of the Land eyther while shee is a Widdow nor her Husband shome
shee shall marry:

Item. I give MABEL MARTHAS, one young Sowe with pigg and one dung-( ) Cock & two
hens:

Item. My will is that my two Sonnes live with their Mother while shee is a Widdow, but
if shee marry & they have cause to complaine, then to be released by ye Court;

Item. I give unto my two Sonnes my spa( ) & all my tooles belonging to my Trade as
Wittness my hand & seale this first day of December 1661

Witnes. CHARLES ASHTON   ROBERT LORD
        SUSANNA LYNDSY

10th March 1661. This Will was proved by the Oath of Mr. CHARLES ASHTON ( )
29th June 1663. SUSANNA LYNDSY ( ) the Probat of this Will ( ) according to order of
Court ( )

p.   KNOW ALL MEN by these pr:sents that I PETER PRESLY for diverse good causes
72   have given & by these pr:sents doe give unto WILLIAM BRADLEY ( ) heyfer
      with her increase shee being ( ) colour black, Witness my hand this 21th of
Aprill 1662
Witness: RI: FLYNT, JONATHAN PARKER   PETER PRESLY
21th Aprill 1662. This Deed of Gift was acknowledged in Court by the sd. PETER PRESLY
& is recorded

p.   I RICHARD WHITE doe give RICHARD SUTTON full power of all my cattell & goods
72   after my decease to dispose of them for the good of my Children and to bee an
      Overseer to them. Item. Three cowes three yearelings one steere I give to my
Sonne, JOSEPH WHITE; one black Sow and a shote one hillinge hoe and weadinge hoe
one greene rug and a blanket, one grisald sow and eight shotes for the good of the
other Children; one pot, one kettle, one greene rug & a blancket, one searge shirte, one
searge fump, six yards of red cloath, nine yards lockrun, six yards of new dowlas, eight
yards of canvas, one tamy wascoate, seaven yards of canvas, seaven yards of canvas &
three quarters; a napkin of sugar, three thousand foure hundred nailes, one axe, one
adce one drawinge knife, one augre, one gouge, one paire of shoes, one paire of
stockins, one paire of drawers, one weadinge hoe, one axe, one dpound of powder, eight
pounds of shott, two thousand & a halfe of pins, one pound black thred, one pound

brown thred; halfe a pound of whited brown thred; two ounces of fine thred, one peece of white tape, one paire of bodies, one white petticoate, two knives, two yards of Lace, one Bill of Foure hundred pounds tobacco; one Bill of Mr. RI: FLYNT of two hundred pounds of tobacco; foure tubs full of Corne, three trayes full of Corne, three hundred & fifty eares of Corne, one skellet, one fryinge pan, three trayes, three hundred pounds of tobacco & caske due from WM: CORNISH; the Last Will & Testamt. of RICHARD WHITE March the 9th 16( )

        JOHN WHITE, his marke   THO: GARRETTs marke
        RICH: WHITE, his marke   RICH: LUGGE
                                           JNO: ABRAREMANs mark

The 21st of Aprill 1662. This Will was proved in Northumberland County Court by the Oathes of RICHARD LUGGE & JOHN ( )

p   KNOW ALL MEN by these prsents that HUGH FOUCH doe confirme unto HUGH
72   MACKREGER, Sonne of JAMES MACKREGER, one Cow comonly called Slow; vizt.,
        chipt & a hole on the right eare & a hole on the left eare, her couller ( ) given
the sd. HUGH FOUCH, To have and to hold the said cow & her increase unto him ye sd.
HUGH MACKGREGER his heires & assignes for ever from me my heires for ever: In
Wittness whereof I have hereunto set my hand this 21th of Aprill 1662
                            the marke of HUGH FOUCH
  21th Aprill 1662. This Deed of Gift was acknowledged in Court by the sd. HUGH FOUCH &
is recorded

p   KNOW ALL MEN by these prsents that I JAMES MACKREGER for & in considera-
73   con of a Cow which was given to my Sonne, HUGH MACKREGER by HUGH FOUCH,
        & by my Servants killed in leiu thereof have given unto my sd. Sonne, HUGH
MACKREGER. one Cowe being of couller black & marked (vizt.) cropt & a hole on ye
right eare & underkeeld. & a hole in ye left eare comonly called Raven, together with
one heifer of couller black about the age of two yeares & of the same marke, the Cowe
above specified is in leiu of a Calfe which was killed belonginge to the said Cowe given
by the sd. FOUCH, To have & to hold the sd. Cowe & Heifer withall there increase unto
him the sd. HUGH MACKREGER his heires & assignes for ever from ye harme of mee my
heires or any prsons whatsoever; In Wittness whereof I have hereunto set my hand this
21th April 1662
Wittness: RI: FLYNT.   the marke of JAMES MACKREGER
        ELEXR: MAXWELL.
  21th Aprill 1662. This Deed of Gift was acknowledged in Court by the sd. JAMES
MACKREGER & is recorded

p.   KNOW ALL MEN by these prsents that I JAMES POPE of the County of Northum-
. 73   berland for diverse good causes & more especially for the vallue of Two thou-
        sand foure hundred pounds of tobco: & caske & one cow & calfe to me already
satisfied & paid. have sould unto WILLIAM & PETER PRESLEY of the aforesd. County and
their heires one thousand ( ) scituate in the County of Northumberland ( ) upon a
Creeke called ( ), Northerly upon the ( ) sd. PRESLY and Coll. TR( ) Land of GERVASE
DODSON ( ) woods towards Coll: ( ) formerly granted to ( ) date the 25th of ( ) warranting the ( ) further oblige my selfe to deliver & assigne a Pattent for the abovesd.
Land ( ) my Wife, DORRIE, shall renounce her Dowry in ( ) demand; by the sd. WM: or
PETER PRESLEY; In Wittness whereof I have hereunto set my hand & seale this 29th day
of Aprill 1662

Signed sealed & delivered in the pr:sence of us
      RICHARD LUGGE,   JAMES POPE, ye Seale
      JAMES HILL
  The 20th of May 1662. This Sale of Land was acknowledged in Court by JONATHAN
PARKER, Attourney of the sd. JAMES POPE, unto the sd. WM: & PETER PRESLEY & is
recorded
       KNOW ALL MEN by these pr:sents that I JAMES POPE of the County of Northum-
berland have & doe by these pr:sents constitute & ordaine my trusty Freind, JONATHAN
PARKER, my lawfull Attourney for me & on my behalfe to acknowledge a Deed for One
thousand acres of land which I have sould to WM. & PETER PRESLEY, beareinge date
wth: these pr:sents; giveinge my sd. Attourney as full power to acknowledge the same
in Court as I my selfe might or could doe beinge p:sonally pr:sent; In Wittness whereof I
have hereunto set my hand & seale this 29th of Aprill 1662
Signed sealed & delivered in the presence of
      RICHARD LUGGE,   JAMES POPE, ye Seale
      JAMES HILL
  The 20th of May 1662. This Letter of Attourney was recorded

p.   To all &c., Whereas &c., Now know yee that I the sd. FRANCIS MORRISON Esqr.
74   give & grant unto DANIELL NEALE three hundred acres of Land scituate in the
       County of Northumberland boundinge vizt., two hundred acres abbuttinge
Southerly upon the Land of ( ); Westerly upon a Creeke issuinge out of ( ) WACOMICO
RIVER Easterly & Northerly upon the maine woods; And one hundred acres the residue,
Southerly ( ) Land of THOMAS KEDBY; South to JOHN JOHNSON, ( ) FORESTs Land, Easterly upon the Land of Mr. ( ); upon the maine woods; the said Land being formerly
granted to THOMAS GARRAT by Pattent beareinge date ( ) of October 1655 & by the sd.
THOMAS ( ) sd. DANIELL NEALE, To have & to hold &c., this ( ) day of June 1661 and in
the Thirteenth year of the reigne of our Sovereigne Lord Kinge Charles ye second &c
              FRANCIS MORYSON   THO: LUDWELL, Secr.
( ) hereunder written doe assigne over all ( ) of this Pattent unto DANIELL NEALE
his heyres or assignes for ever, As Wittness my hand this 20th May 1662
      ( ) MOULTON,   SARAH GERRARDs marke
      ( ) RICHARDSON
  This Assignement was acknowledged in Court ye 20th of May 1662 by the sd. SARAH
GERRARD unto the sd. DANIELL NEALE & is recorded under the Pattent

p.   FRANCIS ROBERTS doe assigne all my right & title of the Pattent wth: the privi-
74   ledges thereon menconed to RICHARD LANSDELL or his heyres or assignes for
       ever, as Wittness my hand this 20th May 1662
Test JAMES AUSTEN   FRANCIS ROBERTS marke
  20th May 1662. This Assignement was acknowledged in Court by the sd. FRANCIS
ROBERTS & is recorded
  (On margin: This Pattent was originally granted to Capt. RICH: BUD and assigned by THO:
WILLIAMS to JOHN HUGHLET and recorded in folio (41) & assigned from HUGHLET to
ROBERTS in folio (59)

p.   This Bill bindes me JOHN MORRIS, Planter, my heyres or assignes to pay or
74   cause to be paid unto RICHARD COLE of SALSBURY PARKE the Lower MACHATICK
       RIVER in the County of Northumberland, Merchant, the quantity of One thou-
sand five hundred pounds of good & merchantable Aranoco bright & large tobco: wth:

sufficient caske to contain ye same accordinge to Act of Assembly to bee paid the 20th
of October next conveniently in consideracon of a Mayd Servant sould me named
KATHERINE MOTT which I JOHN MORRIS ingage to marry or set free & wch: wth all doe
hereby ingage my selfe notwithstandinge other writeinges to serve the sd. RICHARD
COLE or his assignes till the next Crop bee finished & that duringe the sd. terme the sd.
KATHERINE MOTT shall serve the sd. RICHARD COLE or his assignes duringe the sd. term
that I am to serve in consideracon of the lodgeinge washinge diet & furthermore I JOHN
MORRIS doe ingage my selfe to pay sd. RICHARD COLE or his assignes one quarter caske
of good sack for the performacne of all the prmisses I have hereto put my hand & seale
this 20th of March 1661/2 to give security for the debt before marriage.
Signed sealed & delivered in presence of us vizt.
    THO: DARLINGs marke   JNO: MORRIS   ye Seale
  Ye 20th of May 1662. This Bill was recorded

p.   An Obligation of Service from JOHN MORRIS to Mr. RICHARD COLE
74   Wittness: WM: PRESLEY, RI: FLYNT
      20th May 1662. This Obligation is recorded

p.   This Bill bindeth me LEWIS SHEPPARD his heires to pay or cause to be paid unto
74   Coll: RICHARD LEE the full & just sum of 2500 lbs. of good aranoco bright tobco:
      & caske of my owne crop at or upon the 10th day of October next for the true
p:formance whereof ( ) over unto ye Coll. LEE & his assignes all the crop of tobco: &
Corne whereof I shall make or cause to bee made this yeare and further I doe by these
pr:sents oblidge my selfe my heyres unto the sd. Coll. LEE & his assignes ye sume of 5000
lbs. of like good tobco. & caske that I will not dispose or cause any pte: of the crop which
I shall make as aforesd. to bee disposed of untill the sd. sume of 2500 lbs. of tobco: &
caske bee fully & truly satisfied contented & pd., unto the sd. Coll. LEE or his assignes,
And I doe alsoe oblidge my selfe to acknowledge this writeinge in the next Court to bee
held for the County of Northumberland; As Wittness my hand & seale this 25th day of
Aprill 1662
Acknowledged & delivered in ye pr:sence of
    JAMES GAYLARD, GA: KENNADY
  This Writeinge was acknowledged as the marke of LEWIS SHEPPARD ye Seale in Court
ye 20th May 1662 by the above named LEWIS SHEPPARD & is recorded

p.   KNOW ALL whome these may concerne that I RICHARD RUSSELL of NANSEMOND
75   doe hereby assigned unto THOMAS SHIELL of GREAT WICOMICO all my right of
      this Bill of Sale: As Wittness my hand the 8th of March soe called in the yeare
1662
Wittnessed by JOHN WEST   RICHARD RUSSELL
    ROBERT HORRODs marke
  20th May 1662. This Assignemt. was acknowledged in Court by WM. DOWNINGE, the
Attourney of the sd. RICHD: RUSSELL, to ye sd. THO: SHIELL & is recorded
  KNOW ALL whome these presents may concerne that I RICHARD RUSSELL of NANSE-
MOND doe by these pr:sents appoynt my Freind, WILLIAM DOWNINGE of GREATE WICOCO-
MICO my true & lawfull Attourney for to the surrenderinge of all such land as by Bill of
Sale upon Records will make it appeare unto THOMAS SHIELL of the aforesd. WICOCOMI-
CO & what my Attourney shall doe in the premisses I promise to ratifie & confirme as
Wittness my hand & seale this 24th of the month called February 1661
                   RICHARD RUSSELL   ye Seale
  20th May 1662. This Letter of Attourney was recorded

p.   KNOW ALL MEN whome this may concerne that I THOMAS SHIELL doe hereby
75   assigne unto NICHOLAS RISE of WICOMICO the halfe of the Land specified ( ) as
Wittness my hand this 20th of May 1662
THOMAS SHIELL
20th May 1662. This Assignemt. was acknowledged in Court by WILLIAM DOWNINGE,
Attourney of the sd. THOMAS SHIELL to the sd. NICHOLAS RISE & is recorded
KNOW ALL MEN by these pr:sents that I THOMAS SHIELL of WICOMICO in the County of
Northumberland doe appoint my Freind, WILLIAM DOWNINGE my true & lawfull Attour-
ney for me to assigne unto NICHOLAS RISE of the aforesd. WICOCOMICO being halfe ( )
hundred & fifty acres of land as shall bee made appeare by the Bill of Sale & what my
Attourney shall doe in the premisses I doe by these pr:sents promise to ratifie & con-
firme, As Wittness my hand this 20th of May 1662
Wittness JNO: TAILERs marke,   THOMAS SHIELL
     ELIZABETH BENNETTs marke
20th May 1662. This Letter of Attourney was recorded
This Sale of Land was first assigned by GERVASE DODSON & his Wife to Doctr: RICHARD
RUSSELL as in folio (26).

p.   WHEREAS it was ordered at a Court held for the County of Northumberland the
75   21st day of Aprill 1662 that I ABRAHAM JOYCE should forthwith deliver a Cow
ready to calve or a calfe by her side unto ELIZABETH PERRY; Now Know all men
by these pr:sents that I the sd. ABRAHAM JOYCE have given unto the sd. ELIZABETH
PERRY one Cow about the age of seaven yeares of couller browne & marked (vizt.) crop
on the right eare & a nick on the upper side of the same eare & the left eare whole, shee
beinge comonly called by the name of Browninge; To have & to hold unto her the sd.
ELIZABETH PERRY her heires for ever; together wth: all her future increase agt. ye
claime of all p:sons whatsoever to the true performance of the pr:misses I binde me my
heires firmly by these pr:sents; Wittness my hand this 29th of March 1662/1
Wittness: RI: FLYNT, JONATHAN HOWE   ABRAHAM JOYCE
  20th May 1662. This Deed of Gift was acknowledged in Court by the sd. ABRAHAM JOYCE
& is recorded

p.   AN INVENTORY of the Estate of JOHN EARLE deced., Aprill ye 24th Ano: Dom:
75   1662, presented by WILLIAM CLEMENT & ELIZABETH his Wife, who was the Relict
& Executrix of the sd. JOHN EARLE, taken & appraised by us whose names are
subscribed being sworne in Court vizt., 2 cowes each at 400 lbs., 1 cow & 3 heifers; 2
steeres, 4 sowes, a man Servt. haveinge about ( ) yeares to serve, a featherbed, old green
rugg, 4 old feather bolsters, 1 old trunck, dozen of bottles, table & forme; paire of old
canvas ( ), 1 old pillowbeare, a parcell of old pewter, old skillet broken, gimlet, glass
bottles, 2 old guns & 1 pistoll, 1 iron pot & fryinge pan, pot rack, 2 milk trayes, 1 old
pale, 1 Bible sould at 0060; 3 spoones, small parcell of old iron; MARTIN COLE his Accot.,
1100 lbs. of Porke sold att 01100; reced. of JOHN CAWSEY, 2 old diaper napkins, 1 little
ould feather bed wth: old canvas tickin; 1 old flock bed, 1 old cat tayle bolster; 1 old rugg
& blanket, 1 little iron pot & hookes, 1 little fryinge pan; 1 old hoe & 1 old sadle & bridle;
a Mare & a Bull excepted   Summe 9010
    ELIZABETH CLEMENTs marke   RICH: FLYNT
        Sworne in Court   NICHOLAS OWEN
                        ABRAHAM JOYCEs marke
  Ye 20th May 1662. This Inventory was pr:sented to ye Court on the Oath of ELIZABETH
CLEMENT & upon Records

An Account of what debts that hath bin paid out of ye Estate of JOHN EARLE deced. by his Wife & Relict, ELIZABETH CLEMENT. Paid JOSEPH HORSLEY, JAMES CLAUGHTON, JNO: WALKER, Mr. GAYLER, Mr. SPENCER, Mr. CLAY, Mr. FLYNT, Mr. MAUNDER , Mr. ALLERTON, Mr. FRANCIS SIMONS   Summe total: 6492
   Allowed of by ye sd. WILLIAM CLEMENT (   ) 13 lbs. tobco; and (   )

p.   KNOW ALL MEN by these pr:sents that WILLIAM RUST and ANNE RUST his Wife
76   have bargained and sould unto WILLIAM LANDMAN his heires or assignes a
     parcell of land that was formerly (   ) in YEACOMICO upon ye BROAD (   ) con-
sideracon already received (   )selves to acknowledge it in the County Court of Northumberland the next Court, As Wittness our hands & seales the 21th of October 1661
                         WILLIAM RUST
                         marke of ANNE RUST
   20th May 1662 This Sale of Land was acknowledged in Court by Mr. WM. RUST & by
SAMUELL BONAM, the Attourney of ANNE RUST, to ye sd. WM. LANDMAN & is recorded
   KNOW ALL MEN by these pr:sents that I ANNE RUST doe constitute & appoint my Freind,
SAMUELL BONAM, my lawfull Attourney for me & in my name to acknowledge a certaine parcell of land unto WILLIAM LANDMAN the which Land the sd. LANDMAN now
liveth upon, as Wittness my hand this 17th May 1662
Test JNO: TUCKER.   ANNE RUST
   20th May 1662. This Lre. of Attourney was recorded

p.   Debts paid by Mr. EDWARD SANDERS for the Estate of JOHN HUDNALL deced.
76   TOM WATTS for Mr. FOXCROFT, to ABRAHAM ROOME, JOHN LUFFE, JOHN BEERE,
     Major COLCLOUGH. to THO: HOBSON for the use of Mr. FOXCROFT, Mr. BURRELL,
Mr. FLYNT, THO: PAULEY, MRS. WATTS. Mr. WM. BRASEY, THO: WOODWARD for fees; JNO:
LARRET Bill returned; to my owne charges at JAMES TOWNE & else where in my atten-
dance about business relateinge to this Estate of JNO: HUDNALL;   20099
   Wee beinge ordered by the Court to examine Mr. EDWARD SANDERS his Accompt of Mr.
HUDNALLs Estate finde hee hath (   )
   20th May 1662. (   ) was recorded

p.   AN INVENTORY of the Estate of RICHARD WHITE deced. Imprs. 2 ruggs & 1
76   blanket, 1 tin dripinge pan, 1 pint pewter pot, 2 trayes & 5 lbs. sugar; 1 small
     iron kettle; 1 brass kettle, 1 great froe, 1 small iron posset, 1 hoe & an axe, 1 hand
saw, 1 augre & 1 chissell, 1 hammer & drawing knife, 1 old broad axe, 2 saucers, 1 small
fryinge pan, 2 pearcers, 1 pestle, 150 4d. nailes, 5 yards & 1/2 canvas, 1 old blanket, 1 lb.
peper, 1 old searge shute, old tamiwastcoats, 2000 of pins, piece of womens head linen, 6
yards of narrow dowlas, 4 yards of lockrum, 8 yards of fine canvas, 1 paire plaine shoos,
1 paire of old hose, 1 paire of bodies, 1 lockrum shirt, 1 smock, 1 paire of sheepes skin
drawers, 1 womans white coate; 1 lb. black thred, 1 lb. browne thred, 2 quarter pounds
of whited browne thred; 2 ounces of fine thred; 1 small parcell of thred, 2 yards of
broad lace, 1 small p:cell of spice, a small parcell of nailes, peece of tape, paire of Childrens shoos & hose, parcell of coullerd: tape, hand towell, arms length of roanock, set of
hankercher buttons, small box of small things, 1 brush, 2 knives, small stock lock, 6 lbs.
sope, 7 pewter spoones, 1 parcell of rages, 1 peece of broad tape, 2 bowles, 1 ladle, small
balls of cotton weeke (   )   4736   RICHARD SUTTON
   20th May 1662. This Inventory was presented to the Court by sd. RICHD: SUTTON, hee
beinge sworne in Court & is recorded

p.   AN INVENTORY of goods brought before us NICHOLAS JURNEU, JNO: POWELL,
77   THO: PHILLPOT & WILKES MAUNDERS who were appointed to prise the Estate of
            ROB: LAND deced., 5 younge sowes & 6 shotes, 1 cow & calfe, 1 2 yeare ould hei-
fer, 3 3 yeare old heifers, 3 yearelin heifers, 12 steeres, woman servant, 3 guns, 1 brass
paire of spoone moulds, shott, tooles & oald brass, 1 old brass kettle, sawes &c., carpenters tooles, bedding, 2 fryinge pans, caske & earthen pots, pewter kettles & trayes, 2
iron pots & hatt goode, 3 wedges & grubinge hoes, wearinge cloathes   7347
    These are the full of all that was brought before us who was appoynted to appraise the
Estate of ROBERT LAND deced.   THOMAS DUNCKATON
    20th May 1662. This Inventory was recorded

p.   ROBERT SECH his Deed of Gift to ANNE TRUSSELL, Daughter of JOHN TRUSSELL
77   Witnesses FRANCIS CLAUGHTON,   DANIELL ROBERTS
            21th July 1662. This Deed of Gift was acknowledged in Court by the sd.ROBERT
SECH & is recorded
    ROBERT SECH his Deed of Gift of a Cowe to JOHN TRUSSELL JUNR., Son of Coll. JOHN
TRUSSELL deced. In Wittness whereof I have hereunto set my hand this twenty one of
July 1662
Test JAMES CLAUGHTON, DANIELL ROBERTS   ROBERT SECH
    21th July 1662. This Deed of Gift was acknowledged in Court by the sd. ROBERT SECH &
is recorded

p.   To all &c., Whereas &c., Now Know yee that I the sd. RICHARD BENNETT Esquire
78   doe give & grant unto JACOB CONTANCEAN Six hundred acres of Land in the
            County of Northumberland bounded (vizt.) Foure hundred acres of land part
thereof lyinge on the Southermost side of CHICKACONE RIVER and beginning at a small
Creeke that devides the land and Mr. JOHN MOTTRAMs Land & runs West South West
parrellel to the sd. River & unto another Creeke, thence up the sd. Creeke & parrellel to
the Creeke, South South East 32 pole & then East North East 200 poles unto the sd. MOT-
TRAMs Land, & thence North North West parrellel to the sd Land 320 pole unto the pice
where it began. And Two hundred acres the residue abuttinge West upon CHICKACONE
RIVER, North East upon a Creeke that devides this Land from the Land of the sd. JOHN
TRUSSELL granted by a former Pattent, South West & South upon the Maine Woods, the
sd. Land beinge formerly granted unto JOHN TRUSSELL by two severall Pattents dated
vizt., the Foure hundred acres the 14th of October 1649 and the Two hundred acres the
7th of March 1650; both which Pattents are assigned to the sd. JACOB CONTANCEAN; To
have & to hold &c., Dated the 29th of November 1654
                    RICHD; BENNETT   WM: CLAIBORNE, Secr.
    KNOW ALL MEN by these pr:sents that I JACOB CONTANCEAN for good causes & consider-
acons mee thereunto moveinge & ( ) I beare unto my Sonne, JOHN CONTANCEAN & to
his heyres & assignes all my right of the first Fower hundred acres of land menconed;
To have & to hold unto him his heyres & assignes for ever; In Wittness whereof I hereunto set my hand & seale this 20th day of ( ) yeare of the reigne of our Soveraigne
Lord Charles the second 1662
                                        JACOB CONTANCEAN   ye seale
    21th July 1662. This Deed of Gift was acknowledged in Court by THOMAS HOBSON,
Attourney of the sd. JACOB CONTANCEAN to the sd. JOHN CONTANCEAN & is recorded wth:
the Pattent
    KNOW ALL MEN by these pr:sents that I JACOB CONTANCEAN have nominated & make
THOMAS HOBSON my true & lawfull Attourney in my name to acknowledge & confirme a

Deed of Foure hundred acres of Land endorsed on the back of my Pattent, for Six hundred acres. lyinge on the Southernmost side of CHICKACONE RIVER in the County of Northumberland bearinge date wth: these pr:sents unto my Sonne, JOHN CONTANCEAN, his heires &c.. in the County Court of Northumberland aforesd. and what my sd. Attourney shall doe therein these shall binde mee my heyres &c. to ratifie & confirme. In Wittness whereof I have hereunto set my hand & seale this 20th day of June 1662
Sealed & Delivered in the presence of
      JOHN ROGERS,   JACOB CONTANCEAN   ye Seale
      RI: FLYNT
  20th July 1662. This Lettr: of Atturney was recorded

p.   Whereas I PHILLIP CARPENTER of MATTAPANY in the County of Northumber-
78   land & Collony of Virginia for a valuable consideracon to mee in hand paid have
      sould unto RICHARD FLYNT of the County & Collony aforesd.. Fowre hundred & eight acres of land scittuate in Northumberland aforesaid as by a Bargaine & Sale from under my hand & seale bearinge date the 22th day of Xber: 1661 and acknowledged by mee in the County Court of Northumberland abovesd. the 21st of January last past, there recorded more at large may & doeth appeare; NOW KNOW all men by these pr:sents that I the sd. PHILLIP CARPENTER have nominated & appointed JAMES CLAUGHTON of the County of Northumberland aforesd., my true & lawfull Attourney for me & in my name to make a true & absolute assignemt. unto the sd. RICHARD FLYNT his heires & Admrs. forever of the sd. Land & Pattent which beares date the 29th of August 1660 in as large & ample manner as if I were personally pr:sent & did the same as in Law can be required and alsoe to acknowledge an assignemt. in the County Court of Northumberland aforesaid and whatsoever my sd. Attourney shall act or doe in the pr:misses these shall binde mee my heyres to ratifie & confirme; In Wittness whereof I have hereunto set my hande & seale this first day of February 1661
Sealed & Delivered in the presence of
      THOMAS SMITH,   PHILLIP CARPENTER
      DAVID CARTERs marke
  21th July 1662. This Lre. of Attour: was recorded

PHILLIP CARPENTER, his Pattent for Land
To all &c., Whereas &c., Now Know ye that I ( ) give & grant unto PHILLIP CARPENTER of the County of Northumberland ( ) a Branch of the sd. River ( ) N. W. by HENERY TAPPIN ( ) PHILLIP CARPENTER viz., 150 acres ( ) granted unto JOHN CHAMBERS by ( ) GEORGE COLCLOUGH, Atturney ( ) unto ye sd. CARPENTER (p:sons &c., Dated the 29th of August 1657
      Vera Copia   Test FRA: KIRK( )
I JAMES CLAUGHTON, Attourney of PHILLIP CARPENTER, doe hereby assigne over unto RICHARD FLYNT his heyres & assignes the Land menconed in the within written Pattent with warranty agt. all p:sons whatsoever that shall or may lay any claime to the same or any part thereof; In Wittness whereof I have hereunto set my hand & seale this 21th July 1662
  21th July 1662. This Assignemt. was acknowledged in Court by the sd. JAMES CLAUGHTON. Attour: of the said PHILLIP CARPENTER, and is recorded wth: the Pattent, acknowledged in the presence of us   PETER ASHTON,   JOHN ROGERS
                      RICHARD WRIGHT WM: PRESLY
Signed Sealed & delivered in the presence of JAMES GAYLARD,   WM: DOWNINGE

P.   To all &c., Whereas &c., Now know yee that I ye sd. EDWARD DIGGES Esqr. give &
79   grant unto JOHN JOHNSON Two hundred twenty seaven acres of Land scituate in
       the County of Northumberland abutting Southerly upon GREAT WICOCOMICO
RIVER, Easterly & Southerly upon two Creekes issueinge out of the sd. River, Northerly
upon the Maine Woods, the sd. Land beinge formerly granted by Pattent bearinge date
the 21th July 1650 unto THOMAS KEDBY & ye sd. JOHN JOHNSON, which sd. THOMAS KEDBY
hath assigned his right & title to the sd. Land unto the sd. JNO: JOHNSON & consented that
ye same shall bee wholly pattented unto ye sd. JOHNSON name as appeareth by a
certaine writinge upon the Records of the Quarter Courts; To have & to hold &c., Dated
24th of October 1655

                        EDWARD DIGGES,   WM. CLAIBORNE, Secr.
    I JOHN JOHNSON with the consent of my Wife, ANNE, doe assigne all our right to ye land
within specified in this Pattent, and all priviledges thereunto belonginge unto WIL-
LIAM THOMAS & his heyres for ever & doe warrant it from all p:sons whatsoever unto
the sd. THOMAS & his heyres &c., As Wittness our hands this 7th of July 1662
Witnesse ROBERT WILSON   JOHN JOHNSON
                                                ANNE JOHNSON
    21th July 1662. This Assignemt. was acknowledged by JOHN JOHNSON for him selfe &
alsoe acknowledged as to his sd. Wife & is recorded with the Pattent
    KNOW ALL MEN by these pr:sents that I ANNE JOHNSON doe constitute & appoint my
Husband, JOHN JOHNSON, my true & lawfull Attourney to acknowledge to WM: THOMAS
all my right of a Pattent of 227 acres of land; likewise one hundred acres of Land ( )
DANIELL NEALE & my Husband and ( ) Attourney shall doe herein I doe stand ( ) As
Wittness my hand the 20th of July 1662   ANNE JOHNSON
    21th July 1662. This Letter of Attourney was recorded
    KNOW ALL MEN by these pr:sents that I JOHN JOHNSON doe assigne and transferr unto
WILLIAM THOMAS all my title of a Pattent of Two hundred and Twenty seven acres or
thereabouts which land the sd. ( ) formerly seated as also Fifty acres of Land ( ) premisses being Pattented by THO: GERRARD & assigned to DANIELL NEALE; Wittness my
hand ye ( ) of Aprill 1662
Teste SAMUELL GOUCHE   JNO: JOHNSON
       JNO· HAYNIE
    21th July 1662. This Assignemt. was acknowledged in Court by the sd. JOHN JOHNSON &
is recorded

p.   I JOHN KENT have freely given of my owne good will unto THOMAS SHERLY one
79   heifer, ye said Heifer beinge two yeares old marked wth: a crop in the right eare
       & a slitt keeld. on the left eare; As Wittness my hand this 21th of July 1662
Test THO: LEAVETT   JOHN KENT
       sig. of WM: ABRAHAM
    21th July 1662. This Deed of Gift was recorded & acknowledged in Court by the sd. JOHN
KENT

p.   IN THE NAME OF GOD Amen. I EDMOND SINCLER beinge sick & weake in body
79   but haveing perfect sense & memory thanks bee to God for it, have made this
       to be my Last Will & Testamt. viz.
    Imprs. I bequeath my Soule to Allmighty God who gave it mee trusting in him & his
Sonne, Jesus Christ, my Saviour that they will receive it into glory wth: him & his
blessed Angells.
    I bequeath unto Coll JOHN TRUSSELL my fifty acres of Land & my share of the houses
thereupon wth: my Cow & my gunn;

It. I bequeath unto ALEXANDER MACCORTER my Chest & two shirts payinge the man aboard for them;

It. I bequeath unto THO: HASELRIGmy shoates & my three hogs & my shote seeinge mee well buryed;

It. I bequeath alsoe unto ALLEXANDER MACCORTER the Calfe which the Cowe goeth wth; wch: I bequeathed to Coll. TRUSSELL;

It. I bequesth to ANNE, the Wife of THO: HASLERIG, my fryinge pan;

It. I bequeath unto GOODWIFE BEDLAM my iron pot;

It. I bequeath all the rest of my moveable goods equally to be devided betweene GOOD-WIFE BEDLAM & GOODWIFE HASLERIG wth: my Corne equally to bee devided betweene them,

It. I bequeath unto CHRISTOPHER WALKER my stuff breeches;

It. I bequeath my two gall: & 1/2 of Drame which is due from WM: GRINSTED to mee for my funerall to bee delivered to THOS: HASLERIG for the use aforesd.,

I desire Coll. TRUSSELL to bee Exer. of this my Last Will & Testamt. to see it ( ) reversinge all ( ) soever formerly ( ) In Wittness ( ) this nyneth of M( )

Teste DANIELL ROBERTS   EDMOND SINCLER
          JOHN CONTANCEAU

21th July 1662. This Will was proved by the Oathes of DANIELL ROBERTS and JOHN CONTANCEAU and is recorded

p   MRS. BROUGHTON's Accot. of her Husband's Estate
79   The Accompt of MARGARET BROUGHTON of her Husband THOMAS BROUGHTON
        The Estate Dr. Tobco: To soe much paid ( ); more to Mr. BREWER; To Capt. JOHN ROGERS: To Mr. RHODON; To my owne trouble about the Estate severall times; to soe much paid Doctr. BARBERSON -0140;   sum Tobco: totall paid   10833
The Estates Credit accordinge to ye Appraisemt.   10684
            The Estate Debtr: upon Ball: 00149
  This Accompt. was presented to ye Court by MRS. BROUGHTON & allowed of & recorded the 21th of July 1662.

p.   I RICHARD BROWNE doe herein constitute & appoynt my honoured & trusty
80   Freind, Mr. THOMAS HOBSON, to bee my true & lawfull Attourney for mee & in my
        name to acknowledge in Court my Bond unto JAMES CLAUGHTON & alsoe Judgmt.
unto JAMES MACKREGER accordinge to Specialty, giveinge & grantinge unto my said Attourney as full power therein as any Attourney hath or ought to have or be; As Wittness my hand this 21th of July 1662

Teste: THO: BARRET,   RICH: BROWNE
          sig. RICH: LABEN

21st July 1662. This Letter of Attour: was recorded

p.   Whereas I THOMAS WILLIAMS did in my passion scandalize ANTHONY WILKIN-
80   SON sayinge hee was a Rogue & would prove it &c., wth: other such like words,
        I the said WILLIAMS doe acknowledge to have done the said ANTHONY much
wrong & injury by the sd. words and am sorry for itt; In consideracon hereof the sd. ANTHONY doth acquit & discharge the sd. WILLIAMS from all manner of suites & differences from the begininge of the world unto this day, however p:vided the said WIL-LIAMS do ( ) charge belonginge unto the suite ( ) Wittness our hands this ( )th day of March 1661   sig   THO: WILLIAMS
                                          sig   ANTHONY WILKINSON

21th July 1662. This Discharge was recorded

p.   ( ) unto all Men by these pr:sents that I EDWARD COLE of WICKOCOMICO
80   Planter, doe by free Deed of Gift give to ye Sonne of ROBERT CASTLETON of the
       ( ) calfe pied browe & white and ( ) forked & a peece taken off above ( ) &
holes; to him & his heyres for ever ( ) which I confirme as Wittness my hand this 8th
of September 1552 being when ( )   EDWARD COLEs marke
  8th September 1662. This Deed of Gift was acknowledged in Court by the sd. EDWARD
COLE & is recorded

p.   KNOW ALL MEN by these pr:sents that I HENERY WATTS of WICOCOMICO have
80   given made over & graunted and doe by these pr:sents give make over & graunt
       unto ELIZABETH WATTS als. WEBB, my pr:sent Wife, all & singular Cattle & Chat-
tells & goods whatsoever moveables & immoveables which formerly did belonge unto
the sd. ELIZABETH in or during her time of her Widdowhood, And this I doe ratifie &
confirme as a perfect Deed of Gift unto ye sd. ELIZABETH & her heyres for ever; As Wittness my hand & seale this 10th of May 1661
Wittnesseth WILL: NUTT,   HENERY WATTS   ye Seale
       THO: HOBSON
  The 8th of September 1662. This Deed of Gift was acknowledged in Court by the sd.
HENERY WATTS & is recorded

p.   KNOW ALL MEN by these pr:sents that I WILLIAM CORNISH of CHICKACONE in
80   the County of Northumberland for divers good causes & valluable consideracons
       have sold unto JONATHAN ROSTON & to his heyres & assignes for ever a p:cell of
Land beinge twenty acres bee it more or less scittuate & being in the abovesd. County &
upon a Creeke knowne by the name of CHINGOHAN, beginninge at the side of a Sault
Branch at the uper end of a hundred acres of land where the sd. CORNISH liveth on,
runninge from the head of the sd. Sault Branch alonge a valley North North East and
North by East to an old marked Pochickory tree & from thence Northerly or North &
East along the ould marked trees to two marked red Oakes standing neare together &
from thence upon a line of marked trees West & by North to CHINGOHAN CREEKE & soe
up the sd. Creeke to the head of ye Branch which it first began; which sd. tract of land I
the sd. WILLIAM CORNISH my heyres doe warrant to the sd. JONATHAN ROSTON & to his
heyres for ever wth: all manner of hereditaments thereon conteyned, Provided that he
the sd. JONATHAN ROSTON & his heyres shall ( ) what quitt rents ( ) ye holdinge of the
( ) In Wittness whereof I the sd. WILLIAM CORNISH set my hand & seale this ( ) 1662
Signed sealed & delivered in the presence of us
       WM: PRESLY, JOHN CODDINGTON   WILLIAM CORNISH
  The 8th of September 1662. WM. CORNISH acknowledged this Sale of Land unto JONA-
THAN ROSTON & is recorded

p.   KNOW ALL MEN by these pr:sents that I WILLIAM THOMAS of WICKOCOMICO in
80   the County of Northumberland by these pr:sents give unto THOMAS DURANT
       JUNIOR ( ) my Wifes Godsonne, one ( ) of Fower yeares marked & a ( ) eare & a
white udder ( ) & a mealy mouth ( ) to him ye sd. THOMAS DURANT ye Younger & her
increase for ever from mee ye said WILLIAM THOMAS my Exrs. & Admrs. to him ye sd.
THOMAS DURANT the Younger his Exrs. & Admrs. or assignes from any p:sons whatsoever and to the true intent & meaninge hereof I the sd. WILLIAM THOMAS have hereunto set my hand this 8th day of September 1662
Wittnesses.   SAMLL. BONAM,   WM: THOMAS
       WILLIAM COLEMAN

8th September 1662. This Deed of Gift was acknowledged in Court by the sd. Mr. THOMAS & is recorded

p   Wee whose names are underwritten, beinge indifferently chosen to heare &
81   determine a Controversy betweene RICHARD SPANN Plt. and DANIELL NEALE &
        ELLINOR his Wife, Defts., upon an accon of defam: doe conclude determine &
award that the said ELLINOR NEALE (haveinge spoken severall words which doe amount
to slaunder, and not proveinge the same slaunder agt. the sd. SPANN, ( )shall pay all
costs of suite in this behalfe susteyned and see all controversies betweene them concer-
ninge ye premisses to bee fully determined, concluded; In Testimony whereof wee
have hereunto set our hands & seales this ixth day of September 1662 with Court
charges not intendinge any of the Plantiffes expences or any damadges.
                                        WM. THOMAS
                                        JA: GAYLARD
    The 9th of September 1662. This Award was recorded

p.   KNOW ALL MEN by these prsents that I JOHN EARLE hath bargained & sold unto
51   MARTEN COLE his heyres or assignes, one prcell of land lyinge upon the head of
        the LITTLE CREEKE from me to ye sd. JOHN EARLE my heyres & assignes the time
& terme of tenn yeares soe much land as the sd. MARTEN COLE can make use of both for
Timber & Caske, for my owne use of any ( ) and further more I the sd. JOHN EARLE ( )
my selfe my heires firmly warrt. the sd. Land from any manner of psons whatsoever
unto the sd. MARTEN his heyres & assignes and I the sd. MARTEN COLE doe binde my
selfe to leave what houseinge or fenceinge shall be ( ) to leave it sufficient & tenant-
able and if the sd. MARTEN COLE & my Wife doth die then ( ) to have the Land returned
to him ( ) I the sd MARTEN COLE doe ( ) sell nor let the land to any manner of pson
whatsoever if in case I doe not make ( ) againe; And for the true prformance ( ) to pay
unto ye sd. JOHN EARLE two ( ) Feast of Michaell the Arch Angell every ( ) prformance
wee have set our hands this ( ) September 1660
        ( )   JOHN EARLE
                                        MARTEN COLEs marke
    The 8th of September 1662   This Lease was recorded

p.   February 26th 1661. IN THE NAME OF GOD, Amen. I SAMUELL HILL beinge
81   weake of body but of perfect memory doe ordaine this my Last Will & Testament.
        Imprs. I doe bequeath my Soule to God my Creatr: alsoe my body to the earth
from which it proceeded: Alsoe, all my worldly Estate I have in Virginia as Debts or
what else I bequeath unto my loveinge Freind, SAMUELL BONAM, hee seeinge mee decently & Christianlike buryed, & doe make him my whole & sole Exr. of whatsoever I
have here in Virginia to wch: I have set my hand the day & date above written
Test THO: MERTEN   SAMLL. HILLs marke
      JNO: HILLs marke
    The 8th of September 1662. This Will was proved in Court by the Oathes of THO: MERTIN
& JNO· HILL & is recorded

p   IN THE NAME OF GOD Amen. I THOMAS ORLEY in CHERRY POINT NECK in the
81   County of Northumberland in Virginia, Planter, beinge of sound & perfect
        memory praised bee God for the same, yet knowinge the weake & fraile condi-
tion of mans body and the uncertainty of mans life, doe make this my Last Will and
Testament in manner & forme followinge;

Imprs. I doe give & bequeath my Soule unto God my Creatr: hopeinge by the merits of Jesus Christ my Redeemer after the expiracon of my time here to obtaine an eternall waight of glory wth: him in heaven hereafter; And my body I committ to the earth from whence it came; to be buryed in Christian buryall and for my worldly Estate, I dispose of it as followeth:

It. I give & bequeath unto my deare & loveinge Wife, REBECKA ORLEY, after paymt. of my just debts, all that messuage or tenement whereon I now live, together with all the land & priviledges thereunto belonginge, to have & to hold to her and the heires of her body lawfully to bee begotten under the same tenure by which I doe at present enjoy the same:

Next, I doe herein give unto my deare Sister, MARY HARDEN, ye Wife of GEORGE HAR-DEN, Foure hundred ( ) tobco. to bee carefully ( ) decease & deprt: ( ) the first ( ) & soe in case of more( ) moreover it is my ( ) from my Wife as heires ( ) unto JOHN HARDENs Sonne ( ) of MARY HARDEN his Wife ( ) want of such issue unto ( ) ORLEY of WHITECHAPPELL ( ) MIDDLESEX & his heyres;

It. I desire & bequeath ( ) all my goods chattells ( ) else under the rest ( )mediately after m( ) estate bee inventoried ( )ent men & that the ( ) use without controversy ( ) the time of her wi( ) should intermarry ( ) that such Husband ( ) good caution forth ( ) sd. personall Estate ( ) appraysed after my decease ( ) to succeed in the ( ) land, alsoe I doe hereby appoynt ( ), JOHN TINGEY, NICHOLAS OWEN & WALTER WEEKES to bee my Exrs. of this my last Will & Testamt., In Wittness whereof I have hereunto set my hand & seale this eleventh day of August 1662
Signed & delivered in the sight of
    JNO: GARNER. RICH: BROWNE   THO: ORLEY, ye Seale
   The 8th 8ber 1662. This Will was proved in Court by the oathes of the sd. JNO: GARNER & RICHD: BROWNE & is recorded

p   AN INVENTORY indented of all & singular the goods and chattells of Major
62   GEORGE COLCLOUGH deced., taken and appraysed this xith & 7th of September
         1662. At the Plantation of HULLS THICKETT. Imprs. One man servt. named
CHARLES SPARKS haveinge one yeare to serve & 1 moneth at 800 lbs. tobco.; RICH: KEMBALL haveinge 3 yeares 2 moneths; JNO: SANDERS for one yeare 4 moneths; WM. WOOD a boy for four yeares 4 moneths; THO: WARRECK a small boy for about 8 yeares; WM MOSELY a boy for six yeares 2 moneths; an old Negro woman called Joane, a Negro woman called Bess wth: a sucking Child; a Negro man called Tom; WM. TAYLER & his Wife bigg wth: Child for one yeare; 5 cowes & 2 younge calves; 5 yearelins, 1 steere, 1 heifer, 1 pied bull, 1 red bull of 18 moneths old, beddings and other ( ) belongine to the Quarter ( ) & sweete scented tobco ( ) Plantacon   Total 39306
(On margin: A List of Bills & or Accompts in folio 100)

   At the ( ) Plantacon. ( ) SAMUELL EATON, Corne cont: 1/2, old ( ), old hoes, axes with other tooles, ABR: WALLIS for three yeares 4 moneths; ( ) boy for six yeares 3 moneths; ( ) 1 yeare; ( ) yeares very sick; ( ) & a spade; ( ) house plantacon, ( ) brown shirts, 2 canvas smocks, small necessaries in ye Chest; ( ) sheets, bla: arras cover ( ) salt, 12 spoones, 1 porringer, ( ) cupp( ) pr. doggs pr. tonges, small shoes, 2 pillowes, 1 pr. old shoes, needles of severall sizes, p:cell of Physick, 7 haire bedders & horse haltrs:, a few axes, hoes & wedges, In the Ould Chamder: one feather bed bolster & pillowes blanckets, a pr. sheetes, shute of cloathes, 2 ould shutes of cloathes, 2 other old shutes, 2 old coates & one old doublet, 1 new short coate, 5 paire of sheetes, 3 table cloathes, 1 sheete, a p:cell of course napkins & old linen, an old chest & some lumber; old beddinge & coverings for the Servts., 5 pots & iron kettle wth: hangars; 1 fryinge

pan, 2 pestles & a pail, 1 old Gun & a spitt, More in the Old Chamber: 1 lookinge glasses,
1 cubboard cloathe, a cushinge, old chest, pr. of iron doggs, 2 featr: bolsters, 2 pilloves,
pr. old blanckets, flock bed & 1 old chest; In the Kitchinge: a copper kettle, a brasse
kettle, 2 small skillets, a little pot, 1 fryinge pan, 1 old chaffin dish, 1 old brass morter
wth: a hole in it; 3 brass candle sticks, 1 tub, a paile, an old unfixed gun, a chaffin dish,
2 spits, 1 pot, pr. pot racks & andirons, 1 chaire old broken, furniture for the house; 1
flock bed bolster & rug, 3 trayes, 1 cutless, 1 old warminge pan, 104 lbs. of pewter, 1
bason & 2 flagons, the Crop of Sweet scented (   ), a Bull of 3 yeares of age, 4 steares of 2
yeares of age; 15 cowes & 8 calves, a bull of 3 yeares of age, 4 steares of 2 yeares of age,
Servts: JOHN BURCHARD a boy (   ); JOHN ILAND for 1 yeare; JOHN PIRSON sickly; JOHN
ROGERS a sickly boy (   ); THOMAS COLTON for 3 yeares; FRANCK SISCO the INDIAN; JOHN
HICHCOCK a small (   ); MARY LENNAM to bee (   ); SARAH PEIRSON for 4 yeares 6
moneths (   ); JOSIAS BLACKWELL to bee bound at (   ); CONSTANCE COLES for 3 yeares;
PETER HUMPHREYS for 1 yeare; JOHN DAVIS for two yeares; 7 Negroes 3 men & 4 women
at 3500 p. Negro; one Gold Signet   63820
    This is a true & p:fect Inventory of all & singular the goods &
chattles of Major GEORGE COLCLOUGH deced., as it was taken &
appraised by us whose names are underwritten, beinge sworne
& appoynted for that purpose by the County Court of Northumberland at a Court held there the 8th day of September instant
                WM. THOMAS   PETER PRESLY
                EDWARD COLEs marke   RICH: SPANNs marke
    20th 9ber. 1662. Sworne in Court & recorded

p.   These goods not appraised. Imprs. 13 bushells of Salt; 1 pr. of old wheeles;
53   1 Negro man, 2 old coates & a cloake   ELIZABETH COLCLOUGH
        20th November 1662. Sworne in Court & recorded

p.   Mr. SANDERs Deed of Gift
83   Imprs   I give unto PARTAINCE HUDNALL one red Cow called Young Cherry
        wth her female increase marked as in the margent, that is to say, the right eare
cropt & two slitts & the left eare whole only three holes; Likewise, I give unto HENERY
HUDNALL, one younge Cowe called Blossom wth: her female increase marked as in ye
Margent, that is to say, the left eare cropt & two slitts & the right eare only three holes;
Likewise, I give unto MARY HUDNALL two younge cowes & one red cowe calfe the one
of the cowes called Rose being a browne colour & the other a black cowe called Tiedy
and her female increase marked as in the margent, that is to say, both eares cropt & a
peece taken out of the right eare; Likewise, I give unto ELIZABETH HUDNALL two cowes
and (   ) the one female increase they being marked one of the calves being a black (   )
the other a browne cowe called Fence, the other being likewise browne the marke a
peece taken out of the left eare (   ) in the right; (   )male of these above mentoned
Cattle (   ) untill such time as thei(   ) abovesd. Cattle shall remaine (   ) my Wife (   )
appoynt in case of mortality (   )lese Children should dye then (   ) to redowne againe to
me or my heires.
    ((SAUNDERS & (   ) 9ber: 1662   EDWARD SANDERS
    Acknowledged in Court by the sd. EDWARD SANDERS 20th Novembr: 1662 & is recorded

p.   AN INVENTORY of the Estate of THOMAS ORLEY deced., appraised by us whose
83   names are subscribed October the 25th 1662
        Imprs. 1 Servant named EDWARD WHITEY haveinge 2 yeares to serve; 1 Servant

by name THOMAS NASH; 1 Servant by name THOMAS MILLER; 1 Servant by name
RICHARD KNITT, 2 Servant Maides, one yeare each to serve; In the Buttery or Milke
Hosue; 1 small copper kettle, 1 strip pan & cover, 1 brasse drippinge pan, 2 small Childrens skillets and 1 little brasse kettle, old cases milke trayes & other old lumber 5950.
5 Cowes & 3 calves at 400 p Cowe; 3 yearelings, 2 steeres 1 -2 yeare old the other 3 yeares
old, 1 small heifer, 4 sowes & 12 shotes; To the Corne Feild as it now stands 20 barr: at 60
p. barr: Sweet sented tobco: hanginge in ye housinge, to Aranoco tobco: hanginge; to
sweet sented tobco in 16 hogsheads at 400 in a hogsd. wantinge about 100 lbs. in one
hhd. - 6200; To Aranoco tobco: in caske -1600;
   In the Chamber: 1 feather bed, 2 bolsters, 2 pillowes, 1 rugg, 1 blancket, 1 pr. of sheets
& 2 pillowe beares; 2 Russia lether chaires & 2 cushions, 1 old table, 1 press; 1 silke
petticoate, 1 silke wascoat & a large scarffe; 2 small scarffes & 5 hoods, 4 table cloathes, 1
doz. napkins, 6 towells, holland petticoats, 2 smocks, a p:cell of head linen, a paire of
stockings, small womans ( ), peece of tape, a p:cell of wom( )earthern dishes, 4 old
cases & sifter, In the Middle Room. 14 pewter dishes, 2 basons, 1 brass candlestick,
looking glasse, 4 leather chaires, 1 old table, couch & 2 little old ( ); 5 petticoates, 2
waiscoates, pr. of stuff sleaves, 2 paire breeches, pair dimity drawers, 4 knives, small
remnt. of ( ), old coate, old doublet, 4 paire shooes & paire stockings; In the Little Room
1 little old feather bed; 1 paire of canvas sheetes, In the Kitchin: 3 iron potts & hookes,
2 pestles, pailes, tubs, runlet, andirons, In the Little Old Chamber: 2 old feather beds &
bolsters, 2 pillowes, 1 rugg course sheets & 2 Guns; 2 spades & 2 barrills, iron ware & old
iron. JNO: BOGGIS his share in the Crop of Corne & Tobco: is included in this appraysemt
31.998. Left unappraised about 4 Bush. Salt, 1 small Silver Sack Cup & about 15 lbs. of
tobco: Signed: WM. JOLLAN   WM. THOMAS   CHARLES ASHTON
                                       JOS: HORSLEY   NICHOLAS OWEN
   For these goods each specified & doe appraise at 165 lbs. tobco: & caske.
                                       WM. THOMAS   NICHOLAS OWEN
   20th 9ber: 1662. WM. JOLLAN was sworne in Court to this Appraisemt. and Inventory &
is recorded

p.   KNOW ALL MEN by these pr:sents that wee WALTER & ALICE ENGLISH for good
84   causes as alsoe for a valluable consideracon in hand received, have sould from
        us our heyres unto THOMAS ATWELL als. COLLINS his heyres & assignes for ever
all the right & title that wee the sd. WALTER & ALICE have unto a certaine p:cell of Land
(beinge part of a greater dividert) scituate & beinge upon the head of the Lower
MACHATICK RIVER. Begininge at a marked Chesnut standinge upon ye mouth of a little
Branch or Creeke, devidinge this Land from the rest of the Land of the sd. WALTER
ENGLISH. extendinge its bredth from the Forest marked the Chesnut unto the Land of
the sd. THOMAS ATWELL adjoyninge thereto; This sd. p:cell of Land to have & to hold
unto him his heyres & assignes for ever obldginge ourselves or either of us to warrant
& defend from all manner of claimes quarrells or mollestacons that shall arise from the
pretences of any p:sons whatsoever; And in Testimoney to the ( ) wee the sd. WALTER &
ALICE ENGLISH have set our hands & seales this 31th of ( ) our Lord 1662
        ( )   WALTER ENGLISH marke
                                     ALICE ENGLISH marke
   20th November 1662. This Sale of Land was acknowledged by ( ) WATTS, Attorney of
the sd. WALTER ENGLISH and ALICE his Wife. & is recorded
   KNOW ALL MEN by these pr:sents that wee WALTER ENGLISH and ALICE ENGLISH my
Wife doe constitute and appointe our Freind, GEORGE WATTS our true & lawfull Attorney
in our name to acknowledge & ( ) Court at CHICKCONE all our right ( ) to THOMAS

ATWELL or his Attourney ( ) land sould by us unto the sd. THOMAS ATWELL in a Bill of Sale by us unto ( ) what hee our sd. Attur: shall doe in the pr:misses wee ratify as if done by ourselves ( ) this 17th November 1662
                 ( )   WALTER ENGLISH his marke
                                                                  ALICE ENGLISH her marke
KNOW ALL MEN by these pr:sents that I GEORGE WATTS, Attor: of WALTER ENGLISH & ALICE his Wife, doe hereby assigne over unto THOMAS ATWELL his heyres & assignes all my right & title of this Bill of Sale as Wittness my hand this 20th November 1662
       THOMAS SOLLEY, THO: HOBSON   GEORGE WATTS his marke
   20th November 1662. This Letter of Attour: and ye Assignemt. above endorsed was acknowledged in Court & is recorded

p.   AN INVENTORY of the Estate belonginge to ELIZABETH COLCLOUGH as Admrx. of
84   Mr. SIMON OVERSEY deced, viz. 4 feather beds, 3 bolsters, 3 ruggs, 3 blanckets,
          5 feathr: pillowes wth: 3 suites of curtaines & valleynes; 2 greate truncks, 1 case,
3 small tables, 7 leathr: chaires, 2 lookinge glasses, 8 lbs. of plate; 3 paire of andirons, 2 small carpets, 2 dozen of old napkins, 3 old table cloths, 2 paire of old sheetes, 2 window cloths, 2 towells, 30 lbs. of pewtr:, 2 cupboards, 3 beadsteads & 1 truneld. bedstead; 2 small copper & 1 iron kettles, 2 spitts, 1 fryinge pan, 1 chaffin dish, 37 ewes & 2 rams, 4 cowes, 3 calves, 3 mares & 2 mare foales, 3 younge horses of 2 yeares old, 1 old horse, 2 INDIANS, a boy & a girle servants; JOHN PAINE an English Servant for one yeare; a boy goinge by the name of MARY ( ) JACK one yeare; a Servt. maide sould for 188 lbs. of tobco: 2 cupboard cloathes, 2 chests   ELIZABETH COLCLOUGH
   20th 9ber: 1662. Presented in Court & is recorded

p   KNOW ALL MEN by these pr:sents that wee WILLIAM THOMAS & EDWARD COLES
84   doe mutually binde our selves in the sume of ( ) pounds of good ( ) to stand ( )
          at JAMES CITTY ( ) day of September 16( ). Whereas the above menconed ( )
for our selves to ( ) betweene them & that the same which ( )voyed beinge wth:in ( ) same hand bin ( ) COLES his Land by the ( ) as by evidence to ( ) forth belongs & app( ) heyres and assignes in as ( )poses as it did at a ( ) the survey of the ( ) where-on obteyned ( ) Mr. WM· THOMAS his Exrs. ( ) EDWARD COLES or his assignes ( ) ninety & six pounds of good tobco: ( ) the sd. COLES hath bin at in & about ( ) and this our award wee doe order to bee finall determinacon & conclusion of this controversie: Witt-ness our hands this xiith day of September 1662   JOHN CARTER
                                                                  PETER ASHTON

   20th 9ber: 1662. This Award was recorded

p.   Mr. PETER ASHTON his Warrt. for the acquiringe of the Estate of WM.
85   ALDERIDGE.
          Northumberland County. Whereas I am credibly informed that WILLIAM ALDERIDGE who was lately wounded wth: the shott of a Gunn & dyed thereupon, these are forthwith to impannell a Jury of Inquest of Twelve discreet men to veiw the Corpse of the sd. WM. ALDERIDGE & to inquire whether the would soe received was the cause of his death, hereof faile not as you will answer the contrary at your perill; Given under my hand this 17th 9ber: 1662
To the Sheriffe of Northumberland County   PETER ASHTON
his Deputy or Deputies
   The Jurys Verdict 17th 9br: 1662. Wee whose names are underwritten being impan-nelled to open a Jury to veiw the Corpse of WILLM: ALDERIDGE deceased, doe finde &

haveinge seene the wounded body & examined the Chirurgion that the wound was not the absolute cause of his death, but other accidentall causes as an inflamacon in ye throat & a feaver, his wound beinge in ye fleshly part of his thigh

( ) GRAUNT,	JOHN POWELL
( ) GOCKE	THO: MOULTON
( ) HALL	JNO: GIBSON
( )	MATHEW WILLCOCKES
( )	( ) TAYLER
( )	JNO: JOHNSONs marke

The Deposicon of SAMUELL LEGG, Master Katch ( ) & now Ridinge in GREATE WICOCO-MICO taken before us   PETER ASHTON
( ) two of his Maties. Justices of peace in Northumberland County this 19th 9ber: 1662.
( ) examined by what means WM: ALDERIDGE ( ) company acquired that wound in ( ) whereof the sd. ALDERIDGE is since ( ) hee the sd. LEGG with Mr. WM. SAMFORD ( ) of the sd. Katch, & WM. ALDERIDGE ( ) the Cabbin of the sd. Vessell, fixing ( )ells service, the sd Gunn lyinge ( ) in the prsence of mee this Examin( ) all of the psons above menconed & ( )pan, at least, by the examination & drew the stock on the Gun ( ) fired went off & wounded the said ALDERIDGE ( ) ye fleshly part of the thigh
Sworne before us PETER ASHTON   SAMUELL LEGE
        WILL: NUTT

Alsoe DANIELL NEALE & ELINER his Wife, beinge examined saith that WILLIAM AL-DERIDGE haveinge received a wound in the fleshly part of his thigh, was brought to the Examinants house & duringe the time of his beinge there hee did express much of sor-row that ye Master, Mr. SAMLL. LEGE, who was his good Freind, should grieve soe much at an accident; that could not bee helpt; And further these Examinants say that after the second dressinge of his wound, they never heard him complaine of his heart, but did cheerfully say that hee hopt hee should quickly bee well untill a weeke after his cominge a shore & then one morninge hee did complaine that in the night his Cap had fallen off his head & hee had got a great cold & his throat was soe sore that hee could not swallow & this soreness in his throat did continue from Satturday till Sunday night And then these examinants did ask the sd. ALDERIDGE whether they should send for the Doctor & hee said that the Doctor could doe him no good, for his would did not trouble him, but onely the greife in his heart & yt: (as hee said) hee thoush would kill him;
Sworne before us the day & yeare abovesd.   DANIELL NEALE
        PETER ASHTON, WILL: NUTT

The Examinacon of WM. ALDERIDGE, Mercht., of the Katch "Martey," of ROADE ISLAND now ridinge in GREATE WICOCOMICO RIVER taken before us PETER ASHTON and WILLIAM NUTT, Gent., two of his Maties Justices of the peace of Northumberland County this 18th 9ber, 1662.
The Examincon of WM. SANDFORD, the sd. WILLIAM SANDFORD ( ) received aboard ( ) Cabbin of t( ) Master & ELIAS SLEW ( ); WILLM. ALDERIDGE ( ) service the 3d. Gunn ( ) by me the examined ( ) fire at last SAMLL. ( ) drew the Tricker ( ) WM. ALDERIDGE in ( )
The Examinacon of ELIAS SLEW. Alsoe ELIAS SLEW ( ) examined what hee ( ) received aboard the ( ) the sd. Katch, ( ) which after sd. Katch ( ) & vessells servived, yt: ye ( ) divers of the above ( ) fire at last SAMLL. LEGE the tricker of the gun ( ) in the fleshly part of his thigh
The Examinacon of JNO· BEARE. Alsoe JOHN BEARE Chirurgion of ( ) of Bristoll beinge examined sayeth that ( ) tyed above the dessinge of a wound that ( ) dyed had receaved in the fleshly part of the thigh, the sd. BEARE doth testifie yt: the wound received was

not the cause of death; it beinge in the fleshly part, but the temperature of the weather
alteringe the disposicon of his body caused a tumour in his throat wth: an inflamacon
yt:hee could not take any sufficient sustenance & further saith not
Sworne before us   PETER ASHTON   JOHN BEARE
            WILL: NUTT
    20th 9ber: 1662. The Examinacons above menconed were recorded

p.   Whereas it was ordered the Sixth day of August last past by the Comrs:
86   appoynted for the INDIAN AFFAIRES that ROBERT JONES by the Consent of the
             WICOCOMICO INDIANS should enjoy the Neck of Land where hee dwelleth, ex-
tendinge up alonge the Northernmost Branch to the Glade, in consideracon of Twelve
MACHCOATES to be paid at the arrivall of the second Shipp. Now These prsents wittness
that wee the Greate Men of WICKOCOMICO INDIAN TOWNE doe acknowledge to have
received the sd. consideracon in the prsents of Coll. JOHN CARTER and therefore doe
hereby alien, bargaine and confirme the sd. Land wth:all its appurtenances to the sd.
ROBERT JONES his heyres & assignes for ever; And alsoe doe hereby authorise Mr.
THOMAS HOBSON in our names and as our Attour: to acknowledge this in Court as our act
& deed; Wittness our hands & seales this 17th of November 1662
Wittness JOHN CA( )   OWASOWAY   ☙
       GEORGE ( )   CHISTE CUTTEWANS ☙
       JOHN ( )   TATENENOUG ☙
    20th 9br: 1662. This Writeinge was acknowledged in Court by the above named
THOMAS HOBSON unto the sd. ROBERT JONES & is recorded

p.   ( ) for my selfe & my heyres ex( ) give all my right & title of the within ( )
86   to ANDREW PETTIGREW who marryed ( ) Widdow, and his heyres & assignes for
             ever. Wittness my hand the 19th November 1662
                                          JOHN HAYNIE
    20th 9br: 1662. This Reassignement was acknowledged in Court by ( ) Attor. of the sd.
JNO: HAYNIE and is recorded

p   TO ALL THOSE to whom this present writeinge shall come before, Know yee that I
86   RICHARD BROWNE of ( ) NECK for & in consideracon ( ) JOHN RAVEN hath this
             day ( ) LOVETT of Two thousand one ( ) of tobco. & caske in my behalfe ( ) sd.
BROWNE from an execution ( ) layd upon mee at the suite of JAMES MAGREGER, I the
abovesd. BROWNE in consideration whereof doe herein assigne & sett over from mee
and my heyres all my right and interest of my fees in part of the sd. RAVENs Security
to save & keepe harmelesse him him heyres or assignes from the sd. debt as alsoe in the
like kinde for his more security I doe herein binde over as abovesd. one young cow
called Younge Congeduggs & one younge Steere called Old Congeduggs Steare together
wth: one good feather bed and alsoe my ensewinge crop wherever I shall make it & to
acknowledge all here specified upon Record when JOHN RAVEN or his assignes shall
demand the same. my ensueinge crop to bee made in this County of Northumberland;
In Wittness to all herein written, I have set my hand this 21th day of November 1662
Wittness THOMAS LEAVETT   RICHARD BROWNE
       JAMES HOWEEBACKs marke
       RICHARD LABENs marke
    21th 9ber: 1662. This Deed was acknowledged by Mr. BROWNE before us PETER KNIGHT
& WILLM. PRESLY, and is recorded

p.

p.   KNOWE ALL MEN by these pr:sents that I MARY SECH, the Wife of ROBERT SECH,
86   formerly the Wife of Coll. JOHN TRUSSELL, nowe deceased, have deputed &
     authorized my well beloved Freind, JAMES CLAUGHTON, to acknowledge & con-
firme unto Mr. JACOB CONTANCEAN JUNIOR & to JOHN CONTANCEAN their heires &
assignes all the right & title by way of Dower or Thirds that I have or may claime in two
Pattents of Land scituate in Northumberland County on the South side of CHICLACOANE
RIVER containing ( ) my former Husband ( ) JACOB CONTANCEAN ( ) CLAUGHTON to
make ( ) in the Court of the sd. County ( ) & there to release all my ( ) Pattents & Land
(viz.) ( ) one Pattent unto the ( ) hundred acres contain ( ) from the sd: JACOB ( )
CONTANCEAN; In Wittness ( )
Sealed & delivered in the presence of
     DANIELL ROBERTS,   MILES GOREHAM   MARY SECH
  10th February 1662. This Lre. of Attorney was acknowledged in Northumberland
County Court by JAMES CLAUGHTON & is recorded

p.   I doe for my selfe & my Admrs. & assignes transfer all my right & title of the
86   within menconed Three hundred acres of land to DANIEL CROSBY & his heires
     & assignes for ever & in case of any demand in or about ye pr:misses to take
such corse agt. the sd. WATERS within written as hee is by the within conveyance
obliged unto upon the severall circumstances thereof; Wittness my hand the last of July
1662
Wittness JOHN HAYNIE,   RICH: ʃ∕ ILIFFE
        JOHN TAYLER
 10th Febr: 1662. Recognitur in Curia Northumberland & RICHARD ILIFFEs & Record
 This Land was conveyed from ROGER WATERS to RICHARD ILIFFE the 22th of Aprill
1659 & recorded in folio 20 huius libri 20: May 1659

p.   I THOMAS TREIPE doe assigne & transfer all the Land which was assigned unto
87   mee the sd. TREIPE by JENKIN MORGAN & REBECKA his Wife unto THOMAS MOUL-
     TON his heires & assignes for ever as freely and amply as is exprest in this Pat-
tent with all priviledges thereunto belonging. As Wittness my hand this 9th of Feb: 1662
Wit: RI: BROWNE,   JOHN WHITE   THOMAS ─┼─ TREIPE
 10th Febr: 1662. This Assignemt. was acknowledged in Court by Mr. WM. THOMAS,
Attorney of the said TREIPE & is recorded
 The Pattent for this Land was originally granted to EDWARD COLES by him assigned to
JENKIN MORGAN & by him assigned to THO: MOULTON & THOMAS TREIPE 24th Febr: 1661
& is recorded in folio 70 huius libri.
 KNOWE ALL MEN by these presents that I THOMAS TREIPE doe herein constitute & ap-
point my well beloved Freind, Mr. WILLIAM THOMAS, to be my true & absolute Attorney
for mee & in my name ( ) property of Land ( ) in the next Court held for the County of
Northumberland according to my ( ) to him made which land was formerly ( ) the sd.
TREIPE & MOULTON by JENKIN MORGAN & REBECKA his Wife & doe by these pr:sents
make all former Attorneys & Lres. of Attorneys ( ) which are any waies & what my sd.
Attorney ( ) I doe ratify & confirme ( ) as if that my selfe was ( ) to all here written, I
have hereunto set my hand & seal this 9th day of Febr: 1662
        ( )   THO: ─┼─ TREIPE
10th Febr: 1662. This Lre. of Attorney was recorded

p.   TO ALL XPIAN PEOPLE greeting; Know yee that I THOMAS TREIPE of GREATE
87   WICOCOMICO in Virginia, Planter, doe hereby sell unto Capt. DANLL. NEALE, two
     men Servants namely JAMES GARNESBY & EDWARD LUGG, for their respective

times they are to serve according to the custome of the Country and alsoe one halfe part
of that Plantacon which THOMAS MOULTON & I bought of JENKIN MORGAN & which wee
now dwell upon together with all buildings fences and advantages belonging for a
valluable consideracon to mee in hand paid; To have & to hold the sd. Servants & the sd.
halfe part of the sd. Plantacon to the sd. DANIELL NEALE his heires & assignes without
molestacon from any p:sons whatsoever, And I doe further oblige my selfe that my selfe
& the abovesd. JAMES & EDWARD & one able p:son more will (by Gods p:mission) pitch as
considerable a crop of good Oronoco tobacco as wee the said fower p:sons shall be com-
petently able to manage upon the abovesd. Plantacon & the same duly to attend, all
which sd. tobacco I doe hereby binde over & sell & am to deliver well packt. in hogshds.
& that in good & marchantable condicon to him at the abovesd. Plantacon; In Witness
whereof I have sett my hand & fixed my seale the 20th day of January 16( ); The condicon of the above writing ( ) sd. THOMAS TREIPE shall pay unto the sd. DANLL. NEALEs
full order three thou( ) good bright ( ) packt ( ) plantacon upon the ( ) obligacon
shall be ( ) in full force
Signed sealed & delivered before us

THOMAS MATHEW,   THOMAS TREIPE
THOMAS SADLER,   RICHARD LUGGE

I doe hereby appoint THOMAS MATHEW, Marchant, to be my lawfull Attorney to acknowledge the within Deed ( )
Teste RICHARD LUGGE, CHRISTOPHER NEALE   THOMAS TREIPE
10th February 1662. ( ) to DANIELL NEALE ( ) THOMAS MATHEW, Attorney of ( )

p.   I EMANUELL AVERY being ( ) JOHN WATTS doe assigne over unto JOHN WOOD
87   ( ) & title of this Pattent, As Witness my had this ( ) Febr: 1662
                                       EMANUEL AVERY
10th Febr: 1662. This Assignemt. was acknowledged in Court by MATHIAS HOLBROOKE,
Attorney of EMANUELL AVERY & recorded
The Pattent for this Land was originally granted to THO: SAFFALL being 850 acres out
of which 500 acres was assigned to JNO: HUDNALL & recorded in the other Booke in folio
56, the remainder being 350 acres was by the sd. HUDNALL assigned to JAMES
MAGREGER & HUGH FOUCH & by them assigned to JNO: WATTS & recorded in folio 17
huius libri

p.   KNOW ALL MEN by these pr:sents that I JOHN WATTS of the CITTIE of BRISTOLL,
88   Sailemaker, have made & appointed my trusty & welbeloved Freind, EMANUELL
           AVERY of the CITTIE of BRISTOLL, Marriner, my true & lawfull Attorney to take
possession in all that plantacon called by the name of OLD THOMAS his Plantacon being
by the River of GREATE WICOCOMICO in the County of Northumberland within the
Country of Virginia, & alsoe to sue forth a Pattent for the same out of the Court there in
Virginia & the same to deliver over unto PHILLIP GIBBS of BRISTOLL, Merchant, or his
assignes giveing by these presents my sd. Attorney full power to finish all that be
needfull about ye premisses & to receive all such rents as are due for the sd. Plantacon
since the 23th day of March which was in the yeare of our Lord 1658; In Witness I have
hereunto put my hand & seale this ( ) August 1662
                                   JOHN WATTS
10th Febr: 1662. This Lre. of Attorney was recorded
KNOW ALL MEN by these pr:sents that I EM: AVERY being Attorney of JOHN WATTS of
the CITTY of BRISTOLL ordaine MATHIAS HOLBROOKE my lawfull Attorney for mee to
acknowledge the assignemt. of a Pattent to me the sd. AVERY to the sd. ( ) Plantacon is
menconed ( ) from Attorney which is to be ( ) PHILLIP GIBBS or his assignes allowing

whatsoever my sd. Attorney shall lawfully doe in the premisses; Witness my hand & seale this 6th of February 1662/63.
GIFFORD BROWNE   EM: AVERY, ye Seale
10th Febr: 1662. This Lre. of Attor: was recorded

p. 88   KNOWE ALL MEN by these prsents that I ED: SANDERS of the County of Northumberland for a valluable consideracon have sold unto RICHARD DENNIS &
PASCO DENNIS Three hundred acres of land with what houseing there is nowe standing on the sd. Land scituate lyinge & beinge in the County of Northumberland on the head of a Creeke called by the name of DENNIS his CREEKE, likewise the said land is butted and bounded Southerly upon the land of CHRISTOPHER GARLINGTON & Northerly upon the Land which was formerly RICHARD BUDs nowe in the possession of WILLIAM GROFFIN & Westerly upon my owne Land, I the sd. ED: SANDERS doe warrant the sd. Land unto the abovesd. pties according as it is warranted to mee by a Bill of Sale given by JOHN HOPPER as Witnesse my hand this 8th day of Decembr: 1662
Signed sealed & delivered in the presence of
NICHOLAS MORRIS,   EDWARD SANDERS   ye Seale
PETER HULL   MARY M SANDERS, her marke, ye Seale
10th Febr: 1662. This Writeing was acknowledged in Cort: by EDWARD SANDERS & WM: FLOWERS, Attorney of MARY SANDERS & is recorded
KNOWE ALL MEN by these prsents that I MARY SANDERS doe appoint Mr. WM: FLOWERS my Attorney & in my behalfe to acknowledge with my Husband the sale of Land sold to RICHARD DENNIS & PASCO DENNIS, Witness my hand this 9th of February 1662
Test PETER HULL   MARY M SANDERS her marke
EDWD. WITKIN
10th Febr. 1662; This Lre. of Attorney was recorded

p. 88   November the 10th 1662. I JAMES ALLEN of the County of Northumberland
have sold unto RALPH WADINTON his heires for ever being in LITTLE WICOCO-
MICO ( ) marked adjoyning ( ) is in the possession of ( ) trees which was marked all the rest of ( ) to the land of ( ) that did belong to the sd. ALLEN ( ) RALPH WADINTON excepting Fifty acres the sd ALLEN doth give to ELIZABETH WADINTON ( ) not to be molested till his Lease is out; And for the true pformance I the sd. JAMES ALLEN have sett my hand & seale the date above menconed
Signed Sealed & delivered in the presence of us
HENRY WATTS,   JAMES Q ALLEN, ye Seale
FRANCIS BICKLEY
10th Febr: 1662. This Writeing was acknowledged in Northumberland County Court by the abovesd. JAMES ALLEN and recorded

p. 89   KNOWE ALL MEN by these prsents that I HENRY MOUSELEY of CHERRY POINT in
ye County of Northumberland, Planter, with the Consent of my Wife, ELIZABETH,
for a valluable consideracon have sold unto FRANCIS CLAY of ye same County, Gent., from mee my heires & assignes unto him his heires & assignes for ever one pcell of land in Northumberland County bounded as followeth: Beginning at a point upon MOUSELEYS CREEKE soe called running South South West one hundred poles alonge the Branch parting this Land from COPPAGE his Land to a quarter marked tree, from the sd. tree one hundred & sixty poles West North West to a quarter marked tree in the woods, from the sd. tree North North East one hundred poles to a marked tree, from the sd. tree East South East one hundred & sixty poles down to ye Branch & MOUSELEYS CREEKE parting this Land & the Land of Mr. EDWARD MORE to the first station; conteyning One

hundred acres which sd. Land with all its right I HENRY MOUSELEY doe warrant & confirme from any p:sons whatsoever unto FRANCIS CLAY as being his p:per due as may
appeare by this Bill of Sale bearing date ( ) of November 1662; For the true p:formance
wee HENRY MOUSELEY & my Wife, ELIZABETH, sett our hands & seales ye day & yeare
abovesd., Likewise engage to acknowledge the above ( ) next County Court to be held
for Northumberland County to FRANCIS CLAY his heires & assignes

( )　　　　　　　　　　　　HENRY MOUSELEY　　ye Seale
　　　　　　　　　　　　　　ELIZ: E MOUSELEY,　ye Seale
10th Febr: 1662. This Deed of Land was acknowledged in Northumberland County Court
by JOSEPH HORSELEY, Attorney of HENRY MOUSELEY & ELIZABETH MOUSELEY & recorded
　KNOWE ALL MEN by these pr:sents that I HENRY MOUSELEY with the Consent of my
Wife, ELIZABETH, have appointed Mr. JOSEPH HORSLEY our true & lawfull Attorney to
acknowledge a peice of land which by Bill of Sale was sold to Mr. FRANCIS CLAY & his
heires for ever; as by the sd. Bill may appeare; to this Lre. of Attorney wee have subscribed our hands with our seales this 19th day of January 1662, & what our sd. Attorney shall doe wee will ratify & confirme as if our selves were p:sonally pr:sent to act
the same;
Signed sealed & delivered in the presence of
　WILLIAM FREEMAN,　　　　　　HENRY MOUSELEY,　ye Seale
　THO: DANIELL　　　　　　　　ELIZ: E MOUSELEY　ye Seale
　ROBT: X　SELFE his marke
10th Febr. 1662. THO: DANIELL & ROBERT SELFE declared on Oaths in Court this Lre. of
Attorney to be the act and deed of HENRY & ELIZABETH MOUSELEY & is recorded

p.　　I JOHN WOOD doe assigne all my right & title of this Pattent with all the rights
89　　& priviledges thereto belonging unto WILLIAM FLOWER his heires & assignes
　　　for ever; As Witness my hand this 10th of February 1662
Test PETER HULL, WM: DOWNING　　　MARY /U WOOD, her marke
　　　　　　　　　　　　　　　　JOHN +++ WOOD his marke
　10th Febr: 1662. This Assignemt. was acknowledged in Court by JNO: WOOD & PETER
HULL, Attorney of MARY WOOD & recorded.
　The Pattent for this Land was originally granted to HENRY WEEKER being 250 acres
which by him was assigned to JNO: DAVIS 158 acres of which was by GERVASE DODSON
assigned to RICH: GIBBLE & 100 acres the remainder to DAVID ORLAND & the sd. GIBBLE
assigned his right to JNO: WOOD which is recorded in folio 68 huius libri
　This Pattent was assigned to Mr. DODSON by HEN: WICKER in folio 5; huius libri
　KNOWE ALL MEN by these pr:sents that I MARY WOOD doe appoint PETER HULL my
Attorney to a cknowledge with my Husband the sale of One hundred & fifty acres of land
sold to Mr. WM: FLOWER as Witnesse my hand this 9th of February 1662
Test RICH: HARWARD, his marke Ө~　　MARY /U WOOD
　10th Febr: 1662. This Lre. of Attorney was recorded

p.　　BEE IT KNOWNE unto all men I JOHN NICHOLLS for a valluable consideracon sale
89　　unto PETER KNIGHT all my right with warranty from me my heires & assignes
　　　( ) in Court; as Witness my hand this ( ) December 1662
Test JOHN WHISKIN,　　　　　　JOHN NICHOLLS
　JNO: JC CAPE
SARAH NICHOLLS consents to ye above assignemt.
Test JOHN WHISKIN, JNO: J C CAPE
　10th Febr: 1662. Acknowledged in Northumberland County Court by EDWARD SAUN-
DERS, Attorney of JOHN & SARAH NICHOLLS & recorded

This Land was conveyed from the abovesd. PETER KNIGHT to JOHN NICHOLLS & recorded in folio 56: huius libri

BEE IT KNOWNE unto all men by these p:sents that wee JOHN NICHOLLS & SARAH NICHOLLS doe make our loveing Freind, Mr. EDWARD SANDERS, our true & lawfull Attorney to acknowledge in Court a certaine p:cell of Land being Eight hundred acres of land at the head of WICOCOMICO RIVER bought of PETER KNIGHT & nowe sold & re-assigned unto the said KNIGHT & his heires & assignes as by ye conveyance will make to appeare & for the true p:formance of our Attorney wee the sd. JOHN & SARAH doe binde our selves & our assignes to confirme that what our sd. Attorney shall doe shall stand in as full force and vertue as if wee were there pr:sent. Witnes our hands this 12th of December 1662
Test JOHN WHISKIN,
   JNO: I C CAPE, his marke   JOHN NICHOLLS
10th Febr: 1662. This Lre. of Attorney was recorded SARAH C NICHOLLS her marke

(The following material, part of Northumberland County Record Book 1658-1662, was omitted in the typing of this Book.)

p. 24   KNOW ALL MEN by these pr:sents yt: I GEORGE MARSH of RAPPAHANOCK, Mercht., doe hereby ordaine Mr. JNO: SAFFIN, Mercht., my true & lawfull Attorney for me to receive all such tobco: as are due to me in ye County of Northumberland giveing my sd. Attorney as full power as if I my selfe were p:sonally there pr:sent and doe ratify ( ) as if I were p:sonally p:sent; In Witness whereof I have set my hand & seale this 12th of ( )
Signed Sealed & Delivered in the presence of
the marke of GEORGE BRADEN   GEORGE MARSH, ye Seale
20th May 1659. This Lre. of Attor. was recorded

p. 24   Northumberland County the lower bounds thereof by Order of Assembly ( ) the Assembly at JAMES CITTY March ye 20th 1658:
Whereas by Order of ye Court dated the 15th of Decembr: 1656; it was ordered that the TOWNE of WICKACOMOCO should be in & appertain to the County of Northumberland, It is by this Grand Assembly confirmed that ye Land of SAMUELL MATHEWES Esqr., Governr: and Coll. LEE his land & Two hundred acres more be included in the sd. County and the rest excluded   Teste HENRY RANDOLPH, Cl. Assem.
20th May 1659. This Order was recorded

p. 24   BE IT KNOWNE unto all men by these pr:sents that I JOHN SAFFIN of BOSTIN in NEW ENGLAND, Mercht., doe herby constitute & depute & in my place put my loveing Freind, Mr. WILLIAM PRESLY, of CHICACOAN in Virginia my true & lawfull Attorney for mee as alsoe in the behalfe of any p:son or p:sons that I am agent or Attorney for here in Virginia to aske & recover any manner of debts that may appeare to be due to mee the sd. JNO: SAFFIN or to any p:sons as aforesd., within the Land of Virginia giveing my sd. Attorney full power to sue implead deliver upon paymt. to give sufficient acquittances & discharges, alsoe to sell & dispose of any land goods or chattels I shall committ unto his trust & custody for my use and when my sd. Attorney ( ) about the premisses I ( ) confirme & allow as authentique as if I my selfe ( ) In Witness whereof I the sd. JNO: SAFFIN sett my hand & seale this ( ) six hundred fifty nine
Signed sealed & delivered in presence of
PETER ASHTON, WM: ( )   JNO: SAFFIN
20th May 1659. This Lre. of Attorney was recorded

p.   Mr. THO: BROUGHTON of Virginia in Assignemt. of a Patt: & Land to Mr.
24   THO: BROUGHTON in NEW ENGLAND

BE IT KNOWNE ( ) BROUGHTON of CHO( ) alienate & ( ) hundr( ) acres of land
( ) of Pattent from m( ) unto Mr. THOMAS BROUGHTON of ( )rcht., to him his heires
peaceably to be possessed & the true intent of the sd. ( ) confirmation ( ) the sd. THO-
MAS BROUGHTON bind mee my heires firmely by these prsents; In Witness whereof I
hereunto sett my hand this 30th day of March 1659
Witness PETER ASHTON,   THO: BROUGHTON
          JOSEPH HARDY

20th Mary 1659. This Assignemt. was acknowledged in Court by the sd. THOMAS
BROUGHTON & is recorded

The Pattent for this Land was originally granted to JNO: BENNETT & by him assigned to
the sd. BROUGHTON & Mr. CHARLES ASHTON, wch: sd. Assignemt. together with the
Pattent is recorded in the other Booke of Records in fol: 32 Septembr: 20th 1653

MACOTTER. Alexander 53, 63, 69, 93, 112; Rorey (Will of -80)

MADDOCK/MADDOX. Rice 5, (Chyrurgion -15), 88; Richard 76, Mr. 1.

MADESTONE. Thomas 17.

MAGREGOR(Y). Hugh 41, 104; James 1, 9, 11, 17, 26, 41, 31, 53, 93, 98, 99, 104, 120, 122; Mirian 26, 53.

MAHEN. Samuel 87.

MALLERD. Thomas 82.

MALLERY. Mr. 4; Philip (Clerk -4), 5; Roger 5.

MAN(N). Samuell 21, 72; Thomas 12.

MANSOY. Thomas 15.

MAPHEN. Robert 13.

MARKES. George 18, 36, 46.

MARSH. George 125.

MARTHAS. Mabel 103.

MARTIN. Thomas 86.

MARYLAND. Kent 14; Piney Point 21; Province of 11, 50, 51.

MASON. Bill of 13.

MATTHEWES. Esqr. -14; Samuel Esqr. 31, 35, 36, 50, 52, 53, 48-60, 82-84, 86, 91, 92, 98, 125; Thomas (Mercht. -122).

MAUNDER. Mr. 108; Wilkes 7, 12, 16, 28, 35, 39, 77, 84, 85, 109.

MAXWELL. Elexander 104.

MAYES. Diann 44; Henry 44, 71, 85.

MEDCALFE/METCALFE. Ann 2, 43; Elizabeth 2, 43, 90; George 44, 72; Gilbert 50, 51; Henry 2, 43, 67, 90; Jane 3, 43; ( )rine 90; William 13, 43, 90.

MEEKES. John 66.

MERREDITH. Johanna 94; John 93, 94.

MERTEN. Thomas 114.

MICHAELL. Mr. 1.

MIDLETON. Robert 35.

MILLER. Michaell 65; Thomas 117.

MOONE. Abraham 9, 72, 88; Mr. 12.

MOORE. Edward 123; Mrs. 41; Walter 63, 79; William 74.

MORGAN. Henry 12; Jenkin 101, 121, 122; Rebekah 101, 121; Thomas 12.

MORRIS. Comr. -77; John 103, 106; Nicholas 1, 4, 18, 34, 85, 86, 123.

MORRISON. Francis 105.

MOSELEY/MOSELY. Anne 2; Elizabeth 123, 124; Henry 2, 29, 47, 77, 78, 123, 124; Henry (deced. -2; John 2; William 2, 115.

MOTLEY. John 8, 53.

MOTT. Katherine 106.

MOTTROM. Jane 40; John 1, 9, 13, 21, 88, 89, 109; John (Coll.-9), 13, 64, 73, 87; John (Coll. deced. -1), 12-14, 40, 41, 88, 89, 91; Mr. 88.

MOULTON. -105; Joane 64; Thomas 13, 63, 64, 101, 119, 121, 122.

MOUNTAGUE. Peter 72; Peter (deced. ? -72), Sist( ) (Jadwyn) 72.

MOUTON. John 19, 44, 66, 67.

MULTON. John 44.

MUNFORD. William 50.

NASH. Thomas 117.

NEALE. Christopher 122; Daniell 105, 111, 114, 119, (Capt. -121), 122; Ellinor 114, 119; Samuel 11.

NEALMES. Richard 38, 79, 80, 102.

NECKS: Bettys 56; Cherry 46; Cherry Point 61; Morraticoe 58; Upper Machoatick 65; Yeocomoco 8, 38, 34, 71.

NEGROES. -115- 116.

NEPPER(S). Elizabeth 42; James 16.

NEW ENGLAND. -41; Bostin 125; Harfort 16; Salem 46.

NEWMAN. Elizabeth 25, 28, 33; Mrs. 41; Robert 12, 13, 25, 28, 32, 41; Steven 1; William 66.

NEWTON. John 60.

NICHOLAS. Samuel 3.

NICOLLS (NICHOLLS). George 32, 53, 84; John 81, 124, 125; Mordecai 46; Samuell 13, 26, 41, 43, 86; Sarah 124, 125.

NORSWORTHY. George 23; Thomas 23.

NOTT. Anne 57, 79; George 79; John 79.

NUGENT. Neil Marion 72.

NUTT. Phillip 49, 77, (Will of -100); William 11, 19, 20, 53, (Comr.-77), 113, 119, 120.

OBERT. John 36.

ODGER. Gabriel 33.

OLDIS. Thomas 4, 5, Thomas (deced. -4).

ORLAND. David 60, 61, 124.

ORLEY. Rebecca 115; Thomas 7, 22, 46, 92, (Will of -114, 115), 116.

OSBOURNE. William 100.

OVERSEY. Simon 118.

OWEN. Nicholas 2, 43, 46, 86, 91, 96, 107, 115, 117; Walter 49, 89.

PAINE. John 18.

TOPPIN/TAPPIN. Henry 66, 110.
TOWNSEND. Mr. 65.
TREIPE/TREPE. Thomas 13, 101, 121, 122.
TRUSSELL. Anne 89, 109; Coll: 1, 41, 62,
87, 112; Elizabeth 56, 89; John 8, (Coll. -11),
42, 47, 48, (Will of -56), 61, 62, 73, 75, 91,
92, 109, 111, 112, 121; John (Son of John
-56), 109; Mary 56, 121; Mr. 54;
William 56.
TUCKER. John 78, 85, 102, 108.
TURNEY. Mr. 13.

VALONGDEGAN/VANLANDIGHAM.
Michael 53, 63.
VAUGHAN. John 63.
VINCENT. Henry 1, 32; Mr. 1, 10.

WADE. Zacharia 12.
WADDY. John 3, 12, 87, 90.
WADINTON. Elizabeth 123; Ralph 123.
WALE. George 99.
WALKER. Christopher 112; John 21, 22, 36,
49, 85, 108; William 1, 62, 79;
William Junr. 68.
WALLIS. Abraham 115.
WALTERS. Roger 20, 50.
WALTON. John 13.
WARD. John 35, 82, 94; Magdelin 94, 95.
WARDER. Anne 70; William 44, 46, 70, 78.
WARRECK. Thomas 115.
WARWICKE. Alderman 47; Thomas 72.
WATERS. Roger 32, 33, 121.
WATTS. Elizabeth 23, 113; George 117, 118;
Henry 23, 27, 33, 50, 53, 113, 123; John 26,
(Sailmaker of Bristoll -122); Mrs. 108;
Tom 108.
WEBB. Elizabeth 113; Mr. 6; Thomas 33, 71.
WEEKES. Henry 60, 61; Walter 1, 2, 12, 29,
62, 115.
WEST. Elizabeth 3; John 106.
WHEATLEY. William 13.
WHISKIN. John 124, 125.
WHITE. -41; Brent 48; John 104, 121;
Joseph 28, 103; Richard 104; Richard (Will
of -103, 104), 108; Richard (Cooper -72).
WHITEY. Edward 116.
WHITTY. John 40.
WICKER/WECKER. Henry 7, 62, 84, 93, 98, 124.
WIDE. John 45.
WILCOCKES. Mathew 8, 20, 53, 119.

WILDEY. William 20, 22, 27, 44.
WILKINSON. Anthony 112.
WILLIA( ) Auston 32.
WILLIAMS. Charles 12; Edward 55, 57, 58,
60-62, 82, 83, 91; Elizabeth 58; Temperance
57, 58; Thomas 58, 67, 81, 105, 112.
WILLIS. James 1, 71.
WILLISON. Johanis 15; Robert 111.
WINCHESTER. John 12.
WINLEY. Widow 92.
WISE. John 79.
WITKIN. Edwd: 123.
WOOD. John 1, 8, 10, 13, 38, 55, 58, 98, 99,
122, 124; Mary 124; William 115.
WOODWARD. Thomas 108.
WORLICK. William 4.
WRIGHT. Ann 2, 11; Edward 47; Mr. 24, 46;
Nicholas 47; Richard 13, 29, 33, (Capt. -40),
110.
WYATT. William 6.

YARDLEY. Coll: 13.
YARRETT. Adam 64, 65, 76.
YOUNG. Richard Junr. 51.

Heritage Books by Ruth and Sam Sparacio:

Abstracts of Account Books of Edward Dixon, Merchant of Port Royal, Virginia, Volume I: 1743–1747

Abstracts of Account Books of Edward Dixon, Merchant of Port Royal, Virginia, Volume II

Albemarle County, Virginia Deed and Will Book Abstracts, 1748–1752

Albemarle County, Virginia Deed Book Abstracts, 1758–1761

Albemarle County, Virginia Deed Book Abstracts, 1761–1764

Albemarle County, Virginia Deed Book Abstracts, 1764–1768

Albemarle County, Virginia Deed Book Abstracts, 1768–1770

Albemarle County, Virginia Deed Book Abstracts, 1776–1778

Albemarle County, Virginia Deed Book Abstracts, 1778–1780

Albemarle County, Virginia Deed Book Abstracts, 1780–1783

Albemarle County, Virginia Deed Book Abstracts, 1787–1790

Albemarle County, Virginia Deed Book Abstracts, 1790–1791

Albemarle County, Virginia Deed Book Abstracts, 1791–1793

Augusta County, Virginia Land Tax Books, 1782–1788

Augusta County, Virginia Land Tax Books, 1788–1790

Amherst County, Virginia Land Tax Books, 1789–1791

Caroline County, Virginia Appeals and Land Causes, 1787–1794

Caroline County, Virginia Committee of Safety and Early Surveys, 1729–1762 and 1774–1775

Caroline County, Virginia Land Tax Book Alterations, 1782–1789

Caroline County, Virginia Land Tax Book Alterations, 1792–1795

Caroline County, Virginia Land Tax Book Alterations, 1795–1798

Caroline County, Virginia Order Book Abstracts, 1765

Caroline County, Virginia Order Book Abstracts, 1767–1768

Caroline County, Virginia Order Book Abstracts, 1768–1770

Caroline County, Virginia Order Book Abstracts, 1770–1771

Caroline County, Virginia Order Book, 1764

Caroline County, Virginia Order Book, 1765–1767

Caroline County, Virginia Order Book, 1771–1772

Caroline County, Virginia Order Book, 1772–1773

Caroline County, Virginia Order Book, 1773

Caroline County, Virginia Order Book, 1773–1774

Caroline County, Virginia Order Book, 1774–1778

Caroline County, Virginia Order Book, 1778–1781

Caroline County, Virginia Order Book, 1781–1783

Caroline County, Virginia Order Book, 1783–1784

Caroline County, Virginia Order Book, 1784–1785

Caroline County, Virginia Order Book, 1785–1786

Caroline County, Virginia Order Book, 1786–1787

Caroline County, Virginia Order Book, 1787, Part 1

Caroline County, Virginia Order Book, 1787, Part 2

Caroline County, Virginia Order Book, 1787–1788

Caroline County, Virginia Order Book, 1788

Culpeper County, Virginia Deed Book Abstracts, 1795–1796

Culpeper County, Virginia Land Tax Book, 1782–1786

Culpeper County, Virginia Land Tax Book, 1787–1789

Culpeper County, Virginia Minute Book, 1763–1764

Digest of Family Relationships, 1650–1692, from Virginia County Court Records

Digest of Family Relationships, 1720–1750, from Virginia County Court Records

Digest of Family Relationships, 1750–1763, from Virginia County Court Records

Digest of Family Relationships, 1764–1775, from Virginia County Court Records

Essex County, Virginia Deed and Will Abstracts, 1695–1697

Essex County, Virginia Deed and Will Abstracts, 1697–1699

Essex County, Virginia Deed and Will Abstracts, 1699–1701

Essex County, Virginia Deed and Will Abstracts, 1701–1703

Essex County, Virginia Deed and Will Abstracts, 1745–1749

Essex County, Virginia Deed and Will Book, 1692–1693

Essex County, Virginia Deed and Will Book, 1693–1694

Essex County, Virginia Deed and Will Book, 1694–1695

Essex County, Virginia Deed and Will Book, 1701–1704

Essex County, Virginia Deed, 1753–1754 and Will Book 1750

Essex County, Virginia Deed Abstracts, 1721–1724

Essex County, Virginia Deed Book, 1724–1728

Essex County, Virginia Deed Book, 1728–1733

Essex County, Virginia Deed Book, 1733–1738

Essex County, Virginia Deed Book, 1738–1742

Essex County, Virginia Deed Book, 1742–1745

Essex County, Virginia Deed Book, 1749–1751

Essex County, Virginia Deed Book, 1751–1753

Essex County, Virginia Land Trials Abstracts, 1711–1716 and 1715–1741

Essex County, Virginia Order Book Abstracts, 1695–1699

Essex County, Virginia Order Book Abstracts, 1699–1702

Essex County, Virginia Order Book Abstracts, 1716–1723, Part 1

Essex County, Virginia Order Book Abstracts, 1716–1723, Part 2

Essex County, Virginia Order Book Abstracts, 1716–1723, Part 3

Essex County, Virginia Order Book Abstracts, 1716–1723, Part 4

Essex County, Virginia Order Book Abstracts, 1723–1725, Part 1

Essex County, Virginia Order Book Abstracts, 1723–1725, Part 2

Essex County, Virginia Order Book Abstracts, 1725–1729, Part 1

Essex County, Virginia Order Book Abstracts, 1727–1729

Essex County, Virginia Order Book, 1695–1699

Essex County, Virginia Will Abstracts, 1730–1735

Essex County, Virginia Will Abstracts, 1735–1743

Essex County, Virginia Will Abstracts, 1745–1748

Fairfax County, Virginia Deed Abstracts, 1799–1800 and 1803–1804

Fairfax County, Virginia Deed Abstracts, 1804–1805

Fairfax County, Virginia Deed Book Abstracts, 1799

Fairfax County, Virginia Deed Book, 1798–1799

Fairfax County, Virginia Land Causes, 1788–1824

Fauquier County, Virginia Minute Book Abstracts, 1759–1761

Fauquier County, Virginia Minute Book Abstracts, 1761–1762

Fauquier County, Virginia Minute Book Abstracts, 1766–1767

Fauquier County, Virginia Minute Book Abstracts, 1767–1769

Fauquier County, Virginia Minute Book Abstracts, 1769–1771

Hanover County, Virginia Land Tax Book, 1782–1788

Hanover County, Virginia Land Tax Book, 1789–1793

Hanover County, Virginia Land Tax Book, 1793–1796

King George County, Virginia Order Book Abstracts, 1721–1723

King George County, Virginia Deed Book Abstracts, 1721–1735

King George County, Virginia Deed Book Abstracts, 1735–1752

King George County, Virginia Deed Book Abstracts, 1753–1773

King George County, Virginia Deed Book Abstracts, 1773–1783

King George County, Virginia Will Book Abstracts, 1752–1780

King William County, Virginia Record Book, 1702–1705

King William County, Virginia Record Book, 1705–1721

*King William County, Virginia Record Book, 1722
and 1785–1786*

Lancaster County, Virginia Deed and Will Book, 1652–1657

Lancaster County, Virginia Deed and Will Book, 1654–1661

*Lancaster County, Virginia Deed and Will Book, 1661–1702
(1661–1666 and 1699–1702)*

Lancaster County, Virginia Deed Book Abstracts, 1701–1706

Lancaster County, Virginia Deed Book, 1710–1714

Lancaster County, Virginia Order Book Abstracts, 1656–1661

Lancaster County, Virginia Order Book Abstracts, 1662–1666

Lancaster County, Virginia Order Book Abstracts, 1666–1669

Lancaster County, Virginia Order Book Abstracts, 1670–1674

Lancaster County, Virginia Order Book Abstracts, 1674–1678

Lancaster County, Virginia Order Book Abstracts, 1678–1681

Lancaster County, Virginia Order Book Abstracts, 1682–1687

Lancaster County, Virginia Order Book Abstracts, 1729–1732

Lancaster County, Virginia Order Book Abstracts, 1736–1739

Lancaster County, Virginia Order Book Abstracts, 1739–1742

Lancaster County, Virginia Order Book, 1687–1691

Lancaster County, Virginia Order Book, 1691–1695

Lancaster County, Virginia Order Book, 1695–1699

Lancaster County, Virginia Order Book, 1699–1701

Lancaster County, Virginia Order Book, 1701–1703

Lancaster County, Virginia Order Book, 1703–1706

Lancaster County, Virginia Order Book, 1732–1736

Lancaster County, Virginia Will Book, 1675–1689

Loudoun County, Virginia Order Book, 1763–1764

Loudoun County, Virginia Order Book, 1764

Louisa County, Virginia Deed Book, 1744–1746

Louisa County, Virginia Order Book, 1742–1744

Madison County, Virginia Deed Book Abstracts, 1793–1804

*Madison County, Virginia Deed Book, 1793–1813,
and Marriage Bonds, 1793–1800*

Middlesex County, Virginia Deed Book, 1679–1688

Middlesex County, Virginia Deed Book, 1688–1694

Middlesex County, Virginia Deed Book, 1694–1703

Middlesex County, Virginia Deed Book, 1703–1709

Middlesex County, Virginia Deed Book, 1709–1720

Middlesex County, Virginia Order Book Abstracts, 1686–1690

Middlesex County, Virginia Order Book Abstracts, 1697–1700

Middlesex County, Virginia Record Book, 1721–1813

Northumberland County, Virginia Deed and Will Book, 1650–1655

Northumberland County, Virginia Deed and Will Book, 1655–1658

Northumberland County, Virginia Deed and Will Book, 1658–1662

Northumberland County, Virginia Deed and Will Book, 1662–1666

Northumberland County, Virginia Deed and Will Book, 1666–1670

*Northumberland County, Virginia Deed and Will Book, 1670–1672
and 1706–1711*

Northumberland County, Virginia Deed and Will Book, 1711–1712

Northumberland County, Virginia Order Book, 1652–1657

Northumberland County, Virginia Order Book, 1657–1661

Northumberland County, Virginia Order Book, 1665–1669

Northumberland County, Virginia Order Book, 1669–1673

Northumberland County, Virginia Order Book, 1680–1683

Northumberland County, Virginia Order Book, 1683–1686

Northumberland County, Virginia Order Book, 1699–1700

Northumberland County, Virginia Order Book, 1700–1702

Northumberland County, Virginia Order Book, 1702–1704

Orange County, Virginia Deeds, 1743–1759

Orange County, Virginia Order Book Abstracts, 1747–1748

Orange County, Virginia Order Book Abstracts, 1752–1753

*Petersburg City, Virginia Hustings Court Deed Book Abstracts,
1784–1787*

*Petersburg City, Virginia Hustings Court Deed Book Abstracts,
1787–1790*

*Petersburg City, Virginia Hustings Court Deed Book Abstracts,
1790–1793*

Prince William County, Virginia Deed Book Abstracts, 1749–1752

Prince William County, Virginia Order Book Abstracts, 1752–1753

Prince William County, Virginia Order Book Abstracts, 1753–1757

*(Old) Rappahannock County, Virginia Deed and Will Book Abstracts,
1656–1662*

*(Old) Rappahannock County, Virginia Deed and Will Book Abstracts,
1662–1665*

*(Old) Rappahannock County, Virginia Deed and Will Book Abstracts,
1663–1668*

www.ingramcontent.com/pod-product-compliance
Lightning Source LLC
Chambersburg PA
CBHW080334270326
41927CB00014B/3222